SEPARATE

AND UNEQUAL The Inside Story

of Israeli Rule in East Jerusalem

SEPARATE

AND UNEQUAL

The Inside Story of Israeli Rule in East Jerusalem

AMIR CHESHIN

BILL HUTMAN

AVI MELAMED

Harvard University Press

Cambridge, Massachusetts, and London, England

1999

Library of Congress Cataloging-in-Publication Data

Cheshin, Amir.
    Separate and unequal : the inside story of Israeli rule in East
Jerusalem / Amir Cheshin, Bill Hutman, Avi Melamed.
        p.   cm.
    Includes bibliographical references and index.
    ISBN 0-674-80136-9
    1. Palestinian Arabs—Government policy—Jerusalem.   2. Jerusalem—
Politics and government.   I. Hutman, Bill.   II. Melamed, Avi.
    III. Title.
DS109.94.C49   1999
323.1'192740569442—dc21   98-53991

To Mina, Hanit, and Shahar

Contents

Prologue   *1*

1   The Vision and the Reality   *5*

2   Mr. Jerusalem   *12*

3   When Giants Sleep   *29*

4   A Question of Trust   *67*

5   Mr. Arafat, Can You Lend Me a Hand?   *91*

6   The Eagle Has Landed   *101*

7   The Forgotten Ones   *124*

8   Security Breach   *158*

9   Damage Control   *187*

10   A First Friendship   *198*

11   No Judenrein in Jerusalem   *211*

12   A Path to Peace Not Taken   *225*

Epilogue   *250*

Notes   *253*

Maps   *263*

Index   *267*

SEPARATE

AND UNEQUAL The Inside Story
of Israeli Rule in East Jerusalem

Prologue

Why another book about Jerusalem and why now? The question is indeed that simple and poignant, as is the answer. Reams have been written about Jerusalem since it was reunited in 1967. But we believe we are justified in saying that what has been written has not really arrived at the root of the central issue: the failure of Israeli rule in the city. Today, more than three decades after Israel first took control of all Jerusalem, and at a time when the conflict over the city's future appears to be reaching a climax, it has never been more important to understand Israeli policy toward the city.

This was not an easy book to write. Perhaps that is why others in our position—with a behind-the-scenes view of the making of Israeli policy toward east Jerusalem—have preferred to remain silent on the subject. We are Jerusalemites and Jews, and we are deeply connected with the city. We also had a say in forming Israeli policy toward east Jerusalem, which makes us anything but innocent observers. Amir Cheshin was former Jerusalem Mayor Teddy Kollek's adviser on Arab affairs from 1984 until 1993 and then served one year under Kollek's successor, Ehud Olmert. The post put him at the center of Israeli policy-making on east Jerusalem during his tenure. Bill Hutman was a senior reporter with *The Jerusalem Post*. From 1992 through 1996 he covered the Jerusalem beat for the newspaper. Avi Melamed served as deputy adviser on Arab affairs from 1991 until 1994 and as adviser from 1994 until 1996. The three of us literally lived many of the events described, in some instances as observers, in others as participants.

This book has been rumbling in our hearts and minds for years, each of us in our place. We watched with concern as the fragile quiet in Jerusalem was broken again and again. The dreams and images of a united Jerusalem, where different peoples and religions could all make their homes, which guided us and many like us were slowly being destroyed. We talked about the situation with friends and colleagues. We used our professional positions to try to influence things to take a turn for the better, but they only got worse. Ironically, it was a glimmer of hope—the signing of a Declaration of Principles between Israel and the Palestinian Liberation Organization in September 1993—which prompted us to begin to make this book a reality. We reasoned that at such a historic juncture, not only Israelis and Palestinians but all people interested in the fate of Jerusalem would want to know more about this conflict-torn city.

Much of the information contained in this book comes from our first-hand experience. In addition, we have drawn on an extensive archive relating to Israeli policy in Jerusalem since 1967, which we compiled through our work and from various Israeli sources. Included are the minutes of meetings among the most senior Israeli leaders and officials responsible for setting policy in the city; correspondence among these individuals, and in some cases between them and various non-Israelis; and numerous other documents detailing Israel's decision-making process with regard to Jerusalem. Where necessary, we spoke directly with the Israelis, Palestinians, and others involved. Specific references to these materials and interviews can be found in the Notes.

While *Separate and Unequal* begins in 1967 with the aftermath of the Six Day War, our focus is on the past fifteen years—from the rumblings of Palestinian unrest in Jerusalem in the early 1980s, to the intifada, or uprising, that hit the city soon after it broke out in Gaza in December 1987, and finally to the showdown over Jerusalem's future that began after the signing of the Declaration of Principles in 1993. That agreement specifically called for the Palestinians and Israelis to sit down and talk together about the future of the city so dear to them both.

The deadline for those talks to begin—tentatively May 1999—is fast approaching. Thus, some may accuse us of hanging out Israel's dirty laundry at just the time when it could be the most embarrassing and detrimental to the Jewish state and to the man who came to symbolize its rule of the city, Teddy Kollek. To those people we can only say that damaging Israel's claim to Jerusalem is far from our intention. In making public, for the first time, this record of Israeli rule in east Jerusalem, we believe that lessons learned from past mistakes can help build a better future. This chronicle of political intrigue and personal suffering is often an upsetting story for all involved, including ourselves; but it is a story still in the making. Hope remains for a just and peaceful ending, and it is with this hope that we have written this book.

"And my people shall abide in peaceful habitation,
and in secure dwellings, and in a quiet resting place."

ISAIAH 32:18

1

The Vision and the Reality

The Six Day War was still raging. Hours earlier, Jerusalem was taken by the Israeli army. A people whose long history was already filled with miraculous moments was in the midst of an event of biblical proportions. Prime Minister Levy Eshkol prepared to go to the Western Wall—the site of millennia of Jewish longing that had been cut off from the Jewish people since 1948. Before setting out, however, he called together the nation's chief rabbis and other Jewish, Christian, and Muslim religious leaders, "to share . . . the news of the events taking place these last few days in Jerusalem, the Holy and Eternal City."[1]

"Peace has now returned with our forces in control of all the city and it environs," Eshkol told the clergymen.[2] "You may rest assured that no harm whatsoever shall come to the places sacred to all religions . . . With the aid of the Rock and Salvation of Israel, from Jerusalem, a symbol of peace for countless generations, from this Holy City now returned to peace, I would like to have you join me in this call for peace among all the people of this area and of the whole world."

At that moment, it was as if Israel collectively put on rose-colored glasses and turned to view the ancient City of David. Perhaps this was only to be expected. Jerusalem for most Jews was a place seen only from afar, a holy city idealized in prayer and legend. Tradition says King David founded Jerusalem some 3,000 years ago on the slopes of the Kidron Valley. Historically, however, the city's roots go back even further, with the site first inhabited well before 2,500 BCE. For Jews, the city's history began 1,500 years later, when David conquered a Jebusite fortress and declared it the capital. David built a new walled city that remained in Jewish hands until 578 BCE, when the Babylonians conquered Jerusalem and sent the Jews into exile. The city's history since Babylonian times has been one of repeated conquests, spattered with intervals of peace and even disregard. Nebuchadnezzar, Alexander the Great, Ptolemy Soter, Antiochus Epiphanes, Pompey, the Parthians, Herod, Titus, Hadrian, the Persians, Heraclius, Omar, Saladin, the Mongols, Suleiman the Magnificent, General Henry Allenby—they are among the names of the great leaders who led armies into Jerusalem.

The irony of this Who's Who list of conquerors is that for all the city's attraction, Jerusalem remained desolate and isolated for most of its history. It was not a major center of trade. It may have had great religious symbolism, but there were many other far greater centers of learning and religious study than Jerusalem. Even as a pilgrim site, the city just did not seem to get it right. Over the years, Christian, Muslim, and Jewish pilgrims from Europe, Africa, and Asia may have come annually in greater and lesser numbers to the city. But that did not keep Jerusalem from remaining an out-of-the-way place. Few people wanted to live there. Those that did were largely poor and often depended on welfare from various patrons abroad.

Jews became a majority in Jerusalem by the early 1800s. But Jerusalem remained small, more of a village or town than a city, with a population of just 15,000 in 1845.[3] Nearly all of the residents lived in the confines of the Old City. It was about this time that the Zionist movement began to bring Jews to Palestine. The Zionists, however, did not place Jerusalem at the center of their vision; for the most part they chose to live elsewhere. Tel Aviv was founded and quickly became the de facto capital of the Jewish community in Palestine. Still, by 1912 the population of Jerusalem included 45,000 Jews and 35,000 Muslims and Christians, and it continued to grow, largely due to the influx of Jewish immigrants.

Israel's War of Independence in 1948 left much of Jerusalem off-limits to Jews. Historians have spoken of the city as being "divided" in 1948, but this word does not begin to capture the reality in Jerusalem. Historic Jerusalem for the Jews—the Western Wall, Temple Mount, City of David, and Mount of Olives—was part of Jordanian-controlled east Jerusalem. For nineteen years, Jews who wanted to glimpse the Jerusalem of their prayers had to climb atop the YMCA on King David Street, or take their chances with Jordanian snipers at various vantage points near the wall dividing the city.

So it is not surprising that in 1967, still giddy from their lightning-like military victory over their Arab neighbors, Israelis flocked by the thousands to the Old City. They wandered through the narrow streets of the Arab markets, or *shuks*, on their way to the Western Wall. The city was theirs. And in their euphoria over retaking historic Jerusalem, perhaps it is understandable that they paid little attention to the 68,000 Palestinians they had conquered as well, and who also called the ancient city home.[4]

The leaders of Israel, however, cannot be excused for this oversight. They had a clear goal: the reunification of Jerusalem. Ignoring the needs of the city's Palestinian population undermined this goal. The mistakes began immediately after the war and continued, until ultimately they severely threatened Israel's hold on Jerusalem.

In 1967 the image Israel projected to the world of a "united Jerusalem" was that of a body which, though once split in two, had been returned to its natural wholeness. "Jerusalem is rightfully ours again" was Israel's message after the Six Day War. "We will protect the rights of all peoples living in the city, Christian and Muslim. They will be able to worship freely. We will even give them limited autonomy over their holy places. But we will be in charge. This is how it should be."

Israel's great spokesman of the period, Abba Eban, writing to the United Nations just after the war, put the Jewish state's claim to Jerusalem and its plans for the city in much more eloquent terms. In a letter to the secretary-general of the U.N., Eban, Israel's foreign minister at the time, outlined an altruistic and enlightened policy.[5] In retrospect, it is sad to see how far from this vision Israeli policy-makers wandered.

As a result of the aggression launched by the Arab States against Israel in 1948, the section of Jerusalem in which the Holy Places are concentrated had been governed for nineteen years by a regime which refused to give due acknowledgment to universal religious concerns. The City was divided by a military demarcation line. Houses of worship were destroyed and desecrated in acts of vandalism. Instead of peace and security there was hostility and frequent bloodshed. The principle of freedom of access to the Holy Places of all three monotheistic religions was violated with regard to Jews, but not to them alone. On 5 June 1967, the Jordanian forces launched a destructive and unprovoked armed assault on the part of Jerusalem outside the walls. This attack was made despite Israel's appeal to Jordan to abstain from hostilities. Dozens of Jerusalem citizens were killed and hundreds wounded . . . Since 7 June, the entire City of Jerusalem experiences peace and unity. The Holy Places of all faiths have been open to access by those who hold them sacred.[6]

Eban aimed to quell the criticism of Israel's claim to authority. He, along with other Israeli government spokesmen, rejected the term "annexation," arguing that there was no need for Israel to annex east Jerusalem, as that part of the city had been rightly theirs even under Jordanian rule. In subsequent sections of the letter to the U.N. secretary-general, Eban promised an enlightened policy toward the city's religious and ethnic minorities. He stressed that Israel would follow a policy of religious tolerance and that civic understanding between Arabs and Jews would be encouraged, where before the two peoples had been separated by walls and fences. "One of the most significant results of the measures taken . . . is the new mingling of Arabs and Jews in free and constant association," Eban wrote. "There is a profound human and spiritual significance in the replacement of embattled hostility by normal and good neighborly relations. It is especially appropriate that ecumenical habits of thought and action should take root in the City from which the enduring message of human brotherhood was proclaimed with undying power in generations past."

Eban went on to describe the major steps already taken by Israel to improve the poor conditions in east Jerusalem. The Old City was now hooked up to the main water supply of west Jerusalem, ending the acute water shortage Arab residents had lived under during Jordanian rule. New health clinics had been opened in east Jerusalem, and Arab residents could now claim welfare rights equal to those of the Israeli population and far better than they had under Jordanian rule. Compulsory education was extended to east Jerusalem as well. Then, in a triumphant finale, Eban concluded:

> Where there was hostility, there is now harmonious civic union. Where there was a constant threat of violence, there is now peace. Where there was once an assertion of exclusive and unilateral control over the Holy Places, exercised in sacrilegious discrimination, there is now a willingness to work out arrangements with the world's religious bodies—Christian, Muslim, and Jewish—which will ensure the universal religious character of the Holy Places . . . The government of Israel is confident that world opinion will welcome the new prospect of seeing this ancient and historic metropolis thrive in unity, peace, and spiritual elevation.

How far this picture was from reality we can now clearly see. This is not to accuse Eban or other Israeli leaders who presented the rosy outlook in the days after the Six Day War of intentionally painting a false picture. As difficult as it always is to judge intentions, in this case they appear to have been honorable. Victory can bring with it a feeling of magnanimity, and so it was with Israel after the Six Day War. Israel saw itself as a benevolent conqueror and even liberator, and this feeling was strongest with regard to Jerusalem. There, more than in any other territory won in the war, Israelis believed they simply had taken back what was rightfully theirs.

At the same time, the Israeli government was less confident than Eban and other leaders publicly let on that the world would support the Jewish state's claim to Jerusalem. Thus, not surprisingly, while continuing to work to gather international support, Israel at the same time followed a policy aimed at physically strengthening Israel's hold on east Jerusalem. This is the policy that was not announced at the United Nations. Israel's leaders, knowing that their position in Jerusalem was shaky and that they had to act fast to strengthen it, adopted two basic principles in their rule of east Jerusalem. The first was rapidly to increase the Jewish population in east Jerusalem. The second was to hinder growth of the Arab population and to force Arab residents to make their homes elsewhere.

The logic behind this unspoken policy was quite simple: whoever physically dominated Jerusalem would determine the city's fate. If east Jerusalem remained inhabited only, or even predominately, by Arabs, then its chances of re-division would be much greater than if Jews moved in and became the majority of residents. This logic has driven Israeli policy makers from 1967 right up to today. And as we will show in detail in the chapters that follow, it has translated into a miserable life for the majority of east Jerusalem Arabs, many of whom have chosen to leave the city, as Israel hoped they would. At the same time, Jews have moved into east Jerusalem by the thousands. As of 1996, 157,000 Jews lived in east Jerusalem—a number nearly equaling the 171,000 Palestinians who resided there.[7]

To the world, Israel presented itself as an enlightened ruler of a troubled city. In reality, while pursuing what for the Jewish state was the logical goal of fortifying its claim to Jerusalem, the city's non-Jewish residents suffered greatly. Although Israel has gone to great pains to show otherwise, the startling evidence of this policy is obvious to anyone who drives through east Jerusalem, and it is borne out by the statistics on the comparative well-being of Jewish and Arab residents.[8]

Teddy Kollek, Jerusalem's mayor from 1965 to 1993, liked to tell foreign audiences how, "From a provincial backwater in 1967, Jerusalem has become a thriving metropolis" in which all its residents reap the benefits of enlightened Israeli rule.[9] "Projects aimed at improving the quality of life for Jews, Christians, and Muslims in every part of the city have led to the establishment, expansion and improvement of community institutions, centers of art and culture, ed-

ucation and sport, rest and recreation and the preservation and res-
toration of the city's historic heritage, while fostering the theme of
mutual respect and tolerance among the city's peoples," he would
tell them.[10] It was a mouthful of a message, and the audiences ate it
up. This was particularly true with Jewish audiences in the United
States. Kollek's portrait of life in Jerusalem gave world Jewry the
best of both worlds—pride in seeing Jerusalem again the center of
Jewish life, and a clear conscience in being told the Palestinian minority in the city was being treated fairly. This vision, however, was
far from the reality.

2

Mr. Jerusalem

Teddy Kollek was in his element. The main municipal auditorium, which doubled as the City Council meeting hall, was filled with *mukhtars* and other Palestinian notables. Kollek worked the crowd, shaking hands and exchanging greetings with the leading Palestinians of the city. The atmosphere was cordial and relaxed. It was early summer, 1984. On the surface, at least, relations were still relatively good between city hall and the local Palestinian population. But there were also signs of the trouble ahead. This was an important gathering for the mayor, one of a round of periodic, informal, and largely social get-togethers with the city's Palestinian leaders. Sometimes they would even meet in east Jerusalem in the home of one of the Palestinians, before Palestinian nationalistic sentiment made such displays of seeming support—or at least acceptance—of Israeli rule impossible.

Four years later, in December 1987, Palestinians would take to the streets en masse in protest against Israeli rule. This violent uprising—which would become known worldwide by its Arabic name, *intifada*—would spark a complete rethinking of Palestinian-Israeli relations. But Kollek, as early as 1984, was aware that all was not right with the sensitive relations between Israeli authorities and the Palestinian population. "I am sure you have been aware of recent incidents in our city, including the attempt of a fringe [Jewish] group to attack the mosques of the Temple Mount," the mayor wrote in a confidential memo to a Jewish-American associate earlier in the year. "With the increasing tensions throughout the Middle East, the local scene cannot be unaffected, and the Muslim and Christian populations need more attention."[1] But to the Palestinians gathered at city hall that evening, Kollek made no mention of these concerns. His remarks were brief—a few words of praise for his outgoing adviser on Arab affairs and an introduction to the new man taking the post—and were sprinkled with humorous comments in Kollek's characteristic friendly and easy-going manner.[2] The mayor did his best to present a facade of normalcy. As for tensions between Palestinians and Israelis in his city, it was as if, by not talking about them, Kollek believed, they would go away.

Kollek loved to take visitors to east Jerusalem. They would sit in cafes and *kibitz* over Turkish coffee with the locals. One of the mayor's favorite restaurants was the Philadelphia, on Ez-Zahra Street near the National Palace Hotel. This fancy basement restaurant was frequented by the cream of Israeli society. Between the 1967 war and the intifada, Israelis from all walks of life roamed the streets, markets, and cafes of east Jerusalem. To Israelis, the Arab part of the city was exotic and intriguing—and open on the Sabbath. When on Saturdays everything shut down in west Jerusalem, crowds of secular Israelis flocked to east Jerusalem, where they would barter with Palestinian shopkeepers at the *shuk* just inside Jaffa Gate and then pack into Abu Shukri's, in the Old City on the Via Delorosa, or into some other favorite eating spot. People would travel for miles for a plate of Abu Shukri's famous homous and *ful*.

At night, music blared from youth hostels and pubs, where Israelis and tourists from around the world would come to forget their worries with a little help from Lebanese hashish and Israeli beer. On warm summer nights the watermelon market between Mousrara and Damascus Gate would be packed. For just a few lira you could buy an ice-cool slice of fresh watermelon and be entertained by belly-dancers who worked for tips between the stalls. In the winter, hot sahlab, the local sweet tea, was a favorite in the Mousrara market. And year around the aroma of fresh baked bread and pita filled the air. The Mousrara market covered an area that had been no-man's land between 1948 and 1967. It had been desolate, divided by barbed wire and a high wall from which Israeli and Jordanian soldiers looked down on their respective sides of the city.

Immediately after the Six Day War, when Israel pulled down

the physical barriers that divided Jerusalem, Palestinian shopkeepers were at first excited about the opportunity to sell their wares to the crowds of Israeli visitors. Vendors came to east Jerusalem from the West Bank towns of Ramallah and Hebron in hopes of cashing in on the Israeli presence. If business was measured in terms of the number of shoppers, the shopkeepers and vendors should have been doing very well. However, the initial optimism of Arab business-men soon turned to bitter disappointment. Israelis may have been coming in big numbers, but they were hardly purchasing anything. "You watch as the dozens of Israelis pass in the Old City or on Salah A-Din Street, with a cola in one hand and in the other a piece of *cakh* bread," Palestinian shopkeepers would complain to anyone who would listen. *Cakh* is the popular Arab poppy-seeded, donut-shaped roll, traditionally eaten with the spice *zatar* sprinkled on top. It's tasty, and also inexpensive. That was about all the Israeli tourists were interested in purchasing in east Jerusalem, as they continued to do their real shopping in the Jewish sector of the city.

Kollek knew that pulling down the barriers that divided Jerusalem would not be enough to truly unify the city. He quickly realized that, at best, Palestinian Jerusalemites were uncomfortable with Israeli policy and, at worse, were completely opposed to it, and that some-thing needed to be done to make them more accepting. The question was what? A look at one specific answer that Kollek came up with— the revitalization by Israel of one of east Jerusalem's more run-down neighborhoods, Wadi Joz—is telling. Of the dozens of problems in east Jerusalem, from lack of housing to substandard health care, Kollek chose cleaning up the make-shift factories, junkyards, and garages of Wadi Joz as the most important to solve.

Days after he took his post in 1984, the new adviser on Arab affairs was called to Kollek's office to discuss the municipality's agenda for the Arab sector. The mayor went straight to business with his new adviser. "You know Wadi Joz, the area where all the car repair shops are?" began Kollek. "I want to clean the mess up in

Wadi Joz. You should make getting this done a top priority." The mayor wanted the dozens of small factories and garages moved out of Wadi Joz and the area redeveloped with homes, hotels, and commercial space.

A thick file in the adviser's office at city hall was dedicated to Wadi Joz. It was filled with property-owner surveys, surveys of alternative sites for the car repair shops and light industry, cost estimates for the project, and dozens of other documents compiled since the idea was first conceived by Kollek right after the 1967 war. The mayor was after what he and his aides spoke of as a "big success"— something he could show the world as evidence that Israel was doing good for the Arabs of east Jerusalem. With Wadi Joz, however, Kollek and Israel were not able to manage even a little success.

The Wadi Joz file was filled with unrealized plans that had no hope of ever being carried out. There was no hope because the project demanded a major financial allocation on the part of the Israeli government. When it came to helping Jerusalem's Arab sector, Israel was simply unwilling to make such an investment.

By contrast, around the same time a similar project aimed at helping a Jewish section of the city received massive government financial support. The Jewish "Wadi Joz" was Mamilla, a poor, run-down neighborhood of west Jerusalem that straddled the former no-man's land just outside Jaffa Gate. Between 1948 and 1967, any family with the means to do so moved out of Mamilla, because of the dangerous conditions there, and only the poor remained—many of whom were squatters in abandoned houses. But shortly after the Six Day War, Mamilla came to embody the dreams of city planners and investors alike.

The neighborhood stood near the end of Jaffa Road, in the scenic Hinnom Valley that runs along the western side of the Old City. The property was recognized by Israeli policy makers as among the most valuable in Jerusalem. It took years of squabbling between the authorities and private investors, but eventually a semipublic company was formed to oversee the evacuation of the squatters, the buy-out and removal of the other veteran families of the neighborhood, demolition of the dilapidated buildings, preservation of the historic ones, and the start of construction on new million-dollar homes, a five-star hotel, and a shopping district. All the work—much of it subsidized by the Israeli government—was carried out in Mamilla, while in Wadi Joz, just on the other side of the Old City, nothing changed.

In the late 1980s and early 1990s the Israeli government came close to developing Wadi Joz, but not in the manner that Kollek had in mind. Ariel Sharon, Israel's outspoken general who became housing minister under Prime Minister Yitzhak Shamir, tried to evict the Arab residents of Wadi Joz to make way for Jewish development in the neighborhood. Only legal difficulties in evacuating the Arab owners kept Sharon's plan from moving forward.

Kollek managed to initiate several small projects in east Jerusalem—and he is quick to point this out to critics who say Israel has done nothing to improve conditions for Arab residents. A medical center was built in Sheikh Jarrah and a library in the American Colony neighborhood. But these two projects, and a handful of others in east Jerusalem, did not receive their funding from the State of Israel. Rather, a charitable organization, the Jerusalem Foundation, which raises contributions largely from outside of Israel for projects in Jerusalem, backed these projects. Kollek was among the foundation's founders, and he was influential in convincing contributors from abroad who wanted to give only to Jewish projects that it was also in Israel's interest to give to Arab development in the city.

Kollek clearly felt bad about not doing more. He was particularly bitter that even when his own Labor Party associates were in power they only paid lip service to his demands for additional funding for Arab development in east Jerusalem. Some say Kollek himself did not push hard enough, that he should have used his political influence and popularity to do more for Jerusalem Arabs. This point is debatable. What is clear is that, overall, Kollek's priorities were the same as those of other Israeli leaders—to increase the Jewish presence in all parts of the city as fast as possible, while doing for the Arab residents only what was necessary to keep them placated. "We must show them [the Arabs] we are doing something. Even if it is something small, it is important to make a big deal out of it to make it appear like we are working for them," Kollek explained at one meeting between city, state, and security officials on east Jerusalem in July 1985.[3]

The meeting was one of the periodic gatherings called by Kollek to discuss Israel's policy in east Jerusalem. Little new was usually said at these meetings, which were often held late in the evening at Kollek's apartment at 6 Rashba Street in the well-to-do Rehavia neighborhood. The proceedings were generally kept secret, partly due to the presence of representatives from Israel's Shin Bet internal security service. But there was also a sense among Israeli officials that secrecy was required when discussing east Jerusalem, because of the sensitivity of the issue.

This particular July meeting was at the home of city manager Aharon Sarig. The city manager is the most senior nonelected official in the Jerusalem municipality. Also present were Kollek; deputy mayor Amiram Sivan; Ya'acov Pery, the Shin Bet regional commander; Yossi Ginat, the prime minister's Arab affairs adviser; Uzi Wexler, city treasurer; and Rafi Levy, district director for the Interior Ministry. Over coffee and cookies they discussed the latest happenings in east Jerusalem. And as usual, the keen realization of the neglect being shown by Israel to the Arab population clashed with the reality of Israel's priorities in the city. In turn, they reviewed the needs of Arab east Jerusalem, and then they noted that neither Israel's national nor local government was willing to put up the funds needed to meet those needs.

Pery, the security chief, cautioned that this neglect of the Arab population might be dangerous. The poor conditions in Arab east Jerusalem were fueling dissent against Israeli rule. "It's not my job to tell the government what to do with its money, but we need to at least be meeting minimal needs," Pery told the other Israeli officials. "The more the Arabs [in Jerusalem] have to lose [if they rise up against Israeli rule], the more likely they are to remain quiet." Those present generally agreed with Pery. And they came up with a particularly telling proposal to deal with the problem the security chief raised.

The proposal was to continue doing little in the way of developing the Arab sector, but "making a big deal" out of the little that was done. "I think it is fair to say we have come to agreement that it is important that even the little we do in east Jerusalem be given much publicity," said Sivan, the deputy mayor who held the finance portfolio. Sivan was respected as a sharp financial mind with political savvy. He was close to Kollek and normally received the mayor's strong backing. "As for increasing funding. I don't see this happening anytime soon," he said. "I don't see the amount we have been investing in recent years of between NIS 3–4 million [around $1.5 million U.S.] changing."

Israel was not interested in investing any real money to improve conditions for the Arab residents. At the same time, Israeli officials were well aware that conditions in the Arab sector were substandard and that this threatened stability in the city. So the Israeli officials came up with a plan: First, "carry out small projects, using Darwish." This referred to Mordechi Darwish, director of the city's urban improvement department, who was considered the "king" of the little projects that the mayor and others at city hall thought would buy them quiet in east Jerusalem. Second, "ensure that every year there is activity in each area (road construction, school construction, etc.), to make our presence felt, and prevent the Arab residents from feeling the city isn't doing anything."

This was a meeting at which the Israeli municipal and national governments' plans for improving conditions in Arab east Jerusalem were supposed to be consolidated. But no comprehensive plan was offered. In fact, no concrete plan for improving conditions was even discussed. Instead, it was the same each time Israeli policy-makers met to discuss east Jerusalem. They did not attempt to study the situation in order to see what needed to be done. Rather, their aim was to determine how little could be done, without causing too much uproar among Jerusalem's Palestinian residents. In the summer of 1985, when the first ripples of Palestinian unrest were already being felt in east Jerusalem, Israeli leaders remained oblivious to what was happening and continued to ignore the needs of Palestinian residents. This would later cost Israel dearly.

To make matters worse, as the years brought more and more indications that Israel's policy toward east Jerusalem was a failure, still nothing changed. This despite the fact that Israeli leaders recognized the problems—from the lack of housing and infrastructure in Arab neighborhoods to those more "psychological" grievances, such as the feeling among Palestinian Jerusalemites that they were residents of only half the city and were waiting for the day when they would be independent from the Israeli authorities. The city remained divided, although the walls and watch-towers were torn down. In the Jewish sector, new neighborhoods were emerging, roads were being paved, schools and synagogues were opening to meet the needs of the surging Jewish population. Business and culture were also booming in the Jewish sector. In the Arab sector, the only thing booming was the population. Not one new Arab neighborhood had been built, and many of the old Arab neighborhoods remained without sewage and paved roads, not to mention sidewalks and street lights.

What made these differences more startling was the proximity between Arab and Jewish neighborhoods. In north Jerusalem, for instance, new villas and apartments of the French Hill neighborhood are just several dozen meters away from Issawiya, where the stench from the freely running waste is only now being brought under control with the construction of a sewage system. There are few paved roads in Issawiya, no sidewalks, and no parks. Municipal and state funding for such projects was never allocated to Issawiya. Driving up Rehov Lohmei Hageta'ot (Ghetto Fighters Road), passing French Hill's small shopping plaza, and then heading down toward the villas of the Tzamaret Habira section of the neighborhood, no signs are needed to show you that you have left a Jewish area and entered an Arab one. And what makes it obvious has nothing to do with differences between the more traditional Arab and more modern Jewish building styles. At the Tzamaret Habira gas station junction, a well-paved road with sidewalks and shrubbery leads toward the Jewish homes; the road leading to Issawiya is full of potholes, and narrows to barely one lane as it nears the village.

This scene of two realities within one city is repeated throughout Jerusalem: in Shuafat and Beit Hanina, the poor Arab neighborhoods bordering the predominantly Jewish developments of Neveh

Ya'acov and Pisgat Ze'ev, where the government has invested millions of dollars; Jabal Mukaber, a former Bedouin encampment settled by tribal people over half a century ago, with its poor public facilities, next to East Talpiot, the Jewish neighborhood built over the past twenty years with its new roads, parks, and library. The contrasts are testament to a city that remains divided despite the public pronouncements of Israeli leaders that unity prevails. The borders may no longer be drawn on maps, but they still exist on the ground.

The disparities between east and west Jerusalem were well known to the Kollek administration and were discussed by officials in every level of Israeli government. Kollek was a well-connected member of Israel's Labor Party. His nonpartisan style and popularity also gave him leverage with the Likud, the country's other major party. Over the years, Kollek would meet with prime ministers from both parties, asking for more funding for Arab east Jerusalem. He lobbied the many government offices and committees to deal with the issue. But largely to no avail.

Perhaps the most prominent of the Israeli government bodies dealing with Jerusalem was the Ministerial Committee on Jerusalem, which paid much lip service to the importance of making Jerusalem "Israel's eternal capital." The committee was established just after the Six Day War. It received a renewed mandate in the Basic Law adopted by the Knesset on July 30, 1980, which called for its continued operation as the government body overseeing policy in the city. The law was pushed through the Knesset by the government of Prime Minister Menachem Begin. Kollek fought strongly against the article's adoption, on grounds that it was superfluous, only reiterating Israel's long-standing position on Jerusalem. As Kollek predicted, the law merely backfired. It raised the ire of the U.N. Security Council and prompted thirteen countries to move their embassies from Jerusalem to Tel Aviv.[4]

Perhaps most telling, all the good the law promised in the way of additional funding for Jerusalem never fully materialized. The law's final article stated that "the government shall provide for the development and prosperity of Jerusalem and the well-being of its inhabitants by allocating special funds, including a special grant to the municipality of Jerusalem." The special grant, however, was rarely allocated, and when it was, it only went to projects that benefited the Jewish population. The Palestinian population's needs continued to be ignored.

"The level of service given to residents of east Jerusalem is much lower than that given to residents of west Jerusalem," states an internal Jerusalem municipality memo. Infrastructure is lacking in east Jerusalem, there is no garbage collection in many Arab neighborhoods, and schools for Arab children are lacking, the memo continues. "The only place in the entire country where a second-shift is used [because of the lack of classrooms] is in east Jerusalem," it states. If this memo had been written in 1968, one might argue that it was describing a situation Israel inherited. In fact, however, it was written in 1986.[5] And it was damning: "In most east Jerusalem neighborhoods the local roads are no more than unpaved dirt paths without sidewalks or electricity . . . In 60 percent of the east Jerusalem neighborhoods there is no garbage collection . . . The water system in the Arab sector is insufficient . . . There is a shortage of sports facilities both in [Arab] schools and the general [Arab] community . . ." The list goes on and on.[6] Israel had ruled east Jerusalem for nearly two decades, largely neglecting the needs of its Arab residents. More than three decades have now gone by, most of the time with Kollek still as mayor, and little has changed. Israel continues to neglect the Arab sector of Jerusalem.

Kollek certainly must take a good part of the blame. He cannot just be "Mr. Jerusalem" when it comes to the positive things. If he is to be identified with the city, it seems only fair that he be identified with all aspects of the city, good and bad. Kollek was never one to shirk responsibility, but he did often complain that Israel's system of government gave mayors like himself little real power. One of Kollek's favorite stories was how he discovered just after taking office in 1965 that even to put up a new traffic light he needed the government's approval. And what goes for such mundane decisions was even more true with regard to the larger issues of city planning, to say nothing about the funding to realize those plans.

Kollek was well versed on Israel's neglect of Jerusalem's Arab sector. It touched virtually every aspect of the Arab residents' lives. Just how widespread the problem was, and how aware Kollek and other Israeli officials were of the situation, was reflected in the 1986 internal municipal report:[7]

1. Local taxes. The taxes east Jerusalem residents pay are not reflected in the services they receive. There is also a feeling among east Jerusalem Arabs that there is no justification for the taxes in east Jerusalem to be on the same level as those in west Jerusalem, particularly for stores and businesses. Possible solutions—lowering the tax-brackets in which east Jerusalem businesses are classified, or setting up a committee of experts to study the issue.

2. Urban development. The frustration among east Jerusalem residents is even worse in those areas where Jewish and Arab neighborhoods border one another [Issawiya–French Hill, Jabal Mukaber–East Talpiot]. Possible solutions—improving city services in Arab neighborhoods.

3. Education. There is a shortage of classrooms in east Jerusalem. About 200 classrooms are rented, but we still fall far short of the need. No enrichment programs exist for teachers. There is a lack of special programs in Arab schools. Despite all of this, there were recently cuts in the budget for Arab schools.

4. Sport and social activities for youths. A serious budget shortage has caused the closure of many east Jerusalem boys and girls clubs and community centers. Youths who find no place in the public system are being absorbed in private clubs, funded by foreign, and sometimes hostile, sources not within the municipality's control.

5. Housing. The Housing Ministry has failed to help provide housing for Arab residents of east Jerusalem.

6. Police. Arab residents believe the police see them only as a threat. The residents say police ignore crime in their neighborhoods.

7. Social services. The National Insurance Institute has closed its offices in east Jerusalem, making it difficult for Arab residents

to receive the various services and payments to which they are entitled.

8. Shuafat refugee camp. The government is totally ignoring the refugees' needs, on grounds that it is solely the U.N.'s job to take care of them.

This memo, put together by city officials in preparation for a meeting between Kollek and the prime minister, was not unique. It is one of dozens of documents on conditions in east Jerusalem produced by the municipality and other Israeli bodies, making it difficult for Israel to claim ignorance of the problems faced by Palestinian residents of the city. Indeed, the Interior Ministry's indifferent and at times hostile attitude toward east Jerusalem Arabs was addressed in a separate memo attached to the one quoted above. City officials charged that obtaining traveling papers, identity cards, and any of the other services the ministry provided was a bureaucratic nightmare for Arab residents.

To take another example, in 1988 Kollek turned to Efriam Sneh, a future government minister who had just stepped down from the post of government's coordinator in the West Bank and Gaza, to put together a report on conditions in east Jerusalem. There was little new in the report, "The Arabs of East Jerusalem—Positions and Trends," despite its being written nearly six months into the intifada.[8] From the Israeli perspective at least, the problems in east Jerusalem remained the same. "There is little doubt that finding a solution to the building and housing subject is the most important issue for east Jerusalem residents," Sneh found. He suggested "liberalization in issuing building permits; making land available for public housing; speeding up completion of zoning plans for Arab neighborhoods; issuing loans for private construction."

Sneh reported that he had spoken with a number of leading figures in east Jerusalem and that one of their principal demands was that Arab neighborhoods receive services equal to those given to Jewish neighborhoods. Some of the Arab leaders "expressed willingness to accept a level of service that was 50 percent of what the Jews receive." Sneh's suggestions—build sports and youth centers, parks, and clinics, as well as sewage systems and street lights in those areas of east Jerusalem still without. Sneh also touched on the subject of education. "In most of my conversations [with Arab leaders] the issue was raised of the urgent need to improve and strengthen the Arab education system in east Jerusalem," he wrote. There was nothing revolutionary or even new in Sneh's analysis. The issues were raised and possible solutions discussed, and then nothing was done.

In 1990, the well-respected former foreign ministry director-general, Reuven Merhav, tried his hand at the east Jerusalem "problem." Kollek's instructions to Merhav: Determine what can be done in east Jerusalem, without having to invest large sums of money. Merhav, new to the city apparatus and policy with regard to east Jerusalem, quickly put together a team of municipal and academic experts in an effort to meet the challenge Kollek—a fellow Labor Party member and personal friend—put before him. But as quickly as Merhav began work, the veteran diplomat also ran face-first into the reality of Israel's east Jerusalem policy. Merhav asked municipal officials to provide him with a breakdown of city budget allocations to east Jerusalem, only to discover that such a breakdown did not exist. "How can I be expected to make recommendations concerning policy in east Jerusalem when fundamental information like the city's budget for east Jerusalem does not exist?" Merhav asked the officials.

The city officials' answer was in the same Kafkaesque style that the Jewish state's policy toward east Jerusalem demanded. There were no separate financial books on east Jerusalem, the officials explained, because Jerusalem is united. No differentiation was made in allocations between the Jewish and Arab sectors of the city, so there was no need for keeping track of how much money went to each sector. That official reasoning defied the reality of life in Jerusalem, however. It did not take a financial wizard to see that little of the city's budget was going to Arab east Jerusalem, particularly when compared with allocations to the Jewish sector.

Merhav insisted on receiving the breakdown. He eventually got what he wanted. City manager Michael Gal ordered two senior municipal officials to go through the budget books, department by department and neighborhood by neighborhood, and determine just how much was going to the Arab sector. Gal, who first came to work for the municipality in 1987 after a long career in the Israeli army, was himself appalled by the lack of services the Arab sector was receiving from the municipality. On a get-acquainted tour of east Jerusalem when he became head of the city's education department, his first post at city hall, Gal could not believe there was no sewage system or trash collection in many Arab neighborhoods and that this was the case long before the intifada gave municipal department heads the excuse not to provide the services. The education system in east Jerusalem was also a shambles. Gal made it a top priority to bring Arab schools up to standard. But improving east Jerusalem's public school system, along with other public programs and services in the Arab sector, simply was not on the Israeli government's agenda.

Four years later Gal, now city manager, hoped he would have the authority at city hall to change policy on east Jerusalem. He backed Merhav in the demand for a breakdown of the budget. It took weeks for the two officials he appointed to pull the figures together. Their task was not easy. The work they did was historic, confirming in irrefutable numbers what everyone already knew: that Israel discriminated against east Jerusalem in budget allocations.

Palestinians made up 28 percent of the city's population but received between 2 and 12 percent of the budget in the various city departments, according to this report.[9] From education to road construction, funding to east Jerusalem was far lower than it should have been relative to west Jerusalem. If one considers that the conditions in Arab neighborhoods were far inferior to those in Jewish neighborhoods, the vast discrepancy in funding was even more serious. The funding discrepancy created a situation in which the gap between Jerusalem's Jewish and Arab sectors grew more severe each year, as improvements were made in the Jewish sector while the Arab sector was largely ignored.

Merhav passed the figures on to Kollek. The findings caused the mayor great anxiety. Faced with such numbers, he could not deny that city hall was discriminating against Arab east Jerusalem.

Merhav was sensitive to the situation of his friend Kollek and knew that the report, if made public, would hurt Kollek deeply, so the few copies that had been made were quickly recovered and destroyed. Merhav also asked the city officials who compiled the report not to publicize the findings. Kollek was saved from public humiliation, but this was little consolation for his conscience.

The election victory of the Labor Party in 1992 gave Kollek renewed hope that help was finally on its way for east Jerusalem. Soon after the election, the mayor began a lobbying effort with his fellow party members in the newly formed national government to push through his long-delayed plans for the Arab sector. In August, Kollek appealed directly to Prime Minister Yitzhak Rabin.[10] The new prime minister, however, had other things on his mind and pushed off Kollek to the finance minister.[11]

Kollek had little choice but to do as the prime minister instructed. "The level of services and infrastructure in the Arab sector is far below that of Jewish neighborhoods," Kollek told Avraham Shohat, finance minister.[12] "There is a desperate need for emergency allocations to improve the physical and social infrastructure in east Jerusalem, and to begin doing so immediately." Later that month, Kollek also met police minister Moshe Shahal. The mayor touched on a wide range of subjects with Shahal, from the need to ease the passage of east Jerusalem residents over the Allenby Bridge into Jordan, where many of their families live, to security problems on the Temple Mount, to the failure of the National Insurance Institute to provide social and welfare benefits to Palestinians who had been forced to move to the West Bank to find housing. The mayor also demanded that the strict limitations on the number of homes Arabs were allowed to build in east Jerusalem be lifted.

The next month, at Kollek's direction, senior city officials met to determine what needed to be done in the Arab sector. Their conclusion: the physical conditions had become so bad that anything more than token improvements was far beyond the scope of the municipal budget. A sharp increase in government funding was desperately needed, the officials concluded.

Fueled by the findings of his advisers, Kollek continued his road-

show, meeting with the housing, transport, and even religious affairs ministers, trying to convince them all to allocate more funds for
the Arab sector of east Jerusalem. The aging Jerusalem mayor's political clout made it hard for any official or government leader, including the prime minister, to turn him away. So the leaders met
with Kollek, and the mayor and his advisers laid before them the picture of Arab east Jerusalem, neglected by Israeli government after Israeli government since 1967, and appealed to the new ministers to
make a bold change in policy. It did not take long for Kollek to realize he was not getting anywhere. The new Labor government was
not going to be better than any of the previous administrations when
it came to providing funds for development in Arab east Jerusalem.

Not being one to give up easily, Kollek took his fight directly to
Rabin. He demanded numerous meetings with the prime minister
and harried him with countless letters on the dire situation in east Jerusalem. "I am sorry to be bothering you when I know the problems
that you are having to deal with, but I have no choice but to raise
the problems of Jerusalem again and again," Kollek wrote the new
prime minister.[13] He laid out before Rabin the financial needs of east
Jerusalem. In November 1992 the prime minister agreed to set up a
special interministerial committee to oversee development in east
Jerusalem. Kollek demanded an immediate allotment of NIS 30 million ($12 million). But Rabin agreed to only NIS 10 million ($4 million). "The amount will considerably help the municipality," Kollek
told Rabin. "But it is far from what is needed to solve the problems
of such a complicated and sensitive city as Jerusalem."[14] Kollek demanded more money. And he made clear to Rabin what was at
stake—the continued "unity and standing of Jerusalem."

Kollek had been a protégé of David Ben-Gurion, a founding father
of both Israel and the Labor Party, and he had a long list of political
allies in Labor. But with the Rabin government he had an additional
card to play. The municipal elections were fast approaching, and
Rabin was concerned about the results. He wanted a strong showing
for his party as a demonstration of public support for his government's recent peace initiative with the Palestine Liberation Organization. Rabin and other Labor Party leaders' hopes in Jerusalem

were tied to Kollek's agreeing to run again. They believed he was un-beatable in Jerusalem. Kollek tried to use the threat of retirement, which he was seriously considering, to leverage greater government support for his plans, particularly with regard to the Arab sector.

On November 4, 1992, the prime minister's office announced that Kollek had agreed to Rabin's request that he remain in poli-tics. Kollek had agreed to run on the condition that the government would increase its budgetary support of Jerusalem, and he believed his strategy had worked. In the end, however, Kollek was left feeling betrayed. The government balked in its commitment to give more than the originally agreed NIS 10 million. And, according to city officials, even the NIS 10 million never fully made it to the city's coffers.

This was a hard blow to Kollek. In the past, he had fought for and lost similar bids for increased government support for development projects in the Arab sector of east Jerusalem. But in this instance a government led by his own party, which clearly knew what was at stake, was paying little more than lip service to Jerusalem's needs. "With regard to the Arab sector, [the Rabin government] has not even begun to put together a plan," the mayor concluded.[15] "The is-sue will continue to drag on for years without a solution, despite the fact that with some creative thinking solutions can be found." In 1992, Kollek, 81, had expected a different approach from the new Rabin government. Instead, he watched as his country continued to ignore the needs of Jerusalem's Arab population.

3

When Giants Sleep

Hardly anyone was listening as Jerusalem city engineer Elinoar Barzacci walked to the front of the City Council chamber and began to speak. The mayor was taking one of his famous naps. He sat at the head of the large oval table where he and thirty City Council members gathered monthly. Kollek's chin rested on his chest, his arms folded in front of him, and eyes comfortably closed. The loud chattering of the council members was not going to disturb his rest. It never did.

Deputy mayor Amos Mar-Haim, however, would not tolerate the noise. Mar-Haim was Kollek's number two on the council and ran meetings when Kollek was away, or dozing off. Mar-Haim pounded the wooden gavel loudly on the table, but the chattering continued. It took a second round of pounding and a little shouting at several noisy council members and spectators to bring the room to order.

Barzacci, a well-respected Italian-born city planner, began her explanation. She described the proposed zoning plan for the Jerusalem Arab neighborhood of Sur Baher, shown on a map mounted near where she was standing. "The plan will allow for additional homes to be built in Sur Baher, within the government's limitations for the neighborhood," Barzacci said. She told the council members that under those limitations an additional 1,200 units would be allowed in Sur Baher, but no more. Then she went into details about zoning percentages, projected public building construction, and new road plans for the neighborhood. No one seemed to pay any attention. It was nothing personal; City Council meetings often took on a bazaar-like atmosphere, with loud conversation between members, their aides, and the many visitors who came to the sessions—and with little focus on the official business of the day.

One councilperson, Sara Kaminker, of the left-wing Meretz Party, was listening carefully to Barzacci, however. After the presentation, Kaminker, well-known as an advocate of Palestinian rights in Jerusalem, was so enraged by what she had heard that she woke the mayor, demanding an explanation of the limitations on construction in Arab neighborhoods. If there were indeed such limitations, Kaminker said, then it proved Palestinian claims that they were discriminated against in Jerusalem.

Kollek, now well rested, did not miss a beat. He acknowledged the existence of a policy "followed by all governments since 1967" that restricted Arab growth in east Jerusalem by setting a strict limit on the number of new homes built in their neighborhoods. He then brushed aside further questions on the matter, and the meeting moved on to other concerns.

No other council member at the February 1993 meeting took note of the mayor's pronouncement, despite its being the first time an Israeli official—and not just any official but the mayor of Jerusalem himself—had publicly acknowledged the existence of a policy to ensure Israel's demographic superiority in Jerusalem.[1] Twenty-six years after east Jerusalem came under Israeli rule, discrimination against Palestinian development had become a way of life in Jerusalem. It no longer raised eyebrows and only rarely sparked protest from Israelis, except when a few peace activists or left-wingers like Kaminker made a little noise about the issue. Kaminker, a Jewish-American immigrant to Israel who worked as a Jerusalem municipality city planner before being elected to the council, lost her seat after just one term. This served as an important political lesson for Israeli leaders: supporting Palestinian rights in Jerusalem, no matter how worthy a cause, was political suicide. There was no better way to alienate Israeli voters.

The strict limits on Arab housing starts is, in fact, a poorly kept secret in Jerusalem. A good number of city officials make decisions, day in and day out, based on these limits. Most of them, however, do

Neighborhood	Existing units	Potential units	Units planned
Beit Hanina-Shuafat	4,500	12,000	7,500
Issawiya	700	1,500	800
Sheikh Jarrah	1,100	1,900	800
Wadi Joz	900	900	0
A-Tur	1,230	1,230	0
Silwan	1,200	1,200	0
Ras al-Amud	1,240	1,800	560
Abu Tur and Jabal Mukaber	1,400	1,750	350
Arab A-Sawarha	1,120	1,900	780
Sur Baher	990	2,350	1,360
Beit Safafa	800	2,700	1,900
Wadi Hilweh	400	500	100
Shuafat R.C.	1,300	1,300	0
Kafr Akab	590	1,300	710

not even realize it. Take the Jerusalem municipality report, "Potential Housing Construction in Jerusalem," which outlines the housing situation in east Jerusalem.[2] The report includes a one-page, relatively harmless-looking table. Only when one starts inquiring about what exactly the title of the column "Potential units" refers to does one begin to understand Israel's housing policy in Jerusalem.

"Potential units" (see table) does not mean the potential number of units that could be built in each neighborhood, based on certain assumptions about required space, city services, traffic patterns, and so on. The municipality did not carry out an urban planning study to determine such a number. Instead, "Potential units" refers to the maximum number of units the Israeli administration had determined could be built in each Arab neighborhood without precipitating a change in the ratio of Arabs to Jews in the city population.

In Jerusalem, Israel turned urban planning into a tool of the government, to be used to help prevent the expansion of the city's non-

Jewish population. It was a ruthless policy, if only for the fact that the needs (to say nothing of the rights) of Palestinian residents were ignored. In 1967 east Jerusalem was largely without zoning. After the war, when Israel took on the job of adopting zoning plans, in theory this should have been an important step toward improving development and preventing haphazard construction in east Jerusalem. Zoning plans are supposed to reflect the social and economic needs and resources of particular neighborhoods and the city as a whole. There can be differences of opinion about what zoning plan to adopt, if, for instance, there are disagreements over where to allow businesses to be built, how many stories buildings should be permitted to rise, and where roads and highways should go. These issues at times naturally spark disputes between residents and the authorities, particularly when economic or social interests are at stake.

In east Jerusalem, however, the stakes were different. Israel saw the adoption of strict zoning plans as a way of limiting the number of new homes built in Arab neighborhoods, and thereby ensuring that the Arab percentage of the city's population—28.8 in 1967 when Israel took control of the city—did not grow beyond this level. Allowing "too many" new homes in Arab neighborhoods would mean "too many" Arab residents in the city. The idea was to move as many Jews as possible into east Jerusalem, and move as many Arabs as possible out of the city entirely.[3] Israeli housing policy in east Jerusalem was all about this numbers game. Israel believed that the more Jews it moved into east Jerusalem, the stronger its hold on that part of the city. Israel saw each new Jewish neighborhood in east Jerusalem as another insurance policy against the re-division of the city.

The ironic thing, if you can maintain a sense of irony when dealing with such a serious issue, is that Israeli officials today know their job is to limit the growth of the Arab population of the city, but many do not know who gave the original order to do so. They all have seen the reports detailing the limitations on growth in Arab east Jerusalem and even wrote new reports based on the concept that the Arab population must not be allowed to grow in proportion to the Jewish population. But few seem to know the origin of this policy.

It takes some digging, and access to Israeli government documents, to find the answer. An odd secrecy was maintained around Israel's housing policy in the years just after the 1967 war that continues to this day. Dozens of officials were directly involved in the decision-making process, and hundreds more were also indirectly aware of the decisions through involvement in their implementation. But meetings on the subject were top secret. Letters and minutes were classified, and in only very few written documents was it explicitly stated that the development being pushed in east Jerusalem was exclusively Jewish. Not that anyone needed some great source to discover this fact. As the new Jewish neighborhoods went up in east Jerusalem, from Neveh Ya'acov in the north to Gilo in the south, it was clear that Israel was promoting exclusively Jewish development and hampering Arab growth in Jerusalem.

After the war, Israel's housing policy was spelled out clearly in a number of secret reports and correspondences. One report commissioned by the Jerusalem municipality in 1969 gives forecasts for population growth in Jerusalem.[4] The report states that the forecasts are based on the government's policy of hampering Arab growth and encouraging Jewish growth in the city. The report was aimed at outlining future transportation needs, but such predictions also required forecasts on population growth. "The city will have in 1985 a population of about 500,000, of which 80 percent will be Jewish," the report stated. It went on to explain that this prediction was based "on the assumption that the non-Jewish population growth will drop off, and the Jewish population will grow by 3 percent to 4 percent a year, as recommended [by the government]."

An Israeli government report from several years later is even more specific: "Since the Six Day War a great emphasis has been placed on the fast development of Jerusalem. Under the instruction of Prime Minister Golda Meir it was decided that the relation between the Jewish and Arab populations [in Jerusalem] would be held steady. For that reason, an annual growth rate of 4 percent was set for the Jewish population."[5] The report was very specific about Israel's goals for its housing policy in east Jerusalem: "Just as the rate of population growth must be set, so too must the distribution of the population be determined with the aim of establishing a physical reality that guarantees Jewish superiority in the capital. The distribution of the population must be such that it prevents the physical division of the city in any way." In other words, the goal was not simply demographic balance. Israel believed that if Jewish growth was restricted to west Jerusalem, and Arab growth to east Jerusalem, it would set the stage for the city's re-division. Israel wanted Jews to be the majority in east as well as west Jerusalem, hoping this demographic reality would prevent the city from being divided again between Israel and an Arab state.

Kollek himself revealed some of the specifics of Israel's attempt to obtain demographic superiority in east Jerusalem in a letter to a government minister in 1976—at a point when Israel was beginning to realize that it had a battle not only with the Arab sector's housing starts but also with its birth rate.[6] Arab families in Jerusalem were simply outstripping their Jewish counterparts in the number of children they were bringing into the world, and this was creating problems for Israel's housing policy. Kollek noted that the Jewish population was falling short of its targeted growth levels after the Six Day War, whereas the Arab population was growing at a fast clip. He complained to the minister, "It was decided [after the Six Day War] on an annual growth rate of 4 percent for the Jewish sector, but in fact the Jewish population has grown by only 3 percent each year, compared to 5 percent in the Arab sector."

The letter was sparked by the government's decision to begin construction on a new Jewish community to the west of Jerusalem. Kollek charged that the community, Mevasseret Tsion, would draw Jewish families away from the capital. "We talk a lot nowadays about the growth of the Jewish population of Jerusalem compared to the fast pace of the growth of the Arab population. But we are acting in ways that will achieve the opposite of what we want. It is wrong to be encouraging the [Jewish] population to leave Jerusalem," the mayor wrote. He also protested to other ministers. But in the end, he could not stop the bulldozers from going to work on Mevasseret Tsion. Kollek was left to bemoan what he saw as the government's counterproductive housing policies in Jerusalem and its environs, which were endangering Israel's quest for demographic superiority in all parts of Jerusalem.

Hassan Abu Assaleh is a Palestinian who saw from close up Israel's discriminatory development policy in Jerusalem. A quiet, soft-spoken city planner, Assaleh worked for the Jordanian municipality of east Jerusalem before 1967. After the war, he continued working for the city, now under Israeli authority. His philosophy was to leave the major battles to others and use his position to help, as much as he could, individual fellow Palestinians living in the city. Dozens of Palestinian residents frequent his fourth-floor cubicle at city hall daily with questions about how they can realize their dreams of having a home in Jerusalem. Assaleh is from Sur Baher, the Arab neighborhood whose limitations on housing construction were described by city engineer Barzacci.

For Assaleh, the systematic limitations on Palestinian development was old news. He had seen, from the inside, how growth was limited in Palestinian neighborhoods. Usually he kept quiet; as a municipal employee, he was forbidden from taking part in political protests. But on one occasion, he could not restrain himself from speaking out. Not surprisingly, it involved an incident in his own village.

Sur Baher may be a neighborhood from a municipal point of view, but from an architectural, urban, and social perspective it is more accurately described as a village. There are no apartment buildings, row houses, or any other form of urban housing development in Sur Baher. Instead, the community, on a scenic ridge in south Jerusalem, is a collection of Arab-style one-, two-, and in rare cases three-story homes, many surrounded with gardens or small courtyards. The single well-paved road running though the village center is narrow and difficult for opposing traffic to navigate. All the other roads are poorly paved at best, and many are simply dirt paths.

Before 1967, Sur Baher was one of a handful of isolated Arab vil-

lages between Jerusalem and Bethlehem. Then in 1970 Israel expropriated the land around Sur Baher from its Arab owners. The hillsides adjoining Sur Baher where villagers once grazed their livestock
and harvested olive and citrus groves were uprooted by Israeli bulldozers. Ten years later, villagers looked out their windows and saw
the concrete encompass of the new Jewish neighborhood of East
Talpiot, which was built on the bulk of the expropriated land. But
the small tract west of the village remained undeveloped.

The villagers did not allow the land to stand idle. They continued to maintain their family orchards there. The Israeli government,
fearing that the trees would form the basis for the villagers to reclaim
the land, ordered the orchards uprooted.[7] The decision to destroy
the trees was too much for Assaleh. He decided it was time to break
his silence. Using his connections both within the village and among
Israelis he met through his work at city hall, he began to organize
against the expropriation. Assaleh even managed to draw Jewish
residents of East Talpiot into the protest. For the moment, it was forgotten that the East Talpiot residents lived on land that had been expropriated from the village. Palestinians and Jews stood side by side
at the Sur Baher orchards demanding that the trees be left alone.

The joint Palestinian-Israel demonstrations forced the local and
national authorities to rethink the move. Several city officials suggested that as a gesture of good will to the Palestinians Israel should
allow them to build on the land, as they had long demanded. This
view was rejected, on grounds it would create a dangerous prece-
dent. But when the villagers threatened to take their case to Israel's
Supreme Court, the authorities, fearing a court defeat, offered a
compromise. The orchards could remain, they said, but on condition
that the Palestinians acknowledge that this fact did not imply that
plans by Israel to develop the land were scrapped. Assaleh and village leaders—themselves wary of the outcome of a High Court appeal—eventually agreed to the deal. Sur Baher residents were able to
keep their orchards, knowing that some day Israel would again try
to destroy them.

Development in Sur Baher was closely watched by the Israeli authorities, as it was in the rest of Arab east Jerusalem. The urban planner hired by city hall to come up with a zoning plan for the village was given strict orders not to go beyond the permitted number of new homes.[8] He was told—in accordance with the "Potential Housing Construction in Jerusalem" report—that the limit on new homes was set at 2,350. He was also given another strict limitation: only build in already built-up areas. Arab housing could not be expanded to land surrounding the village.

Planners with the city's engineering office, when drawing the zoning boundaries for the Arab neighborhoods, limited them to already built-up areas. Adjoining open areas were either zoned "green," to signify they were off-limits to development, or left unzoned until they were needed for the construction of Jewish housing projects. The map the Sur Baher planner received from the city engineer's office reflected this policy. The only open areas he was given to zone were those between already existing homes in Sur Baher.

The planner was infuriated by the guidelines. By confining Sur Baher to such a small area, the only way 2,350 homes could be built would be too add extra stories on existing buildings. He believed this would destroy the village's charm, and so he went to Barzacci, the city engineer, and asked that he be given several dunams of "green" land nearby. Barzacci's answer was an emphatic no.

The reason for her refusal goes back to the first years of Israeli rule in east Jerusalem. The newly annexed part of the city provided challenge and adventure for Israel. East Jerusalem was Israel's Wild West. The hustle and bustle of the Old City and adjoining business district of Salah A-Din and Sultan Suleiman streets stood in sharp contrast to the undeveloped and largely barren outlying areas that had also been annexed to the city. Israel had purposely drawn the city's new, expanded boundaries to include the maximum territory possible, with the minimum possible Palestinian population. Israel foresaw the potential the undeveloped land held for building homes for tens of thousands of Jews in east Jerusalem. Israeli officials rushed to put together development projects aimed at achieving these goals. Both the local and national government were in-

Name	Total area (dunams)*	Jewish-owned (dunams)	Arab-owned (dunams)	State-owned (dunams)
East Talpiot	4,400	500	3,400	500
Neveh Ya'acov	700	150	500	50
Kalandia A	1,300	0	0	1,300
Shema'ah neighborhood	120	50	0	70
Tel-Ful	2,500	550	1,500	450
Shuafat and Beit Hanina	4,000	0	3,000	1,000
Beit Safafa	150	25	125	0
Malha and Sharafat	3,500	250	2,000	1,250
Kalandia B	1,100	0	0	1,100
Total	17,700	1,025	10,525	12,925

*A dunam is equal to one-quarter acre.

volved. There were differences of opinion, but overall there was agreement on the need to build quickly and move as many Jews as possible into east Jerusalem.

Kollek spearheaded the effort by Israel to settle east Jerusalem with Jewish families. In 1970 Kollek coauthored the proposal for development in east Jerusalem that became the basis for Israeli policy for the next decade.[9] Indeed, the 1970 Kollek plan contains the principles upon which Israeli housing policy in east Jerusalem is based to this day—expropriation of Arab-owned land, development of large Jewish neighborhoods in east Jerusalem, and limitations on development in Arab neighborhoods. In the 1970 proposal, Kollek recommended the expropriation of land at nine different locations in east Jerusalem (see table). "This proposal is based on the need to prepare a reserve of suitable land, in addition to the land already in the hands of the [Israel Lands] Authority today that included over 4,000 dunams for housing construction, public buildings and industry, that will be needed for the coming 10 to 12 years," Kollek wrote in the proposal.

Though the fact that the vast majority of the land proposed for expropriation was Arab-owned was clear from the figures, what was not stated was that all the development would occur in the Jewish sector. In all, Kollek wanted some 17,700 dunams expropriated, 12,925 of it Arab-owned. He singled out four sites as being the most urgent for development: Neveh Ya'acov, in north Jerusalem, where the land was slated for a new Jewish neighborhood; East Talpiot, next to the former U.N. headquarters in southeast Jerusalem, for another new Jewish neighborhood; Kalandia, a refugee camp also in north Jerusalem, the adjoining lands of which were earmarked for an industrial area; and the Shema'ah neighborhood, near Mount Zion and the Old City, for the development of a park. Kollek emphasized in presenting the plan that all the land was within Jerusalem's new city limits and that none of it apparently belonged to city churches or the Wakf—the Muslim religious authority—which might have the influence to torpedo an expropriation plan by rallying international condemnation.

Kollek was not alone in pushing the 1970 proposal, or other plans for Israeli development in east Jerusalem after the 1967 war. The Israeli government set up a variety of forums to coordinate development in Jerusalem. The most influential was the Ministerial Committee on Jerusalem, which was headed by the prime minister and included the ministers holding central portfolios related to development. Kollek was a nonvoting member, as he was not a minister, but his influence there was great. Just two months after Kollek presented his proposal to the government, it was brought before the Ministerial Committee for discussion. Prime Minister Golda Meir resided over the meeting, on May 12, 1970.[10] Without opposition, the four sites earmarked for immediate expropriation in the proposal were accepted by the committee.

Some government ministers wanted more. Agriculture minister Shimon Peres suggested that a fifth site, Kalandia B in north Jerusalem, be expropriated. Peres said the 1,300 dunams at the site could provide a possible new home for Israel Aircraft Industries (IAI), at the time located near Tel Aviv. Kalandia B was named for the nearby refugee camp, Kalandia, which adjoined Jerusalem's Atarot Airport. Peres told the committee it was the ideal location for the IAI factory, the pride of the Israeli war machine that had helped secure the devas-

tating victory in 1967. Kalandia was in areas annexed to the city after the war. By moving the factory there, Peres believed that Israel
could further demonstrate its intentions of never giving up east Jerusalem.

Kollek did not say anything immediately about Peres' comments.
He remembered seeing a map of the area and believed that Kalandia
B was not as close to the airport as Peres reported to the committee.
But he sat quietly. No decision was taken on Peres' proposal, and it
was decided to discuss the matter further at the upcoming cabinet
meeting. The next day, Kollek checked the maps again and consulted
with city officials familiar with the area. Peres, it turned out, was
badly mistaken. Kalandia B was 3 kilometers from the airport. The
mayor sent an urgent message to the prime minister: "There is no
possibility for creating a continuous band [of Israeli control] between the site [of Kalandia B] and the airport, as the land in between
is owned by [Muslim] welfare and religious organizations," from
whom the government would have difficulty expropriating. "The
only way to expand in areas adjoining the airport is in land that is
part of the [occupied] territories, outside the city's boundaries. In
light of this, I believe we must rethink the matter of the area
called Kalandia B, and I myself recommend we not expropriate the
area."[11]

Kollek's recommendation was accepted by the prime minister. IAI
remained where it was. Years later Israel discovered that it was
saved a lot of headaches by those 3 kilometers that made it undesir-
able to move the aircraft industries to north Jerusalem. In principle,
Kollek supported Peres' proposal to move IAI to Jerusalem. The
mayor's objection at the time was purely a planning consideration,
and he continued to push for the government to move one of its large
military factories to the Atarot Industrial Zone, which adjoined the
airport.

The industrial zone was surrounded by Arab neighborhoods and
villages. Israeli workers driving to their jobs in the zone frequently
found themselves the target of attack by stone-throwing Arab
youths. Given these conditions, Israel had difficulty convincing businesses to set up shop at Atarot. Major tax breaks were offered to

attract the few factories that would even consider the move. The military industries had strong unions, and their workers were not interested in moving to Jerusalem. No one in the government was particularly keen on the idea either, at least not keen enough to make it happen.

It took a tough U.S. stand on Israeli development in east Jerusalem to finally put the idea to rest. In 1987, U.S. Ambassador to Israel Thomas Pickering informed Israel of his government's firm decision that aid to Israel not be used to build or operate factories located in the occupied territories. In the U.S. view, east Jerusalem was included in that definition. "The U.S. had adopted measures to implement our long-standing policy against use of United States government funds for contract performance in the occupied territories," Pickering informed Israel.[12] Pickering made clear that this U.S. policy was not new but in the future would be more strictly enforced. The message was first sent to the Israel Defense Ministry, and from there to Kollek. "In light [of the U.S. policy], moving IAI to Atarot would greatly hurt our ability to sell and market in the United States," the ministry informed the mayor, burying a project he had pushed for nearly two decades.[13]

Little stood in the way of Israel's developing east Jerusalem as it saw fit, in the years directly following the Six Day War. Construction crews worked throughout east Jerusalem on new Jewish neighborhoods, as the government cleared the way for building by cutting bureaucratic red tape that in normal circumstances made development a slow process in Israel. The government put its full weight behind the 1970 Kollek plan. Senior officials from an array of government ministries also ensured that the plan got off the ground quickly and smoothly. The prime minister was firmly supportive. Meir Shamgar, the attorney-general, took personal charge of the expropriations; he would later become the president of Israel's Supreme Court and one of the most respected legal figures in the country. Few people associate him with the now often condemned expropriation of Arab land in Jerusalem. Meron Benvenisti, Kollek's close assistant who helped the mayor shape his overall policy on east Jerusalem, also played a key role. Benvenisti, too, is known as a champion of Palestinian rights, not as an implementor of Israel's controversial expropriation policy.

In mid-May 1970 Shamgar gathered senior government officials in his Jaffa Street office in central Jerusalem to discuss the pending expropriation of Arab land in east Jerusalem. Kollek and Benvenisti were also present.[14] The meeting was shrouded in secrecy, and the minutes were stamped "classified." Shamgar opened by noting that "in order to put together concrete proposals to implement the government approved expropriations, we need more details concerning the designated areas and their boundaries, including details on land ownership and the funds necessary to carry out the expropriation." The Housing Ministry and Israel Lands Authority were delegated the job of drawing up the maps and locating the owners. The two bodies, together with the chief state assessor, were to determine the costs of the expropriations. The maps and figures compiled were to be presented to the Finance Ministry, and only afterward to the government for final approval. Shamgar left nothing to chance.

Shamgar also touched on another controversial issue at the meeting—the severe shortage of housing for Arab residents of Jerusalem. Shamgar broached this delicate subject by noting that "it would be desirable that in the housing plans being drawn up projects designated for Arab residents of Jerusalem be included." But he did not push the point. There was no further discussion of the issue at the meeting.

The official protocols of the various government committees and subcommittees discussing development in east Jerusalem during this period did not explicitly mention that all the work being done was for Jewish development. But the fact was that the Housing Ministry was building infrastructure for Jewish housing projects, not Arab housing projects. The new roads being built by the Transport Ministry were meant to serve the new Jewish neighborhoods. Development for the Arabs in east Jerusalem was an afterthought, at best. The Israeli government sponsored only two small housing projects for Arab residents of Jerusalem. One was outside the city, and it reflected Israel's desire to get Arabs to move to the West Bank more than any concern to ease their housing crunch. The other was the Nusseiba Project in east Jerusalem. The approximately four hundred apartments in these small projects were plenty for the Arab population of the entire city, according to Israel's thinking. This, while thousands of apartments were built for the Jewish population.

Israel even insisted on having a say as to who would live at the Nusseiba Project.[15] Israeli Arabs were given preference over Arabs from the West Bank and east Jerusalem who did not have Israeli citizenship. Israel wanted tight control of even the little bit of development it allowed for Arabs in east Jerusalem. In particular, Israel did not want to undermine its basic strategy of trying to force Palestinians living in Jerusalem to move to the West Bank by allowing Arabs already in the West Bank to move to the city.

Another in the series of secret meetings on east Jerusalem development occurred in August of 1970. Shamgar called together the same forum that met in May, this time to discuss the payment of compensation to Arab landowners whose property was being taken by the government. "In previous expropriations in Jerusalem no one was ever compensated," Shamgar noted.[16] "The major reason for this was that the Arab landowners were not willing to request compensation. But even given this, we must take into consideration that no action was taken to encourage landowners to receive the compensation they were due." Shamgar wanted the government to initiate payments and not wait for the Arab landowners to request money.

The attorney-general called on the government to set up an office in east Jerusalem to be responsible for notifying the owners of their rights to compensation, and to establish a 2 million lira ($60,000) fund to cover payment costs. Shamgar did not leave any detail untouched. He even insisted that the government make arrangements for payments in Jordanian dinars, as many of the landowners resided in Jordan, and in other denominations for owners elsewhere. But this special arrangement never really materialized—and not because of any failure on Israel's part. Arab landowners in east Jerusalem for the most part continued to refuse to accept compensation for their expropriated property. In the eyes of the Arab world, acceptance of money from Israel constituted recognition of Israeli rule in east Jerusalem, which amounted to treason.

Several days after the August meeting, the Israeli cabinet convened to discuss ways to further speed up construction of Jewish neighborhoods in east Jerusalem. The cabinet decided to establish a special ministerial committee with the authority to issue building permits, thus avoiding delay in the various local and national planning boards. Shamgar called his forum on east Jerusalem together the next day, to fine-tune the government's decision. The forum decided to set up a shadow committee of local and ministerial building and planning officials to advise the government committee. Shamgar also ordered his own office to begin drafting the necessary legislation that would allow the new government committee on building in east Jerusalem to circumvent the normal building approval process.

Kollek was appointed to head this new committee. This move put Kollek at the forefront of Israel's housing policy in east Jerusalem, at a time when the biggest wave of Israeli development in lands annexed to the city after the 1967 war was about to begin. The appointment solidified Kollek's central position in implementing Israel's expropriation and development policy in east Jerusalem.

Everything was now set for work to begin. It was indeed remarkable. In the years just after the 1967 war Israel remained a heavily centralized, bureaucratic society. But the nation's leaders knew how to get things done within this bureaucracy when they wanted. Nowhere in the country were Israelis more excited by the 1967 victory than in Jerusalem. In Jerusalem in particular Israel was determined to act quickly and prevent a reversal of the gains made in the war. The vigor and intensity with which new Jewish neighborhoods were built in east Jerusalem echoed that shown by the nation when it fought the war itself.

By 1968, work had began on the first of two new Jewish neighborhoods in east Jerusalem, Ramot Eshkol and Ma'alot Dafna. A little over a year later, in March 1970, Kollek made his recommendations on east Jerusalem to the government. In May 1970, Kollek's recommendations were adopted by the ministerial committee and then passed on to the government for final approval. By September, detailed plans for two more new Jewish neighborhoods in east Jerusalem were completed. The one in the north, Neveh Ya'acov, was meant to house some 50,000 Jewish residents.[17] The one in the south, East Talpiot, was earmarked for 15,000 Jewish residents.[18]

Neveh Ya'acov was slated to be built on 3,200 dunams of land, most of which was expropriated from Arab residents of nearby Shuafat and Beit Hanina. Some 14,500 homes, mostly apartment units, were planned. All of the new Jewish neighborhoods were designed down to the last details—although for budgetary reasons the plans themselves were never followed through completely. The intention was to build not only homes but everything else a neighborhood needed. Nothing was left to chance—or even the market—to determine. "The Program," as officials called the detailed neighborhood plan for Neveh Ya'acov, called for the construction of 40 kindergarten classes, 11 elementary schools, 10 day-care centers, 10 mother and infant centers, 4 clinics, a community center, central park, soccer field, synagogues, post office, gas station, and a movie theater. The location of each building was mapped out. A timetable was established for construction.

East Talpiot was a smaller neighborhood, covering 1,800 dunams. Nevertheless, "The Program" for East Talpiot was as detailed as the one for Neveh Ya'acov: 24 kindergartens in 12 two-classroom buildings, 4 elementary schools, a high school, a library, 3 day-care centers, a community center, park, shopping area, and gas station. Even a wedding hall was included in the plan. Israel wanted to establish well-rounded communities with everything residents might require.

Meanwhile, government officials said that there was not enough money available for developing Arab neighborhoods. That was hard for Arab residents to accept, when they saw the beautiful communities being built for their new Jewish neighbors.

Kollek was more concerned with international reaction to Israel's rushing to build Jewish neighborhoods in east Jerusalem than with complaints by Arab residents. He invested much time and effort into trying to put Israel in a good light. He had good reason to be concerned. In general, the world condemned the occupation of lands taken in the 1967 war, including east Jerusalem. At the United Nations, the Arab states together with other nonaligned nations had an easy time passing a series of resolutions after the war calling for Israel to return the land. The United States and many European nations tacitly and sometimes openly supported the resolutions.[19]

Israel had hoped the international community, and particularly the United States, would at least differentiate between east Jerusalem and the West Bank. The U.N. partition plan of 1947 placed Jerusalem under international rule, and Jordan's conquest of east Jerusalem in 1948 never received the international legitimacy the Hashemite Kingdom wanted. In 1949 the U.N. even adopted a resolution, General Assembly Resolution 303, calling for Jerusalem to be put under international auspices. Jordan ignored the resolution.

After 1967, Israel went ahead with development in east Jerusalem despite repeated calls by the U.N. to halt, on the grounds that such action was forbidden by international law. U.N. Security Council Resolution 267, adopted on July 3, 1969, explicitly "censures in the strongest terms all measures taken to change the status of the City of Jerusalem."[20] The resolution also "urgently calls once more upon Israel to rescind forthwith all measures taken by it which may tend to change the status of the City of Jerusalem, and in future to refrain from all actions that are likely to have such an effect." The resolution singled out expropriation of land for condemnation and even warned it would take undisclosed action if Israel did not comply.

Several days before the resolution was adopted, the U.S. ambassador to the U.N. again made clear the United States' disapproval of Israeli policy in east Jerusalem. "We understand the deep emotional concerns which move the parties to the Arab-Israeli dispute on the subject of Jerusalem," the ambassador said in a statement to the U.N. Security Council. "We do not believe, however, that any of those concerns are served by what is now taking place in east Jerusalem . . . The expropriation and confiscation of land, the construction of housing on such land, the demolition or confiscation of buildings, including those of historic or religious significance, and the application of Israeli law to occupied portions of the city are detrimental to the common interests in the city." The ambassador's statement continued:

> The United States considers that the part of Jerusalem that came under the control of Israel in the June 1967 war, like other areas occupied by Israel, is occupied territory and hence subject to the provisions of international law governing the right and obligations of an occupying Power. Among the provisions of international law which bind Israel, as they would bind any occupier, are the provisions that the occupier has no right to make changes in laws or in administration other than those which are temporarily necessitated by his security interests, and that an occupier may not confiscate or destroy private property. The pattern of behavior authorized under the Geneva Convention of 12 August 1949 and international law is clear: the occupier must maintain the occupied area as intact and unaltered as possible, without interfering with the customary life of the area, and any changes must be necessitated by the immediate needs of the occupation. I regret to say that the actions by Israel in the occupied portion of Jerusalem present a different picture, one which gives rise to understandable concern that the eventual disposition of East Jerusalem may be prejudiced, and that the private rights and activities of the population are already being affected and altered.

The U.N. and the United States—which to this day do not officially recognize Israeli rule in east Jerusalem—were not going to stop Israel, however. Plans moved forward in Jerusalem for additional expropriations and new construction of Jewish neighborhoods. Kollek, knowing that the plans for new Jewish neighborhoods in east Jerusalem would be met with a wave of international condemnation, recommended that the foreign ministry prepare its officials for the onslaught.[21] Ever conscious of world opinion, Kollek suggested that the exact figures on the expropriations be gathered, as well as details about the plans to compensate the Arab landowners. Kollek wanted to emphasize to the world that some of the land being expropriated was slated for factories that would also provide jobs for Arab residents. He offered to put the municipality at the ministry's service for any information needed about building plans in east Jerusalem.

Kollek believed that Israel was particularly justified in its expropriations of the East Talpiot area, because between 1948 and 1967 the area was part of the demilitarized zone. Jordan and Israel had divided the zone into two parts, with Israel getting the western half and Jordan the eastern. Kollek reasoned that as the area had never been under Jordanian rule, there was no reason why, even under Geneva Convention regulations concerning occupied territory, Israel should be prevented from developing the area. Indeed, this was in general the Israeli defense of its development in east Jerusalem—that Jordanian rule in the city was never recognized internationally, which meant Israel could not be accused of occupying another country's territory.

Rather than slowing Israel's building efforts in Jerusalem, the international condemnations seemed to speed them up. Israel did, however, show sensitivity to Muslim and Christian interests in Jerusalem. When Israel discovered its planners had included lands and even buildings belonging to religious groups in its expropriations, attempts to make amends were swiftly undertaken. For instance, the Foreign Ministry in May 1970 sent an urgent message to the Ministerial Committee on Jerusalem requesting the reversal of an expropriation of a 35-dunam tract that belonged to an Italian doctor, Professor Luigi Gidada, on the Mount of Olives. Professor Gidada was a personal acquaintance of the Pope. The Vatican had lodged a protest over the move with the Israeli Embassy in Rome. The Israeli foreign ministry was also concerned with the possible international repercussions of the planned expropriation of a lot belonging to the Latin church on Mount Scopus, and land belonging to Frères College for Boys.

At the end of June, Shamgar called a meeting at his office to discuss the protests against the expropriations by various Christian and Muslim organizations. Kollek was present.[22] Shamgar, Kollek, and the other senior government officials were sensitive to the protests but at the same time did not want to allow them to wreck their development plans in east Jerusalem. It was decided that, with regard to Frères College for Boys, talks would be initiated in which Israel would take the position that the land was already slated for expropriation during the period of the British Mandate, before 1948, and that under Jordanian rule it was zoned off-limits for development. If the college insisted on holding onto the land and refused an offer of another lot in exchange, the expropriation would not be carried out, Shamgar's forum decided. They also decided to cancel the expropriation order for the Latin church's land on the Mount of Olives.

In the case of claims made by the Syrian Patriarch, however, they had a problem: Israel had already built on land expropriated from the church. The only option was to offer the church another plot elsewhere in exchange, or financial compensation. The Israeli authorities also recognized that they had made a mistake when expropriating an old Ottoman-period building in the Old City that later turned out to belong to the Muslim Wakf. The mistake was made during the expropriation and eviction of Arab families in the Old City to allow for the Jewish Quarter to be rebuilt. But the Wakf building was not part of the plan, and there was no reason to keep it, so it was returned to the Muslim authority. Such mix-ups are not surprising if one considers the speed with which Israel's development plans in east Jerusalem were carried out.

The fast pace of development was creating serious problems for the Jerusalem municipality. "The Program" for each of the new Jewish neighborhoods spoke of the importance of building self-sufficient new communities. In reality, however, the government was putting most of its money into building homes. Other projects, such as schools, community centers, commercial centers, and parks, were put on the back burner. The goal was to bring as many Jewish families to east Jerusalem as quickly as possible. The government was less concerned that these families would be without some basic services for awhile.

For Kollek and the municipality, however, this was a big concern. Complaints about the lack of schools and synagogues were being lodged with city hall, not with the national government. The residents were pressing the municipality for action, and the municipality in turn tried to press the national government, largely to no avail. The government's priorities were in building homes for Jews. The extras, in the government's view, could wait.

In 1992 the Jerusalem municipality hired a leading Israeli urban planner, Ze'ev Baran, to draw up a zoning plan for the north Jerusalem neighborhood of Kafr Akab. Baran was given the number of "potential units" allowed and was sent on his way to begin work. He quickly discovered, however, that already more homes existed in Kafr Akab than were officially permitted. If he held to the strict municipality guidelines, he would have to draw up a zoning plan for the neighborhood that allowed for no more home construction.

How had Kafr Akab managed to surpass its limitation of homes without the Israeli authorities noticing? Officially, construction in neighborhoods without zoning plans, such as Kafr Akab, was forbidden. There were many Arab neighborhoods in this category. But the Arab residents still built. Mostly, they did so illegally, without obtaining building permits. In a few cases exceptions were made and permits were granted, using a loophole in the building code which allowed permits to be issued when a neighborhood had no zoning plan, so long as the process of drawing up a zoning plan had not yet begun. But if the process of drawing up a zoning plan was under way, it was then forbidden to make any exceptions to the no-permit policy. In another neighborhood, Jabal Mukaber, the city had begun drawing up a zoning plan in 1984 and had stopped issuing permits. Over a decade later, the zoning plan had yet to be approved, meaning that for over ten years there had been no way to build legally in the neighborhood. Still, the loophole provided relief for some Palestinian residents, and in fact became so popular that the municipality had maps drawn up indicating where zoning work had not begun and special permits could be issued.

The municipality had originally informed Baran that there were 590 housing units in Kafr Akab and that the limitation was 1,300. Baran, however, had bad experiences in the past with the city's es-

timates, and so he checked for himself. He sent in a team to literally count the number of housing units (including both single-family
homes and apartments) in Kafr Akab. The team was aided by ae-
rial photographs of the neighborhood. The total number of units
counted came to 1,300. Kafr Akab had indeed reached its limit.

Baran—who over the years had become a close associate of the
mayor—was furious. He knew that the reasoning behind the numbers had nothing to do with the traditional urban planning considerations for setting limitations on growth. Under normal considerations, many more homes would have been permitted in Kafr Akab.
The neighborhood had great growth potential, and there was no reasonable argument for blocking all new housing development. Baran
took his case directly to Kollek, and a meeting was called in Kollek's
office.

Barzacci, the city engineer, and Avraham Kahila, deputy mayor
for building and planning, also attended. The problem was especially difficult to solve because any step taken by city hall had to go
before the regional planning board, which was controlled by the
government. In the past, when the city approved zoning plans that
went above the limitation, the regional board rejected them. Kollek
and the city officials, however, also recognized that there was no
way a zoning plan could be adopted for Kafr Akab that allowed for
zero growth.

Barzacci suggested a possible solution: divide the neighborhood
into two parts, apply the limitation and new zoning plan to only one
part, and leave the other section for future zoning. The mayor and
deputy mayor bought the idea. But they knew it would be difficult
convincing the regional planning board. There were obvious holes in
the idea. It clearly meant exceeding the limit for the neighborhood
and creating an absurd situation in which development would be allowed in one half of the neighborhood. But Kollek believed he had
no choice but to try, and in the end the board approved. One half of
Kafr Akab was zoned, and construction was permitted. The other
half remained unzoned, and construction was forbidden. It took
four years for approval to be received, but that was not such a sur-

prise, as development plans in Arab neighborhoods were never a priority for the board.

The regional planning board—made up of representatives of several government ministries—was famous for blocking development projects in Palestinian communities in east Jerusalem. The board was the guardian of the limitation system. In Kafr Akab, it showed some compassion, but that was an exception. Most of the time the board was ruthless in its application of the policy to limit Arab housing construction in Jerusalem.

The residents of Beit Hanina and Shuafat learned the hard way about the regional planning board. The board, in its handling of the Beit Hanina–Shuafat zoning plan, also taught Kollek a lesson. Kollek knew full well when the neighborhoods' zoning plan was first presented to the board in 1980 that it violated the limitation system. The zoning proposal called for some 17,000 new units, while the limitation system capped the number of new units at 7,500. But the mayor reasoned that the area, in north Jerusalem, was the last large reserve of land left for Arab development in the city (as other Arab lands had been expropriated), and the most should be made of it. Kollek's thinking was that rules are often bent as circumstances dictate. In a country where "no" is never a no, the mayor felt there was room for an exception to be made with Beit Hanina–Shuafat. Plan Number 3,000, as the proposal was named, was also the first major zoning plan for east Jerusalem to be presented to the board, and the limitation system had not really been tested yet.

But when it came to helping Arabs in Jerusalem, Kollek and others at city hall quickly realized, the policy of "demographic balance" was unbending; no matter how good they believed the justification, no fudging would be tolerated.

Kollek wanted to believe that the zoning plan for Beit Hanina–Shuafat would prove to the world, and to east Jerusalem Palestinians, that he was indeed also working for their good. He was eventually beaten in 1980, when the board rejected the zoning plan allowing 17,000 new housing units in Beit Hanina–Shuafat, because the limitations system permitted only 7,500 new homes. But Kollek did not give up. He tried again four years later, cutting the total number of units by several thousands in the belief that this would satisfy the regional planning board. After the city's planning board approved the proposal—now listed as Plan 3000A—Kollek was so confident of victory that he threw a party to celebrate. Arab notables from east Jerusalem were invited to the City Council chambers for an official reception. Among those present was Sayid Amouri, from Shuafat, who had been an outspoken critic of Israel's housing policy in east Jerusalem. Kollek convinced Amouri that the authorities this time had done something good for the Arabs of east Jerusalem. With some coaxing from his host, Amouri agreed to be interviewed by one of the foreign television news teams that were present, and he put in a few good words about the Israeli authorities. The party was a success. Kollek and his aides foresaw a breakthrough in Arab-Israeli relations in the city.

Where Plan 3000A might have led we will never know, because the bubble burst a few months later. The regional planning board rejected the proposal, again on grounds that it violated the limit on new housing starts for the area.

Kollek was furious. The government had ripped an important victory for coexistence in the city out of his hands. At first, he would not take the district committee's no as an answer. He fought to push through the original plan. Then the bartering began. Kollek, who in 1980 started at 17,000 units and had already dropped to 14,000 in the second version of the plan presented in 1984, was forced to go lower. The mayor found a partner in these negotiations in the housing minister. The two sides exchanged proposals, haggled, and resubmitted positions again and again, until they finally reached a compromise: the zoning plan would allow for the construction of 10,000 new units.[23] This was considerably less than the city originally wanted but still more than the limit.

In return for being allowed to surpass the limit, Kollek agreed to remove about 20 percent of the area in the original plan. At issue was a strip of land bordering the neighborhoods to the west. The Housing Ministry was toying with plans to build Jewish housing projects there. The official reason given for removing the land from Beit Hanina–Shuafat was that it was along the city's border with the

West Bank and should therefore be kept off limits for Arab construction. Kollek agreed to the compromise. A letter was exchanged between the mayor and minister making the agreement official, and city planners went back to work on a new zoning plan, this time based on allowing 10,000 housing units in Beit Hanina–Shuafat.

The local planning board, which Kollek presided over, approved the plan, which kept its old title, 3000A. But the regional board again rejected it. Kollek had made a grave mistake. He forgot that while the Housing Ministry had much influence on the regional board, it did not have the final word. There were other ministries represented on the committee with which to contend, and enough of them were against breaking the limit to again defeat the plan.[24] So it was back to the drawing board at city hall. A disappointed Kollek was left with little choice. The Beit Hanina–Shuafat zoning plan was again revised, this time to include only 7,500 potential new homes, the maximum permitted under the limitation system.

It was not until 1994 that a new zoning plan—3000B—for Beit Hanina and Shuafat was approved by the district planning board. But residents still could not build legally. Israeli bureaucrats found another way to slow down construction for Arabs—by holding up implementation of the "detailed zoning plans" that must be drawn up after the overall zoning plan is approved. Those plans cost money, and not until 1996 was money allocated to begin working on them. Today, final approval is still awaited for the Beit Hanina–Shuafat zoning plan, over twenty years after it was first proposed.

To a small degree, delays were caused by Shuafat and Beit Hanina residents themselves. They petitioned the planning boards and courts, drawing out the approval process for Plan 3000B but in the end not getting anything changed. They were particularly upset with Kollek, who haggled with the government while the infrastructure and basic public services of their communities remained underdeveloped and growth was stunted.

Shuafat and Beit Hanina make up the northern finger of Jerusalem, reaching the city's border at A-Ram. The main road linking

Ramallah and Jerusalem runs through the heart of the two neighborhoods. Residents are among the most affluent in the city's Arab sector. The neighborhoods also have a large population of Israeli Arabs, who have come to live in Jerusalem since 1967. The Israeli Arab residents were at the forefront of the fight over the zoning plan. But their wealth and connections in Israeli society could do little when faced with the harsh policy of demographic balance. Where Kollek could not make much headway, the residents of Beit Hanina and Shuafat could not even get a hearing.

What made the case even more painful for the residents was that as they lost battle after battle in getting the plan approved, they watched two massive new Jewish neighborhoods go up on land expropriated from them just after the 1967 war. The neighborhoods, Pisgat Ze'ev and Neveh Ya'acov, were planned, constructed, and inhabited, with the eager support of the government, while neighboring Beit Hanina and Shuafat struggled to get a plan approved that would allow them merely to build their own homes. This was Israel's reunified Jerusalem—Pisgat Ze'ev and Neveh Ya'acov with new schools, parks, and synagogues to go along with the thousands of new apartments and homes, next to Shuafat and Beit Hanina, where for lack of a zoning plan it was difficult to get special permission to put up a single home.

Whether one agrees with the policies that stemmed from the numbers game Israel played in east Jerusalem, the logic in the equation, at least in the minds of Israeli policy-makers, is hard to deny. Since the time of the early Zionist movement, Jewish leaders have stressed the importance of physically staking claim to the land. The Zionists called this "putting facts on the ground," an expression which Israeli policy-makers continue to use to this day. The early Zionists were experts at putting up a "wall and watchtower" settlement under the cover of night, which Arab residents would discover the next morning. In east Jerusalem, Israel did not have to build in the dark. One new Jewish neighborhood after another has cropped up—from Ramot, Ramot Eshkol, French Hill, Pisgat Ze'ev, and Neveh Ya'acov in the north to East Talpiot and Gilo and now Har Homa in the south, again putting "facts on the ground" that the Arabs must face when making their claims on the city.

Israel used the bulldozer to stake its claim to east Jerusalem. But we have seen that it had another, even more powerful tool: the expropriation order. In 1967, just after the war, when Israeli Defense Force officers toured east Jerusalem, maps in hand, marking down the new borders of the united city, they had this tool in mind. The Israeli officers aimed to draw the city's new borders so as to include the maximum territory with the minimum Palestinian population. The undeveloped territory was where Israel wanted to settled tens of thousands of Jewish families. Before 1967, east and west Jerusalem together covered 38 square kilometers.[25] After the war and Israel's expansion of Jerusalem's borders, the city covered 108 square kilometers.[26] But there was still a problem. Much of the undeveloped land was owned by Arabs. This fact, however, did not slow the efforts of Israel to develop the land for Jewish growth. The government simply issued orders to expropriate much of the land, taking advantage of a legal system in Israel that gives owners little recourse against the authorities taking away private property, ostensibly for public use.

In January 1968 Israel carried out its first major expropriation in east Jerusalem. Some 3,345 dunams were taken from largely Arab landowners to build the Jewish neighborhood of Ramot Eshkol; 486 dunams were expropriated for Ma'alot Dafna.[27] Four months later, another 900 dunams of land was expropriated by the Israeli government in east Jerusalem—the bulk in the north for the Neveh Ya'acov neighborhood, and a smaller tract in the Old City.[28] But Israel's land grab in 1968 was nothing compared with the one that occurred at the end of August 1970, when eight separate expropriation orders were carried out, covering over 10,000 dunams of land in east Jerusalem. The largest expropriation was for the Ramot and Shuafat Ridge neighborhoods, which totaled 4,840 dunams, followed by 2,700 dunams for Gilo and 2,400 dunams for East Talpiot. The August 1970 expropriations also included 1,200 dunams for the industrial area in east Jerusalem, just north of Beit Hanina, which was later named Atarot, and a few small expropriations of several hundred dunam tracts at Mamilla, Ramat Rachel, and in the Hinnom Valley just outside the Old City.[29]

With that, the land grab halted for ten years, until March 1980, when Israel carried out its single largest expropriation in east Jerusalem, taking some 4,400 dunams from Arab landowners in Beit Hanina and Shuafat to build the Jewish neighborhood of Pisgat Ze'ev.[30] The move allowed Israel to complete a continuous line of Jewish settlement in northeast Jerusalem from Neveh Ya'acov to Pisgat Ze'ev to French Hill. Just over ten years later, in April 1991, Israel carried out its last major expropriation in east Jerusalem—taking some 1,850 dunams of land at Har Homa.[31]

Unlike in the previous expropriations, most of the land at Har Homa was owned not by Arabs but by a Jewish entrepreneur, David Meir, who had purchased a large tract with the hopes of developing it. There were also a number of other Jewish owners of small tracts. The government, however, preferred to expropriate the entire area—taking land from both Jewish and Arab landowners—to build a new Jewish neighborhood on the hilltop overlooking Bethlehem. Meir, a businessman with profit and not politics on his mind, over the years entered into an unofficial partnership with Palestinians whose land had also been expropriated, as well as with left-wing Israeli groups and Palestinian leaders in Jerusalem, in order to oppose the government's Har Homa project. They used every tactic imaginable, from staging demonstrations to Supreme Court appeals, in the effort to halt the project. They succeeded at first. But by spring 1996, the authorities gave the go-ahead to construct a Jewish neighborhood at Har Homa, and the bulldozers were brought in to begin work.

The Har Homa affair, at face value, seems like a clear-cut issue of balancing the needs of the state and the private entrepreneur. The government argued in the courts that it had no choice but to expropriate the land to carry out the large-scale development. The argument is a fair one. The large number of property owners in the area were not able, on their own, to agree on a joint building project.

Meir says that he has now done this, but that is arguable. In any event, viewing the issue at this level, it seems to be a simple case of state versus a private entrepreneur. But the question of Har Homa is in fact much more complicated.

The first question that must be asked is why were 1,850 dunams expropriated, instead of 1,200, or 800, or 2,000 even? Officials involved in the project say the consideration was never connected with the planning of the neighborhood. Rather, the idea was to expropriate as much undeveloped land as possible in the area, to prevent Palestinians from building. Israel was particularly concerned that Palestinian construction would eventually link up Palestinian villages in southern Jerusalem with the nearby West Bank towns of Beit Sahur and Bethlehem.

Publicly, Israel has portrayed Har Homa as an innocent development project, like the kind any city around the world would carry out to provide housing for its residents. Israeli leaders even hinted that part of Har Homa might go to homes for Arab families. Privately, however, Israeli officials have made clear that Har Homa will be the latest of the Jewish-only new neighborhoods built since 1967. The expropriation of 1,850 dunams at Har Homa was not meant just for the new neighborhood, which required far less land, but to prevent Palestinian development.

The planners have declined to speak on the record about this subject, but the protocols and correspondences between them on Har Homa dispel any doubts about the site's role in the larger Israeli policy of Palestinian containment. An example is a letter dated April 4, 1992, from Uzi Wexler, a senior local official close to Kollek, to then housing minister Ariel Sharon:

Honorable Minister,
As you recall, parts of Har Homa have been owned by Jews for dozens of years, but still not a single project that was initiated there was carried out. At our initiative, we arrived at an agreement with Himunata [a quasi-state-run property holder], which holds most of the Jewish owned land at Har Homa, and we developed a plan that could close a serious hole in south Jerusa-

lem. During the planning work, it turned out that Himunata indeed held most of the land, but there was still no choice but to expropriate about 225 dunams, in order to allow for a continuous strip of [Jewish] development . . . At a certain stage, the [Israel Lands] Authority . . . decided to expropriate 1,850 dunams, including several hundred dunams that cannot even be developed, but was done in order to "straighten the line" of the Jerusalem municipal border, as some of the land that was expropriated was in Jewish hands, but not a single holder. We believe that . . . only a minimal expropriation of around 275 dunams is necessary . . . As you know, the immediate battle is over the connection of Gilo with East Talpiot, via Givat Hamatos. If not, Beit Sahur and Sur Baher will become connected. This is not just another site that we can wait ten years to develop, in order to maximize profits, but a project that must be carried out immediately, this year.
With great respect,
Uzi Wexler

Israel's position on Har Homa is clearly defined in the letter. The threat was seen that Palestinian development would link a West Bank village (Beit Sahur) with a Jerusalem Arab neighborhood (Sur Baher), and every effort was made to prevent this. Israel instead wanted "a continuous strip of [Jewish] development" connecting the Jewish neighborhoods of East Talpiot and Gilo, by building new Jewish neighborhoods at Har Homa and the adjoining Givat Hamatos site. The decision to expropriate 1,850 dunams stood.

By the summer of 1996, with the strong support of the new government of Prime Minister Binyamin Netanyahu, it appeared the Jewish neighborhood of Har Homa would be built, and Israel would succeed in putting another "fact on the ground" in east Jerusalem.

In twenty-five years of rule in east Jerusalem, Israel expropriated a total of 23,378 dunams for the construction of nine Jewish neighborhoods. To understand the extent of the expropriations, consider that the total area of Jerusalem, west and east, is 123,000 dunams, of which over half, or 70,400 dunams, are lands annexed by Israel in 1967. Thus Israel had expropriated 33.2 percent of the territory of east Jerusalem for the construction of Jewish neighborhoods.

As with Har Homa, Israel, claiming that it was expropriating lands for construction, took large tracts of Arab land and then left them undeveloped for decades. The aim was not only to build homes for Jews in east Jerusalem but to prevent the Palestinians from building homes. For instance, in East Talpiot, the land that in 1970 was ostensibly being expropriated for the project covered some 2,240 dunams, but the amount of land to be used for the new neighborhood was substantially less—only 1,800 dunams.[32] Similarly, 4,840 dunams were expropriated for the construction of Neveh Ya'acov, but only 3,200 dunams were used.[33] The rest of the land was left undeveloped—until Israel saw a need for additional Jewish expansion.

The legal justification for the expropriations was that they were going for public use. This is a legitimate reason for the state to use private land. The reality, however, was that the land was going exclusively for the use of the Jewish sector. The new neighborhoods built on the land were specifically earmarked for Jewish families. If this sounds like a throwback to the "Whites Only" days of segregation in the United States, it should. Israel was a little more subtle than the segregationists in America—there were no signs stating "Jews Only" at the sales offices of the new neighborhoods being built in Jerusalem. But only Jews were eligible for the low-interest loans and other incentives subsidized by the state for purchasing the homes in these neighborhoods. This policy raised few eyebrows in Israel. For the average Israeli, it seemed fair. The Palestinians of east Jerusalem were not citizens of the country and were therefore not eligible for the state subsidies that made the new home purchases possible. This was the justification for the de facto "Jews Only" policy.

It is important to note that the issue of the division or segregation between Jews and Arabs in Jerusalem, and throughout Israel, from the local perspective is not one that raises the moral and social questions that the issue implies for Americans or others in the West. There is no battle in Israel between the segregationists and integrationists. Coexistence, for both Israelis and Palestinians, means living in peace, apart. Each side, at least for the moment, wants to live in its own communities, go to its own schools, and marry from within its own group.

There are several exceptions to this segregation. In the Abu Tur neighborhood just outside the Old City, for instance, there are both Jewish and Arab residents. It cannot really be said that they live together: the neighborhood was split by the 1948 war, with Jewish families occupying the homes in the western part and Arab families in the east. When the city was reunited in 1967, Abu Tur became a joint Jewish-Arab neighborhood, although within the neighborhood itself the old division between east and west remained in effect. In other areas of the city, particularly in east Jerusalem, the fast pace of Jewish development has encompassed what were once several lone homes of Arab families. The homes of these Arab families now are like islands in the middle of the Jewish neighborhoods that surround them. Relations between the two sides have their ups and downs. Sometimes the two peoples live in peace, with the Arab families using the superior social services of the surrounding Jewish neighborhoods. At other times, when relations turn violent, the homes of both Arabs and Jews become the targets of attack by hoodlums.

Kollek liked to describe the separate ethnic and religious neighborhoods in Jerusalem as exemplifying "self-segregation." He advocated the continuation of the ancient model of the Old City—where there are separate quarters for Muslims, Jews, Christians, and Armenians—throughout the city. His argument is that self-segregation is a cultural and historic, rather than a political phenomenon, noting that there are even separate neighborhoods in Jerusalem for Ultra-Orthodox and secular Jews. The Israeli Supreme Court has upheld the policy of allowing Jews-Only neighborhoods. The test case involved the Jewish Quarter of the Old City, rebuilt after the 1967 war. An Arab family that had owned a home in the quarter before 1948 petitioned the Supreme Court that it should be allowed to purchase a home in the new Jewish Quarter. The court, however, rejected the petition, on grounds that homogeneous neighborhoods were a historic reality in Jerusalem. The Jews have their quarter of the Old City, the Muslims theirs, and this is how it should remain, the Israeli government convinced the court. The catch, of course, is that when it came to Jews purchasing homes in the Muslim Quarter the Israeli courts looked the other way (see Chapter 11).

The building of new Jewish neighborhoods in east Jerusalem was aimed at more than ensuring Israeli demographic superiority in the city. Israel also hoped that the new neighborhoods would serve as a physical barrier cutting Jerusalem off from the West Bank. Har Homa, for instance, is meant to separate the Arab neighborhoods of Sur Baher and Umm Tuba from the West Bank towns of Beit Sahur and Bethlehem. Gilo, Neveh Ya'acov, and Pisgat Ze'ev serve the same purpose with regard to adjoining Arab neighborhoods. Israel hoped to isolate east Jerusalem Arabs from those in the West Bank and to unite east Jerusalem Jews with those in west Jerusalem. In some areas, however, it was impossible to build Jewish neighborhoods as physical barriers with the West Bank, because there was simply no room for development between the Palestinian neighborhoods of Jerusalem and Palestinian communities in the territories. For instance, there is a continuous stretch of Palestinian communities from the Shuafat neighborhood of Jerusalem to Ramallah in the West Bank.

Even without a wall of Jewish neighborhoods dividing Jerusalem from the West Bank, Israel could have perhaps still succeeded in creating the separation it wanted. If Jerusalem Palestinians were treated like Jerusalem Israelis, Israel might have made them feel some positive sentiments toward the country, as Kollek so dearly wanted them to feel. But in housing, we have already seen that the Palestinians were treated at best as second-class citizens. The Palestinians also saw this for themselves. One had to be blind not to see what was happening.

If Israeli leaders had their way, most of the Arab population of east Jerusalem would have left the city long ago. This is a harsh statement, but it is the truth. Policy decision after policy decision on east Jerusalem showed that Israel was doing everything possible to encourage, and at times force, east Jerusalem Arabs to leave the city. This was particularly true with regard to housing and land policy. Publicly, Israeli leaders deny this, but privately they speak differently. Particularly in the first years after the 1967 war, Israeli leaders seriously considered ways of literally transferring Arabs out of Jerusalem. During a meeting with Kollek in December 1992, Moshe Dayan, the Israeli war hero and renowned political leader, brought up the idea of building housing projects for Jerusalem Arabs in villages just outside the city limits, as a way of moving Arabs out of Jerusalem.[34]

Dayan, then defense minister, was in a decisive position with regard to any such plan. The West Bank was under Israeli military rule, and Dayan was at the top of the Israel's military hierarchy. Even civil affairs in the West Bank needed Defense Ministry approval. Dayan told Kollek that he strongly supported the building of inexpensive homes for Arab Jerusalemites. The homes would be most attractive to Arab families recently evicted from the Old City, due to the rebuilding of the Jewish Quarter, as well as to other Arab families hard pressed by the housing shortage in the Arab sector. The minister told Kollek that Azariya or Abu Dis, villages literally straddling Jerusalem's borders on the southern and eastern slopes of the Mount of Olives, were the best candidates. Israel already controlled land in both villages that could be allocated for housing projects, the minister reasoned.

During this same period, there were also discussions among Israeli leaders about the possibility of expanding Jerusalem to include Azariya and Abu Dis. The proposal was rejected on the grounds that Israel was not interested in including in Jerusalem the large Arab populations of the villages. The annexation of Abu Dis and Azariya would have wreaked havoc on the policy of demographic superiority, as Israeli policy makers were well aware. At the meeting with Kollek, Dayan was outspoken in his opposition to the annexation.

But in an effort to make the plan to move Arab families out of Jerusalem work, Dayan suggested that the Jerusalem municipality could continue to extend its authority to the proposed Arab housing projects in Abu Dis and Azariya. As bad as the services east Jerusalem residents received from the Jerusalem municipality were, they were nowhere near as poor as those received by Arabs in the West Bank from the Israeli authorities there. Dayan reasoned that Arab families from Jerusalem would be more likely to move to the West Bank if they knew they would still be receiving their basic services from the Jerusalem municipality. Kollek agreed with the minister on both the concept of building for Jerusalem Arabs outside the city limits and extending municipal services as a way to encourage Arab families to move out of the city.

The Abu Dis–Azariya plan, however, would have to wait. Building homes for Arabs outside of Jerusalem was no more of a priority for Israel than building homes for them in Jerusalem. It was only years later, in 1982, that the first stage of the project finally got off the ground. A several-dozen-unit housing project was built in Azariya for Jerusalem Arabs, with Israeli government support. It was a great success. Arab Jerusalemites, after receiving promises they would not lose their Jerusalem identification papers and would continue to receive services from the municipality, rushed to purchase the units. The second stage, involving several dozen more units, also sold fast. East Jerusalem Arabs had needed some convincing from the Israeli authorities that their rights would not be affected by the move into the occupied territories. Kollek even managed to get written promises to that effect from some of the Israeli authorities.

But in the end, it turned out that the Palestinian residents probably should have followed their instincts and not listened to the promises of Israeli authorities. Eventually, the welfare benefits were taken away from the Palestinian families who relocated to Azariya, on grounds that as residents of the occupied territories they were no longer entitled. Someone forgot to tell the authorities in charge about the promises made to the families before they moved. Luckily, however, Kollek had the deal in writing, and the authorities were forced to back down—but not until the new Azariya residents appealed to Israel's High Court of Justice to prevent their entitlements from being taken away.

The matter of the future of their all-important identification papers was more problematic. Israel stood by its promise not to take away Jerusalem identification papers from those residents who chose to move to the Azariya project. However, Israel refused to grant Jerusalem identification papers to additional children born after the families moved out of the city, although the parents, brothers, and sisters had them. In addition, the Azariya project residents found they had difficulties obtaining visas for relatives living abroad to live in or even visit Jerusalem. Jerusalem Palestinians are entitled to the visas, called "family reunification permits," under certain conditions. But on matters of family reunification, the Azariya project residents were looked upon by the Israeli authorities as no longer residents of Jerusalem and therefore no longer qualified to receive the visas for relatives.

Despite all these difficulties, the Azariya residents were the lucky ones. They were only a few hundred in number, and they had some of their rights in writing. But the thousands of Palestinian families who left Jerusalem for other "suburbs" in the West Bank quickly discovered that Israel did everything possible to cut them off them from Jerusalem. The housing for Palestinians in Jerusalem, however, was so grim that many families felt they had no choice but to take their chances and move to the occupied territories in order to find a home.

The Nusseiba Housing Project in Beit Hanina—one of only two small housing projects for Arabs that Israel has sponsored in Jerusalem since reunifying the city in 1967—took nearly a decade to get off the ground. The project was initiated by a well-known Palestinian engineer in Jerusalem, Mohammed Nusseiba. His brother, Anwar Nusseiba, was a senior Jordanian official in Jerusalem before the 1967 war, and the family, which had lived in the city for generations, remained after the war. Israel agreed to subsidize the construction by Nusseiba of 500 units in the northwestern section of Beit Hanina. But the money was held up by the Israel government until 1980. To this day, the project stands out. It remains the largest public housing project for Palestinians in Jerusalem—although it was not local Palestinians but Palestinian families from northern Israel who purchased most of the homes. It is also one of the few multi-storied apartment projects in Arab east Jerusalem, which otherwise is characterized by single-family homes in the traditional Arab style.

A smaller multistory apartment complex was also subsidized by the Israeli government in the mid-1980s for Palestinian residents of Jerusalem. The project consisted of 50 units in the Wadi Joz neighborhood, just outside the Old City. The tract where the project was built could fit several hundred units, but the Israeli authorities refused to provide the approval or funds for a larger project. Even private Palestinian developers were prevented from building on the land.

The irony of Israel's housing policy in east Jerusalem is that despite all the effort to contain Palestinian growth, the Palestinian population in Jerusalem continued to rise in proportion to the Jewish population. Official statistics show that by 1996 the Arab population in the city had risen to 180,000, or 30 percent of the total population, while the Jewish sector had grown to just over 420,000, or 70 percent; this compares with 28.8 percent and 71.2 percent, respectively, in 1967.[35] Those numbers, however, are somewhat deceiving, because they include as residents the tens of thousands of Palestinians who are now living in the villages in the occupied territories just outside the city's limits but still hold Jerusalem identification cards. If they were subtracted, it would likely show that Israel is succeeding in keeping down the Palestinian population in Jerusalem. The more important point for Israeli policy makers is that nearly half of east Jerusalem's population is Jewish. Israel's plan to bring Jews to east Jerusalem, and keep the Arab population down or out, seems to have worked.

4

A Question of Trust

Darwish Darwish did not want to push his new friends at city hall too hard. All he wanted was a soccer field. For a Jewish neighborhood, approval would have been granted without a second thought. In fact, most of them already had soccer fields and even more luxurious sports and recreation facilities. But in the early 1990s when Darwish approached city hall, parks, playgrounds, and sports fields were virtually nonexistent in Arab neighborhoods in east Jerusalem. Even at Arab public schools, recreation facilities were minimal.

An exception was the multipurpose sports park in Sheikh Jarrah. The fanfare surrounding its opening in 1993 is perhaps the best testimony to the bleak reality elsewhere in Arab east Jerusalem, where nothing even close to it exists. When there are few things to celebrate, even a little good news can be cause for a big party, like the one the municipality put on at the opening. One should not get the wrong idea about what was built in Sheikh Jarrah. This was no large, or for that matter even small, covered complex with an indoor gym and swimming pool. The Sheikh Jarrah sports park consisted simply of a fenced-in open area, with pavement designed for outdoor athletic activities. There were a couple of basketball hoops on the side, and soccer goals. But that was it. Which brings us back to Darwish, who was not even looking for something as "grand" as Sheikh Jarrah had received. He just wanted a soccer field.

Darwish lived in the village of Issawiya, where his ancestors had first settled about five hundred years earlier. One of the oldest Arab villages in the Jerusalem area, Issawiya lies on the eastern slope of Mount Scopus. Village homes on the hillside overlook the Judean Desert. On a clear day, the Dead Sea and Hashemite Kingdom of Jordan can be spotted easily from Issawiya. Residents trace their roots back to the time of Jesus. They are Muslims, however, not Christians.

Darwish's family is one of the largest and oldest in Issawiya. His ancestors apparently arrived in the village about the time of the great Arab conqueror Salah A-Din in the twelfth century. Being in his early fifties, Darwish was neither a village elder or a member of the more militant younger generation. Perhaps this is what enabled Darwish and a handful of other Issawiya residents of his standing in the early 1990s to form a village committee whose expressed purpose was to bring the village's needs to the awareness of the municipality and provide a line of communication between city hall and residents.

These were no easy tasks. The intifada was still raging. Issawiya was one of the hot points of unrest in east Jerusalem. Police and the paramilitary border police generally stayed out of the village. When they did enter, the *shabab* or "youths" would often pelt the Israeli policemen with stones and bottles, and in more extreme cases even fire bombs. To be caught working with the Israeli authorities was to risk being branded as a collaborator and face exclusion from the community or worse—a violent death at the hands of the organized movement of young intifada activists known as the *shabiba*. Darwish, however, was willing to take the risk. He believed that he could walk the fine line between the dangerous realm of collaboration and the legitimate domain of meeting the basic needs of the community, even if that meant dealing with the "occupying authority."

Darwish looked older than his age. He had led the tense and at times frightening life under Israeli rule that most Palestinians experienced. He watched as friends and family were detained for their opposition to the occupation or were injured and killed in the clashes between villagers and Israeli police and army. But there was another, positive, side of Israeli rule that Darwish and other villagers had also known. The Israelis brought jobs and with them a higher standard of living. The limited contact with Jews who had moved into the new neighborhoods built near Issawiya after 1967 had even led, in a few instances, to real friendships between Palestinians and Israelis.

But most importantly, there was the reality of daily life and its demands. The promises of Palestinian leaders that one day they would be free of the occupation became hard to stomach as the years of Israeli rule turned into decades. There were children and grandchildren to feed and clothe, who needed a place to go to play and learn, and the reality of life in east Jerusalem left only one place to turn to—Israel. This reality motivated many Palestinian Jerusalemites, like Darwish, to risk being labeled collaborators and to work together with the local municipal authority to solve their day-to-day problems.

Darwish also took out an insurance policy. He called upon Faisal Husseini at the PLO headquarters in Orient House to see whether he supported the formation of a village committee that would work together with the Israeli municipality. Orient House, an old three-story Arab home in the American Colony neighborhood, attracted many east Jerusalem Arabs looking for an official blessing to their relations with Israel. Darwish received what he was looking for from Husseini—a clearly defined go-ahead to set up an Issawiya village committee that would work in conjunction with the Jerusalem municipality to advance local development and promote improvement in municipal services. There was a strict limitation, however, on the relationship Palestinian leaders would allow between the village committee and city government. Husseini warned Darwish to keep to village issues and to avoid any action that could be used by Israel to justify its occupation of east Jerusalem.

Husseini's message was not meant just for Darwish. In other Arab neighborhoods of the city the municipality was also working to establish village committees. But the going was slow, because of insecurity on both sides about how the move would be interpreted politically. This made the first projects that much more sensitive. Each side was feeling the other out, and testing itself. The concept of village committees was grassroots on both sides. The idea was the brainchild of the office of the mayor's adviser on Arab affairs. Kollek, and for that matter senior municipal and Israeli government officials, had no word of this new experiment until it was well under way. Similarly, Palestinian residents approached by the adviser's office at first discussed the idea among themselves. Only after they believed that the idea was workable did residents go higher up—in Darwish's case to Husseini.

Darwish along with other committee members would hold frequent meetings with members of the adviser's office. The meetings were cordial, and a strong working relationship developed between the Israelis from the office and the Palestinian villagers. During one meeting the issue of the soccer field was raised by Darwish. It was only a small matter on the day's agenda. Most of the talk had been about a major project the two sides hoped to get off the ground, the building of a sewage system in Issawiya. The municipality refused to pay for the system itself, saying the residents also had to contribute, as they did elsewhere in the city on public works projects. An agreement was eventually reached under which the municipality would provide the materials for the sewage system, such as the pipes and cement, and the residents would pay for the construction. The committee was to help oversee the work, as well as collect the money from residents for the project.

Darwish and his colleagues were somewhat apprehensive about this plan, however. They were worried about being seen as doing the dirty work of the city—collecting fellow residents' money, even though it was going to the good of the village. Clearly, the sewage project would take several years to work out, if it worked out at all. Darwish was looking for more immediate results, and the proposed soccer field offered one possibility that on its face appeared to be easily doable.

The adviser's office immediately agreed that the project seemed feasible. While the committee's strategy was to use the new soccer field to show Issawiya residents that the committee was for real, the adviser's office had an ulterior motive. The soccer field would be used by the village soccer club, many of whose members were actively involved in the shabiba. The shabiba set the tone of the intifada and its violent assaults on Israeli targets and received the brunt of the retaliation by the Israeli police and army. The soccer field project offered a way for the adviser's office to open up channels of communication with the young people of Issawiya. There were no misconceptions about reforming the shabiba. That was not even a consideration for Israel. But the importance of establishing various lines of communication with the Palestinian population was not underestimated.

At Jerusalem city hall it was one thing to discuss and agree in principle on a project. It was quite another to find funding and implement it. The city's sports department turned down the soccer field project on the grounds that the department was already running a deficit. A direct appeal to the national government for funding of an array of projects in east Jerusalem, including the soccer field, also turned up only a rejection. This is where Mayor Teddy Kollek's connections inside and outside government could be critical. Kollek was an unparalleled pro at raising money for the city. Normally, whether the money coming into Jerusalem was from the national government or foreign donors, little of it trickled down to the Arab sector. But 1993 was an election year and Kollek needed the Arab vote, so he played that card to his advantage.

Just two months before he was up for reelection, Kollek confronted the finance minister with a demand for an emergency outlay for east Jerusalem. Kollek was desperate for the funds, but the finance minister was busy and kept putting off a meeting. Kollek was persistent. One day, he got word that the minister was on his way to Ben-Gurion Airport, about 30 miles from Jerusalem, to fly to the United States for the historic signing between Israeli Prime Minister Yitzhak Rabin and Palestine Liberation Organization Chairman Yasser Arafat of the Oslo Peace Accord at the White House. Kollek caught the minister on his cellular phone. He agreed to meet the mayor at the airport, as he waited for the flight to Washington.

Kollek rushed off the airport, imploring his driver to make good time. In the end, it was worth the trip. The minister agreed to a one-time "emergency" allocation, but he wanted to leave the details until his return. Kollek would not have it. He wanted at least a guarantee of NIS 10 million ($3.3 million), and he wanted it right away. The election was fast approaching. He needed something to show the Arab residents now. The minister was convinced. He agreed to an immediate allocation of between NIS 5–6 million. The head of the Bank of Israel, Ya'acov Frankel, who was flying together with finance minister Shohat to the United States, was in the room also. Kollek turned to him and asked him to be witness to the minister's promise. The mayor had been burned too many times in the past by unfulfilled promises. He did not want to be misled again, particularly at such a crucial time in his political career.[1]

The mayor was euphoric upon his return to city hall. He informed his advisers about the promised funding, and they began making plans for its use. The Issawiya soccer field was among the east Jerusalem projects at the top of the list. The city's sports department estimated the cost for the new field at around NIS 240,000 ($80,000). The mayor informed the engineering and transport department, which was to oversee construction, that the funding was on its way. When the Issawiya committee heard about the approval, it did not hesitate to spread the word in the village. It was good news for all. A great sense of optimism overtook the committee. The soccer field appeared to demonstrate that the municipality and Palestinian residents could work together in a nonpolitical framework.

The optimism was short-lived, however. The money never made it to the project. And instead of becoming a symbol of cooperation, the project turned out to be yet another source of frustration and disappointment for Jerusalem's Arabs under Israeli rule. The head of the engineering and transport department, Michael Nackman, openly admitted that he unilaterally scrapped the Issawiya soccer field plan. He had decided that other city needs in the Arab sector took precedence and failed to understand the full implication of the move. Kollek found this out only after he had lost the election and it was too late for him to do anything. It was yet another blow to the Israeli authorities' image in east Jerusalem, and it badly damaged an important attempt to improve local Israeli-Palestinian relations in Jerusalem by establishing village committees.

The village committees of Issawiya and elsewhere in Arab east Jerusalem arose in part from the vacuum created by the collapse of the mukhtar system. The mukhtars for centuries were the central figures in Arab societies, not only in Palestine but in much of the Arab world. In its heyday during the Ottoman period, the mukhtar was the village sheriff, tax collector, and judge. Mukhtars—their name taken from the Arabic word meaning "elected one"—were not restricted to Muslim communities. Christian and Jewish communities in the Arab world also had mukhtars.

In general, the weaker the national authority, the stronger the mukhtar. If the national authority was strong, it carried out many of the local tasks, such as keeping marriage records and conscripting young persons in the army, that otherwise would have been left to the mukhtar. At the turn of the century, Jerusalem was under Ottoman rule, with the central government in far-off Constantinople. The city was poor and its population, while growing, was small. In this geopolitical backwater, local affairs were generally left to mukhtars.

The mukhtars of the Ottoman period had much authority. They acted as judges in disputes between the large families, or *hamulot*, of the village. Sometimes they were called to a neighboring village to make peace, or *sulha*, between hamulot when the nearby village wanted an impartial judge. Their responsibility for conscripting young men into the army was a lucrative business—with families paying large sums in exchange for an exemption. Families without the means to pay, or those whom the mukhtar turned down for one reason or another, had other ways of keeping their sons out of the army, such as chopping off their trigger finger.

The power of mukhtars declined considerably after the British conquered Jerusalem and the rest of the Holy Land in 1917. During British rule, the central government was strong and took on many of the responsibilities the Turks had left to the mukhtars. Socioeconomic changes that the Arab communities of Jerusalem and elsewhere were undergoing during the period also contributed to the mukhtars' downfall. The traditional Arab family structure was experiencing severe stress, as was the power structure in Arab society as a whole. Young people were more educated than their parents and less willing to accept the authority of the mukhtar. Traditional patriarchal values were crashing head on with new, liberal values.

The mukhtar, however, did not totally disappear during the British Mandate. The British found that the local mukhtar was a good avenue for keeping in touch with the population. Regulations were even drawn up to define the process and criteria by which an appointment to mukhtar would be made. Despite this formalizing of the mukhtars' position, however, their heyday was long over. A strong government, even a foreign one, in Jerusalem left the mukhtars with little real authority.

The mukhtars experienced a slight revival after 1948. The Hashemite Kingdom of Jordan, for all its stated affection and connection to Jerusalem, generally ignored local affairs there. The mukhtars filled in where the Jordanian authority left off. Following the British lead, the Jordanian government, which sat in Amman, appointed mukhtars and provided them with identification cards, making their position official.

When Israel conquered east Jerusalem in 1967, the mukhtars were, once again, the natural channel for contact with the Arab population. Israel put much faith in the mukhtars, believing they had influence in their communities. The Jerusalem municipality began issuing identification papers to mukhtars, while Jordan continued to issue its own IDs to mukhtars, as a symbolic show of its claim to authority in east Jerusalem. With two authorities issuing a mukhtar ID, there was potential for conflict. But the Hashemite Kingdom, acknowledging Israel's de facto rule of the city, decided to grant identification papers according to the Jewish state's lead. A mukhtar would have to present an Israeli mukhtar ID to the authorities in Amman in order to be granted a Jordanian one.

The mukhtars quickly discovered that the Israeli ID was a must. A mukhtar could flash it at a police or army checkpoint and be waved through, while their fellow Palestinians had to endure long and sometimes humiliating searches. At various government offices the official mukhtar ID was an important tool in cutting through Israel's infamous bureaucracy, which drove not only Arabs but also Jews crazy. The mukhtars also received from Israel a small monthly stipend, ostensibly to cover "travel expenses."

The benefits Israel gave the mukhtars were small but significant, particularly considering that their status had been waning for most of the century. Israel wanted to strengthen the mukhtars' standing, and the few benefits they received helped, to a degree and for a short period, to return their authority. Villagers knew that they needed their mukhtar, and if they did not remember, the Israeli authorities did their best to remind them. Virtually every official matter an Arab resident of east Jerusalem needed to have done required the mukhtar's signature. From marriage licenses to building permits, the Israelis made sure that everything went through the mukhtars' hands. The municipality also provided the mukhtar with an official stamp, in addition to the ID. The stamp, with the mukhtar's signature on top, was required on official forms residents presented to city authorities.

Until the early 1980s, the mukhtars were even responsible for delivering the mail in east Jerusalem. The Israeli Postal Authority wanted nothing to do with east Jerusalem. The Arab neighborhoods there were unknown and somewhat intimidating, and there were few street names and addresses in many of the villages. The traditional Arab way of naming children, with only a few common names repeated in many families and even within the same families, made it more difficult to determine where to deliver the mail, especially since extended families with the same names often lived in the same area. There were ten people named Ibrahim Aliyan in Beit Safafa and twenty named Mahmoud Abu al-Hawa in A-Tur and a dozen named Jamil Siyaj in Abu Tur.

Using these arguments, the Israeli Postal Authority stuck to its guns and refused to deliver in east Jerusalem. Instead, the mukhtars would come to the main east Jerusalem post office on Salah A-Din Street and pick up their community's mail at most two or three times a week. They would normally drop off the entire load at one of their local grocery stores, where the residents would have to stop by to see if they received any letters. The mukhtars did not complain about the system, which gave them at least a little authority in their communities. They also received a stipend for their work from the Israeli Postal Authority.

While the system was convenient for the Postal Authority, it did not always work to Israel's advantage. One example: the mukhtar would return to his village with the mail, and at the local grocery store, he would meet a resident:

"Ahalan, Mukhtar," the resident would say.

"Ahalan," the mukhtar would respond.

A short exchange of additional greetings and small talk would follow. "Is there anything for me?" the resident would ask, pointing at the mail bag.

"Aywa, I saw several letters addressed to you."

"Who were they from?"

"Here, look. This one is from your uncle in America; here's a telephone bill, and another letter from the Income Tax Authority."

The resident would then decide what he wanted to take. There was no question about the letter from his uncle. He'd have that one. It was also worth his while to receive the phone bill. If he did not pay, his phone would be cut off. Now, with regard to the letter from the Income Tax Authority—it could only want money. So the resident would ask the mukhtar to put it back into the mail bag and return it to the post office. "Tell them you couldn't find the address," the resident would say.

It is unknown how much money various Israeli private and public companies lost because the bill "never reached its address." Not that Palestinians simply got away without paying their bills. But with the mail service not regular, it simply made dodging payments attractive. The Israeli authorities were forced to use various payment agencies and legal proceedings—which themselves cost money—to make sure bills were paid.

A solution was eventually found for mail delivery. Not that one had to look far. Young men were hired from the different Arab communities to distribute the mail to the residents' homes. Still, it took a decade and a half for Israeli authorities to come up with and implement a system for home mail delivery in east Jerusalem.

Israel also found another job for mukhtars. Desperate to show the world that Jerusalem was united, Israel needed representatives of the Arab community present at the official ceremony held to welcome foreign dignitaries to the city. Mukhtars were chosen for the job, after real Palestinian notables in the city repeatedly declined. "Make sure the mukhtar you bring wears a kafiya, so he stands out," was the order given to city officials helping organize the welcoming ceremonies. It was no coincidence, then, that the more traditional mukhtars who wore the Arab head-dress were the ones who were always invited. The mukhtar would shake hands with the foreign dignitary and exchange a nod and brief hello. The foreigner did not know the mukhtar was not widely respected in his community.

Not only city hall but various Israeli government bodies relied on mukhtars when operating in Arab east Jerusalem. The army and Shin Bet, for example, were heavily dependent on the mukhtars for gathering intelligence on the Arab sector of the city. Israeli policy makers—from the mayor's office on up—thought they could reinvigorate a system of local authority, beholden to Israel, that had long ago proven obsolete. Meanwhile, in the late 1970s and early 1980s, a new, young Arab leadership was emerging in the city which Israeli authorities largely ignored until it had no choice but to pay attention. When the stoning, fire bombing, and strikes of the intifada broke out in east Jerusalem in December 1987, Israel quickly realized its mistake.

In early 1988, just after the start of the intifada, Hader Dabash, Mohammed Fawaka, and Ahmad Dajala came to city hall looking very concerned. The three were mukhtars from Sur Baher. Hader Dabash was the senior of them. Dabash was among the slickest of all east Jerusalem mukhtars. A former municipal worker, Dabash knew his way around city hall, as well as most of the local government institutions in east Jerusalem, better than any of the other mukhtars. He could frequently be seen hurrying from one city hall office to the next, using his connections to get a villager a break on his property tax payment or obtain a building permit. Like other mukhtars, Dabash had not been risking his life for nothing. He had helped the residents the Israelis wanted him to help, but at a price. The income he received as mukhtar, added to his minimal pension from his city hall job, had left him and his family among the most well-off families in the village.

Dabash and his two fellow mukhtars came to city hall that day to give up that good life. The expression on their faces said everything. They did not have to say a word for anyone to know something terrible had happened. The three presented a letter to the office of the mayor's Arab affairs adviser. It was simple and to the point. The mukhtars of Sur Baher were quitting. To make their resignation official, they attached their mukhtar identification papers to the letter. What they left out, however, was the reason behind the unexpected resignations. Dabash had decided that he would deliver the details personally.

"We have been humiliated in our own village," he began, unable to hide his distress. "Yesterday, some of the youths started throwing rocks at the border policemen who entered the village, and they tried to make us stop them," Dabash said. "The border policemen called us out of our homes and wanted us to sit in their jeeps and drive around the village using loudspeakers to call on the youths to stop throwing stones." The mukhtars refused, on grounds it was not their job to contain the youths. But the damage to their image had already been done. The border police were seen coming to their homes asking for help. The three mukhtars, always suspected of aiding the Israeli authorities, had been dealt their death blow, perhaps literally. Intifada justice demanded the death of collaborators.

The incident occurred during the first days of the intifada. The event Dabash described as involving just a couple of stone-throwing kids was in fact a full-scale riot. The scope of the unrest caught Israeli security forces by surprise, and the reaction of the border police at Sur Baher was one of the results. A local border police commander, not really knowing how to react to the rioting, decided to try to use the mukhtars to quell the unrest. When the mukhtars refused, he at first threatened to arrest them. But this tactic also failed to get results, and the mukhtars stood firm in their opposition to being used by the border police.

The commander eventually backed down and let them go. Having no insight into the sensitive position mukhtars were in, the commander did not realize what damage he had caused. On top of that, the commander, unprepared for the rioting, simply did not realize that even if he had succeeded in forcing the mukhtars into the jeeps, he would have just brought on more trouble for himself and his men. The shabiba had never thought much of the mukhtars; seeing the mukhtars working with the Israeli border police would only have incited more unrest.

The city tried to convince the three mukhtars to stay at their posts. The intifada had left city hall in dire straits. It was fast losing a grip on east Jerusalem, and city officials saw the mukhtars, no matter how bad, as their last hope for restoring some line of communication with Jerusalem's Arab community. But the mukhtars remained firm in their decision to resign.

Just how weak the intifada left Jerusalem mukhtars is reflected in the story of Mohammed Shahin, an Old City mukhtar. Shahin and his brother ran a homous and kebab restaurant on the corner of David Street and the Butcher's Market Alley in the Muslim Quarter. This was not just another homous and kebab restaurant. Traditional Arab cuisine was a delicacy at Shahin's. The mukhtar and his brother attracted business from all over the city, including Jews from west Jerusalem. But that was before the intifada. The rioting turned east Jerusalem—and in particular the Old City—into territory off limits to the Israeli public.

Shahin's son worked with him at the restaurant. Even before the outbreak, the teenage boy often skipped work, without ever explaining why. These absences increased after the intifada started. One day, in the first months of the intifada, Shahin rushed to city hall. "My son has been arrested," he announced, as he barged into the office of the mayor's adviser on Arab affairs. "You must help me," Shahin said. "My son has done nothing. He is by my side at the restaurant all day. You know how tough things are these days. He never leaves me." Shahin, like many a father, was not above lying for his son. "There is no way he could be involved in something criminal, or in some sort of terror activity," Shahin said. He concluded with a series of oaths, including the most sacred any Muslim could make: "I swear in the name of the Koran, in the name of Allah, in the name of my son, that all I say is true."

The average Palestinian could never get help from city hall with this type of trouble, but a mukhtar was not an average Palestinian. A city hall official picked up the phone and called Russian Compound Police Station, the central police headquarters in the city. The call went through directly to the minorities division. It did not take long to get an answer. The mukhtar's son was suspected of throwing a fire bomb on Eid el-Kurd's money-changing business, just inside Damascus Gate. Police believe the money-changer was attacked for opening his business on a day that intifada leaders had called for a strike. The mukhtar's son, police believed, was a member of an intifada "shock squad," or gang of youths employed by intifada leaders. Fire-bombing was one of the shock squads' tactics to intimidate Palestinians into obeying the intifada leaders' orders, such as what days to close their businesses in protest of Israeli occupation.

Shahin did not sound surprised when he heard the news. He had known his son was on an intifada shock squad. He had turned to city hall hoping his connections there might get his son off. In this case, it did not. But in numerous other instances, city hall intervened with the security services—the army, Shin Bet, and police—to request lenient treatment for relatives of mukhtars or other Palestinians who were helpful to the Israeli authorities.

The intifada made crystal-clear to the local Israeli authorities in Jerusalem that the mukhtar system was a failure. Mukhtars in the West Bank and Gaza were being killed by fellow Palestinians who accused them of collaboration. The east Jerusalem mukhtars feared a similar fate. They no longer represented their communities. They had no control or influence on the Palestinian population of the city. Their time had passed.

As the intifada intensified, the mukhtars simply stopped working with city hall. It was too dangerous for them. On a few occasions, there were apologetic phone calls to the office of the mayor's adviser on Arab affairs. Not that the absence of the mukhtars really changed anything. In the past, when mukhtars contacted city hall, it was normally on personal business: an uncle needed a building permit; a son has to be registered for school; a relative living in Amman wanted a visa to come to Jerusalem. After the intifada, the mukhtars' families may have felt the absence of contact with city hall, but the rest of the population did not.

Just as the mukhtar system was collapsing, village committees like the one in Issawiya arose, giving Israeli authorities a new opportunity to improve relations with east Jerusalem Arabs. Issawiya was the site of the first village committee, which was established about a year after the outbreak of the intifada. The municipality was behind the project, quickly seeing what political rewards it could reap by helping foster a Palestinian leadership in the city that was willing to work with the local Israeli authority.

The Issawiya committee managed to get off the ground—despite the soccer field fiasco—largely because another city-sponsored project, the construction of a new sewage system, eventually did succeed. Other villages watched as bulldozers rolled into Issawiya and the pipes were laid for the sewage system, and then they decided that they too wanted committees that would coordinate such projects with city hall. Committees were soon established in Kafr Akab, Ras al-Amud, and Sawarha. The principle in each case was the same. The municipality, holding out the possibility of funding for public works projects and improved services, encouraged the cooperation of Arab villages.

For Israel, the issue went far beyond improving living conditions in east Jerusalem. The committees opened avenues for dialogue between the Israeli authorities and Arab residents. Those avenues at times proved very fruitful. The killing of 29 Palestinians by a Jewish settler in March 1994 in Hebron, for instance, set off a wave of rioting throughout the West Bank and east Jerusalem, which also hit Issawiya. A youth was shot dead by police trying to quell the unrest. The youth was the grandson of one of the most respected village residents, Abu Tarek, who had headed the Village Council before 1967. The youth's funeral was the scene of even greater unrest. Thousands of Palestinians took part. The police, hoping to avoid a provocation, kept out of the village. It was a smart move. Without a target for the anger, the funeral passed quietly.

The Israeli police, however, were concerned about what would happen in the village at the memorial service traditionally held by Muslims forty days after a death. Intelligence reports indicated there would be trouble. The police turned to the adviser's office in the hope of finding a way to reach the shabiba in Issawiya and calm the atmosphere. The request was rare. In general, the Israeli police did not like to look outside its own ranks for help, in particular in its operations in east Jerusalem. But the police had heard of the city's new contacts with the Issawiya village committee and hoped this connection would pay off in keeping the peace during the upcoming memorial service.

The adviser's office did not turn to the committee, however. There was no need. Improved relations between the municipality and the village allowed the adviser's office to go directly to the shabiba. The youths promised that as long as the police kept clear, the memorial service would pass quietly. They also promised that the event would be confined to the village, giving the police even less reason to enter. The office relayed the shabiba's promises to the police, and the promises were kept.

The make-up of each village committee reflected the political faction that dominated the village. If a village was a stronghold of Hamas, so too would be the committee. The same if Fatah was the major force. In most cases the various political factions had varying degrees of support, and no one group dominated, and this too was reflected in the village committees. The common purpose among all the committees was to improve city services in their communities, even if this meant cooperating with the Israeli authorities. Palestinians had come to terms with the fact they had to deal with Israel on a local level to improve the quality of life in east Jerusalem. Conditions even before the intifada were atrocious, and after the outbreak of the unrest the situation on the ground in Arab east Jerusalem only grew worse. Most city services were halted. Schools were shut down for long periods by the Israeli security forces. Roads were not repaired, and new development came to a standstill. The committees aimed to end this freeze, by completely separating the national political issues that divided the Palestinians and Israelis from the day-to-day matters that concerned east Jerusalem Arab residents, even if "in the meantime" (at least in Palestinian eyes), they had to turn to Israel for help.

A Hamas activist headed the village committee in Nazlat Abu-Sweh. At the time Hamas did not have the bloody reputation it acquired after it masterminded numerous suicide bombings and other acts of terror that killed dozens of Israelis. But in Israeli eyes this Islamic fundamentalist group was already known as an extremist organization that advocated the annihilation of the Jewish state. The city was apprehensive about working with the Hamas leader. There were a series of meetings at city hall to determine what to do.

The village is in effect a section of the larger community of Ras al-Amud, along the old Jerusalem-Jericho road straddling the eastern border of the city. Ras al-Amud was considered, along with Silwan and Issawiya, to be among the most unruly areas of east Jerusalem. The community was a hotbed of anti-Israeli activity. The municipality initially saw it as a positive sign that a committee had been set up there. Only after it was discovered that the committee was headed by a Hamas activist were there second thoughts. City officials knew that any project the committee together with the municipality was able to get off the ground would be seen as not only the committee's success but also a success of Hamas.

This was the case with all the committees. While they were ostensibly nonpolitical, villagers were well aware of their membership and who headed them. The city had this information, too, and was at first unsure whether to proceed. But a decision was finally taken to move ahead. With Kollek's approval, it was decided that the city would deal with committees no matter the organization with which they were linked. The political implications of the city's relations with the committees would be overlooked. The intifada had disrupted normal life in the city, and Kollek was desperate to find some avenue to restore at least a semblance of order, even if that meant doing business with what, in Israel's eyes, was the devil.

Hamas was not singled out for concern. Working with Fatah supporters in Issawiya was seen by Israeli authorities as being just as risky as cooperating with Hamas affiliates in Ras al-Amud. In this respect, the municipality was breaking new ground and making important inroads in Palestinian-Israeli relations in Jerusalem that surpassed the efforts of the national government. Kollek's pragmatism should be credited. He had his mind set on one thing: improving local Palestinian-Israeli relations and running a normal city. The emphasis for Kollek was always on the "local," that is, on avoiding national issues that bogged down attempts to improve Palestinian-Israeli relations elsewhere.

Kollek's paper, "Sharing United Jerusalem," which appeared in the winter 1988/89 issue of *Foreign Affairs*, centered on the premise that the Israeli municipal government, by sticking to local issues, could make progress with the Palestinians that the national government had not been able to make. Kollek was always willing to ignore the national politics of the Palestinians in Jerusalem, for the sake of coexistence. With the emergence of the village committees, the Palestinians showed a similar willingness.

How much could be read into this relationship, however, remained to be seen. In retrospect, it appears that expectations were too high on both sides. The Palestinians hoped the city could deliver improved conditions for Arab neighborhoods, ignoring the fact the municipality could do little without the approval of the national government. The municipality, for its part, was looking to the committee members as partners in a dialogue that went beyond how to improve the sewage system, ignoring the fact that the committee members were incapable of delivering anything more than improved contact in local affairs in east Jerusalem. The committee members may have received a political go-ahead for their work, but that did not make them leaders in any sense of the word.

As village committees began to spring up all over east Jerusalem in the early 1990s, meetings were set up between committee members and heads of various city departments, such as sanitation, water, engineering, and education. It sounds absurd, and it should, that these city departments previously had virtually no direct contact with the Arab population of east Jerusalem. But that was the situation. The little contact that had occurred was handled by the office of the mayor's adviser on Arab affairs. Palestinian residents would approach the office, and the office would forward requests to the various municipal departments. This was the method under the mukhtar system, and the department heads preferred it. They were somewhat wary of the Palestinian population. If a department head entered a Palestinian neighborhood—even in the days before the intifada—they demanded to be led there by the Arab affairs office. The system was a disaster, for both sides. It was ineffective, accentuating the division that continued to exist between Jewish and Arab Jerusalem.

The emergence of the committees offered a great opportunity to break down some of the barriers between the two populations. Committee members were eager to meet with the department heads directly, and when the initial meetings took place, understandings were reached on how the members would be in direct contact with the various municipal professionals responsible for city services. But the understandings were never realized. Before long, the department heads refused to be in direct contact with the committees and insisted on reverting to the old relationship in which everything went through the Arab affairs adviser's office.

Direct contact did not work because it turned out to represent only a cosmetic change. The view city hall took toward Arab east Jerusalem remained the same: Arab residents' needs can be ignored. The office of the adviser on Arab affairs served as a buffer between the Arab residents and city hall. Municipal department heads knew that priorities were not going to change at city hall and that the committees' demands for services comparable to those the Jewish neighborhoods received would never be met. But city officials could not look the committee members in the face and tell them. They preferred hiding behind the office of Arab affairs.

The municipality passed up a great opportunity. A new leadership—no matter how weak and "local"—was emerging, but city hall failed to break with its old ways. The failure was particularly harsh for Kollek. The committees had opened a back door to his much-talked-about "boroughs plan" for Jerusalem. The City Council had blocked the plan, rejecting Kollek's argument that Palestinian self-governing boroughs in east Jerusalem would be set up only to deal with local issues and that broader, national implications should not be read into the plan. Consequently, the issue of the committees was never even brought before the council. The committees were the card Kollek held close to his chest, hoping to show it only after he was sure he had a winning hand. The time, however, never came. The committees, while doing some good, turned out be disappointments, through no fault of their own.

Not surprising, the major reason the committees failed to reach their potential was money. The committees faced the same reality other Israeli initiatives for the Arabs of east Jerusalem confronted. Israeli policy makers, in this case the mayor and his advisers, may have been well-intentioned. Indeed, many senior officials spoke positively about the opportunities the committees offered. But when it came to allocating funds, no one with the authority was willing to put up the money needed to make the committees work. Large sums were not demanded for the enterprise. Money was needed to rent each committee a small office, install and operate a telephone line, and purchase a few pieces of furniture. But even this basic funding— not to speak of the large investment that would be needed for the projects the committees were supposed to carry out in conjunction with the city—was not available. There were times when the city could not pull together the two hundred dollars a month needed for the Issawiya committee office to operate. City officials had to literally search through municipal warehouses to find abandoned furniture for the committee's office. An education department official, when he heard about the needs of the Issawiya committee office, offered several chairs. It was discovered only later that the chairs he had in mind were sized for second graders.

Kollek and other city leaders simply did not do what was necessary to make the committees work. Kollek always spoke favorably, and with excitement, about the opportunities offered by the committees. He would repeatedly tell advisers that he hoped the committees would be the first stage toward new neighborhood councils in east Jerusalem, which in turn would provide the basis for implementing his boroughs plan. "I want us to establish a new council in east Jerusalem every year," Kollek said. But when it came to turning that excitement into concrete plans, Kollek failed in the most elementary ways. The aging leader's plans were nothing more than empty pronouncements.

Israeli apologists prefer to put the blame on the Palestinians. The Palestinians, these defenders say, failed to take advantage of the opportunities offered to them by Israel, beginning with joining the Jerusalem City Council after the 1967 war. The argument continues that Israel was in a no-win situation in east Jerusalem because of the Palestinians' refusal to cooperate even in local affairs. Furthermore, there was no real Palestinian leadership in east Jerusalem; even if Israel had wanted to, there was no one it could really speak with on the Palestinian side who truly represented east Jerusalem.

But a closer look shows the weakness in the argument that puts the blame on the Palestinians. It was Israel which forcibly disbanded the east Jerusalem City Council just after the war and deported many Arab leaders from east Jerusalem, branding them as terrorists and inciters. The move depleted the city of many of its leading Arab citizens. When new Palestinian leaders emerged, nowhere at city hall was there a concerted effort to locate and make contact with this young Palestinian leadership. As early as the mid-1970s the Shin Bet had identified Faisal Husseini, Sari Nusseiba, and other activists affiliated with various Palestinian groups who were considered to be pulling the political strings in east Jerusalem.[2] Shin Bet, however, did not see its job as promoting relations with these emerging Palestinian leaders. On those occasions when Shin Bet did try to encourage one or another of the Palestinian leaders in the city, it found that it was working in a vacuum.

"We never saw the need to make contact with the young Palestinian leaders in the city, to encourage the development of a local Palestinian leadership in the city," says Kollek's former adviser, Aharon Sarig. He gives two reasons for the failure: First, not only at city hall but also on the national level, the Jordanians, not the Palestinians, were seen as a partner, at least until the outbreak of the intifada. Second, "the idea behind any political [dialogue] would be that there was something to talk about, that there would be some real possibility for compromise. That clearly did not exist. We all know that Israel was not really offering the Palestinians anything of any substance," Sarig says.

In this atmosphere of poor Israeli attention to political developments in Arab east Jerusalem, Israel suddenly woke up in 1988 to discover that the PLO had a headquarters at Orient House, in the heart of the city; the intifada leadership was based in the city, and even the Islamic fundamentalists had established deep roots there. The Palestinians, it seems, had stolen a page out of the Israelis' book—establishing their own "facts on the ground" with which Israel was forced to contend. Israel, however, tried to ignore this new reality. Only in 1993, five years after the outbreak of the intifada, was Faisal Husseini, the senior PLO official in Jerusalem, who had long since become a political force, approached by Kollek.

A secret meeting was held at the home of a close associate of Kollek on the morning of January 18. The meeting lasted an hour and a half. Husseini demanded a complete media blackout and Kollek was sensitive to the demand. Only two of the mayor's closest aides were present in an effort to ensure that it remained secret. Minutes were kept of the meeting, but no copies were made and the original was stored in one of the mayor's personal files.[3] Husseini and his aides who attended were not named and were referred to only as "the guests" in the minutes.

The atmosphere at the meeting was generally upbeat. Husseini said he hoped that the meeting would be the first of many. He was interested in finding out about the status of various zoning plans in Arab east Jerusalem. He also asked about the workings of city hall, and how Palestinian residents could get more out of the municipality.

Overall, it was the type of down-to-earth meeting that Kollek had wanted. Instead of getting bogged down in the bigger political issues, the participants stuck to local affairs. The immediate aftermath of the meeting seemed to confirm Kollek's upbeat feeling. Husseini, in an interview with the *Al-Quds* newspaper, announced that he met Kollek. Husseini said he was confident the meeting would be well received by the Palestinian public and viewed as an important discussion of local affairs and not a sell-out to the Israelis. "Over there, there are developments like the elections in addition to the many other questions on the present situation that we wanted to find out about. All these things prompted the meeting, which we believe was important and necessary." The meeting had positive results, Husseini proclaimed in the interview, such as Kollek expressing willingness to redo existing zoning plans that had greatly limited Palestinian development.

The cooperation on the local level Kollek had long hoped for appeared possible. Husseini and Kollek agreed to set up a follow-up committee to improve communication between Orient House and city hall. The central role of the committee was to help Palestinian residents in their dealings with the municipality. This is exactly what Kollek had been looking for—a concrete avenue of communication between city hall and Palestinian residents on local issues. The mayor believed Israeli-Palestinian relations in Jerusalem were on the verge of a major breakthrough. And he was right. But it was not the breakthrough he had expected, and the implications for Jerusalem were far different than he had hoped.

The Kollek-Husseini initiative never got off the ground. The Palestinians, at least on the subject of cooperation, were never heard from again. No committee was ever established. There was one additional meeting between Kollek and Husseini, in August 1993. The meeting was again held in secret, and this time it remained that way. The Oslo Accord was in its final stages of completion, and both sides were sensitive about any move that might derail the process. Kollek himself was not fully aware of what was happening. He had heard about the secret talks in Norway but was not privy to the details. Others at the meeting were—particularly Husseini and Uri Savir, Israel's Foreign Ministry director-general and chief negotiator at Oslo.

The months that followed turned out to be a time of great change in the leadership of the city's Palestinian and Israeli communities. In November Kollek was ousted after nearly three decades in office and replaced by a Knesset member from the right-wing Likud Party, Ehud Olmert. Husseini was promoted to minister without portfolio in the new Palestinian government of PLO leader Yasser Arafat. In 1996, six other leading Palestinian Jerusalemites were elected to seats in the Palestinian council or parliament. Together with Husseini they called on Israel to relinquish control of east Jerusalem, declaring east Jerusalem the Palestinian capital. They were not interested in local issues. For them, such proposals as Kollek's "Sharing United Jerusalem" were acceptable only if the two sides were equal partners, with east Jerusalem declared the Palestinian capital and west Jerusalem the capital of Israel.

The Husseini-Kollek initiative was already a distant memory. The time had passed when any legitimate Palestinian leader would set as a goal improving conditions for Palestinians living under Israeli rule in Jerusalem. Now Palestinians and their leaders simply wanted Israel out of east Jerusalem, and they believed the Oslo Accord has set the stage for this.

What sort of reality would the sides be facing today if Israel had done more to foster the village committees, or tried to reach out to Husseini and other local Palestinian leaders in 1973 or 1983, instead of waiting until 1993? No one will ever know. But what is clear is that there have existed in Jerusalem Palestinians with whom close ties could have been developed, based on a common goal of making Jerusalem more livable for all its residents. The committees, for instance, if properly fostered by Israel, could have become the basis for the self-rule borough system much talked about by Kollek. This would have greatly strengthened Israel's hand in negotiations over the city's future. Instead, the committees and the failure to reach out to the local Palestinian leadership in a timely and effective manner represent additional missed opportunities for Israel in Jerusalem.

5

Mr. Arafat, Can You Lend Me A Hand?

Israeli officials at the time called it the rumor mill. If the correct hints were given to the right people in east Jerusalem, a good rumor could do more to influence public opinion than a thousand public statements by an official at any level. In this case, the idea was to get east Jerusalem Arabs to the polling stations to vote in the municipal elections—the first since the Six Day War. It was 1968, and Israel was still struggling to solidify its hold on the city. Israeli officials, particularly Kollek, looked to a large turnout in east Jerusalem as evidence that life had returned to normal in the city and that Arab residents accepted Israeli rule.

There was only one problem: the Palestine Liberation Organization and other Palestinian nationalist groups had called for a boycott of the election. The Jordanian authorities in Amman had also called on Arab Jerusalemites not to participate. Both the Palestinian nationalists and Jordanian government foresaw Israel trying to use a large Arab turnout in the election to its advantage. A clear message from the Palestinian and Jordanian leadership was sent to Arab residents of the city: Don't vote, and anyone who does will be branded a traitor.

The Israeli authorities, however, were still determined to persuade Arab residents to participate in the election. The Israelis wanted an Arab list to run for City Council. Immediately after the war, Israel had disbanded the old Jordanian east Jerusalem City Council but had encouraged the Arab council members and Arab mayor of east

Jerusalem to join the Jewish council of west Jerusalem. The Arab council members and mayor had refused.

The Israeli authorities believed the only way to overcome the heavy pressure to boycott was through counter pressure on Arab residents. That is where the rumor mill came into play. In various forums with leading Arab figures in the city, Israeli officials hinted that Arab residents would "suffer" if they did not vote. Just how would they suffer? Different rumors were spread by the Israelis. One rumor was that Arab residents' Israeli identification cards would be taken away if they did not receive a stamp at the polling stations indicating they had voted. The rumor played on the Arab residents' fears that Israel would try to evict them from the city and take their property. Another rumor used against the 1,500 Arab residents who worked for the municipality was that they would lose their jobs if they and their family members did not vote.

Israeli officials spread the rumors and then were careful to hint of their truthfulness in all sorts of unofficial ways. Officially, Israel insisted no one was being forced to vote, and this was in fact true. But Israel also knew the rumors were being taken seriously, and they hoped this would bring tens of thousands of Arab residents to the polling stations. The rumor mill was something only a few of Kollek's closest aides knew about, and which they kept secret. Israel, and the mayor's, images were at stake. Not just in 1968 but also in every local and national election since, Kollek aides and Labor Party activists have spread unfounded stories about the ill consequences of not voting, in hopes of bringing Arab residents to the polling stations.

Israel was greatly disappointed with the results of the 1968 City Council election. The Arab residents took their chances that they would lose their Jerusalem residency rights and for the most part boycotted the election. Only a handful of eligible Arab voters showed up—7,500, or approximately 20 percent.[1] In subsequent years, even fewer Palestinians took part in elections.

In 1973 the percentage of Arabs who voted dropped to 8 percent.[2] In 1978, 15 percent of eligible Arab voters went to the polls, after a leading PLO official, Ramin A-Tawil, publicly came out in favor of participation several days before the election.[3] A-Tawil did not exactly jump up and down with excitement over Arab residents participating in the election. In an article in the weekly *Al-Awda* newspaper, A-Tawil described Kollek as "the best of all evils" for Arab residents. The mayor was not at all upset over the swipe and hoped it would work to his favor.

But the turnout was still small. So Kollek used some innovative arithmetic to make the number appear more significant. He declared that "despite the constant threats of PLO violence against the Arab populace, 40 percent of the male electorate did vote."[4] Kollek came up with the higher figure by not counting women, or men between 18 and 21, on the grounds that those Arab residents were not used to voting. He also did not count an undefined number that was meant to reflect Arabs who did not pay taxes and may have therefore thought they were forbidden to vote, as had been the case under Jordanian rule. That reasoning helped him declare the 1978 election a victory for Israeli rule in east Jerusalem. In later elections, however, Kollek found that even creative arithmetic was not enough to make Israel look good.

The stakes became higher in subsequent elections. In the 1980s, the Arab vote was no longer just a matter of Israel's image but of Kollek's political survival. Kollek was finding it increasingly difficult to muster a majority on the council. Starting with the 1983 election, the mayor and his aides looked to the Arab vote as a way to save his slowly dwindling public support in the Jewish sector. The Labor Party took it for granted that the only issue was convincing Arab residents to vote, and that if they did vote they would surely vote for Labor or a Labor-supported candidate. The right-wing Likud Party also took this for granted.

As the electoral importance of the Arab vote grew, so did the effort that Kollek and the Labor Party made to convince Arab residents to go the polls. Party officials divided the city into districts before each election. One party activist was put in charge of each district. A central task was arranging parlor meetings at which Arab residents would raise their concerns and the activists would encourage them to vote in order to make their voices heard. The housing shortage in the Arab sector that forced many Jerusalem Arabs to move to Azariya, A-Ram, and other Arab suburbs in the West Bank forced the Israeli political apparatus to expand beyond the city limits. Parlor meetings were held in those towns as well.

Kollek ran at the head of a list, called "One Jerusalem," that was ostensibly independent. But the mayor was a Labor Party member, and One Jerusalem was in effect Labor's list in Jerusalem. National party leaders called many of the shots when it came to election campaign strategy, and Kollek tried to use his close connections with the national party to his political advantage and the good of the city. Jerusalem, however, was not a Labor city. The city's relatively poor Jewish population, including a large percentage who had immigrated to Israel from Arab states, did not identify with Labor, which was seen as the party of Israelis of European descent. Particularly after the Likud's rise to power in 1977, the city became a bastion of support for the right-wing Likud Party. Kollek's political future depended heavily on his ability to distance himself enough from Labor to attract voters who would not vote for a Labor candidate. Kollek played this "independent" status to the hilt when appealing to Jewish voters.

The status of "independent" was also an important element in Kollek's appeal to Arabs. He knew that an important step in getting Arab residents to vote was to persuade them that their participation was a local issue—independent of the larger question of Jerusalem's political future. The mayor was always emphasizing that the municipality was a *local* authority, and that election issues in the City Council race did not involve national, politically charged issues, such as Palestinian claims to the city.

Oddly, however, Kollek chose figures identified with one of the national Israeli authorities most hated by the Arab population—the Shin Bet internal security force—to run his campaign in the Arab sector of east Jerusalem. In 1983 Yitzhak Tsur, who had headed the Jerusalem district for the Shin Bet, ran One Jerusalem's Arab sector campaign. In 1988 the campaign was run by Rueven Hazak, former Shin Bet deputy directory. Only in 1993 was a politician put at the head—Benvenisti, the former Kollek aide and city councilor. But even then a former Shin Bet officer, Shimon Romach, was director of operations for the Kollek camp.

Kollek thought Shin Bet officers knew east Jerusalem best, and he banked on their contacts within the Palestinian population to help his campaign. He appeared to have forgotten what sort of contacts the Shin Bet actually had. Tsur, Hazak, and Romach were great at setting up the parlor meetings in east Jerusalem at which party activists would try to drum up support for Kollek. The former internal security officers also brought Kollek the reports he wanted—showing Arab residents willing to vote for him. It is little wonder that these optimistic reports turned out to be unfounded. The Arab population was well conditioned when it came to dealing with Israeli security officers. Arab residents knew that it was always best to be agreeable and cordial. Tsur, Hazak, and Romach may have left the security service when they were working for Kollek's campaign, but in the residents' eyes, "Once a Shin Bet officer, always a Shin Bet officer." They told the retired officers what they wanted to hear, and then proceeded not to vote.

Kollek never seemed to learn from past electoral failures in the Arab sector. Neither did the senior Labor Party officials who were pulling many of the strings in his campaigns. The mayor was already in political trouble long before the 1993 municipal election. The right-wing Likud Party put up the strongest candidate it ever had to challenge the incumbent mayor, sensing the opportunity for victory. That candidate, Likud Knesset member Ehud Olmert, was a nationally known political figure who lived in Jerusalem. With his party out of government at the national level, Olmert saw the possibility of becoming Jerusalem mayor as a great political opportunity. So did the party. The power the post lacked in real terms—which Kollek had always lamented—was in many ways offset by its national and international prestige.

The Jerusalem race was to be held a year after Likud took a beating in the national election, and the party wanted badly to win it. The race was viewed by both parties as their first major test since the national election. Kollek had seriously considered retiring and allowing a younger Labor-affiliated candidate to run in what was expected to be a grueling race. Several key Labor Party officials in the city were also pushing for a change. Among the alternative candidates was a popular Israeli army general, Yitzhak Mordechai, who was considering retiring from the military and entering political life.

Israel has a long history of former army officers moving on to political careers. Prime Minister Binyamin Netanyahu was the commander of an elite Israel Defense Force commando unit. Prime Minister Yitzhak Rabin, whose assassination in 1995 brought about the early election Netanyahu won, had an illustrious army career during which he reached the highest rank in the Israeli Defense Force, chief of general staff. A long list of other Knesset members and ministers entered politics after making names for themselves in the military. Officially, army officers in Israel were not supposed to have any political contacts until they retire. But many officers considering a political career met with officials from the various parties while still serving. Both sides would try to keep the meetings secret, and Mordechai's meeting with Haim Cohen, the Labor Party secretary in Jerusalem, was no exception. Cohen saw Mordechai as Labor's best bet if Kollek retired, and Mordechai was interested in the post.

However, Rabin, then prime minister and party head, rejected the idea and pressured Kollek not to retire. Rabin saw the five-term mayor as his party's best chance for maintaining political control of the city. After extracting promises from Rabin for greater financial support for the city, Kollek announced that he would try for a sixth term. (Mordechai eventually joined the Likud Party and became defense minister in the Netanyahu government.)

In 1993, Labor was counting on the Arab vote to lift Kollek to victory. The old rumor mill first put to work for the party in 1968 was rolled out again. It had not worked well in the past, but this time, party officials believed, an added twist to the campaign made things different—the perceived "threat" of a Likud victory in Jerusalem. Labor portrayed Likud as a right-wing extremist party that would be bad for the city as a whole, and particularly for the Arab community of east Jerusalem. Labor charged that Olmert would take away Arab lands to build Jewish housing projects, move more Jewish families into the Muslim Quarter and other Arab neighborhoods, and invest little in development for the Arab sector.

Benvenisti, an outspoken supporter of Arab rights in Jerusalem, was brought aboard to help in the effort to get the Arab vote. Benvenisti promised party leaders victory. He predicted that tens of thousands of Arab residents would vote for Kollek, easily enough to ensure the incumbent mayor a victory. At party headquarters on Emek Rafayim Street, Benvenisti mapped out the party's east Jerusalem election strategy. The Arab sector was divided into areas, as in past elections, and Jewish and Arab party activists were assigned to each area and given the task of drumming up support for Kollek and spreading "the word" that an Olmert win would be a disaster for east Jerusalem.

Kollek did not stop there. He knew the Palestinian vote would be essential in the 1993 election, so he turned to the Palestinian leadership for support. At the time, the PLO was an illegal terrorist group in the eyes of the Israeli public and Israeli law. Consequently, all of Kollek's contacts with Palestinian leaders occurred under great secrecy. Kollek met twice with Faisal Husseini, the senior PLO official in Jerusalem, in 1993.[5] Both meetings were held in secret in the homes of close friends of the mayor (see Chapter 4). Kollek also spoke with other Palestinian leaders in the city.

But with a close election anticipated, Kollek decided to go higher. In June 1993 he appealed indirectly to PLO Chairman Yasser Arafat in Tunis. Abi Nathan, an Israeli peace activist, had recently served a jail term simply for meeting with Arafat. Kollek was not so daring as to speak with Arafat face to face, but he was willing to use a go-between to transfer a message to the PLO leader. The go-between was Omar al-Khatib, a Palestinian businessman from east Jerusalem with close ties to the PLO and to Kollek. The mayor asked Khatib, also known as Abu Khalid, to see if Arafat would be willing to give his approval for Palestinians in east Jerusalem to vote in the mayoral election, or at least not make any statement or take any action preventing such participation. In return, Kollek held out the promise that he would try to push through his plan for granting greater self-rule to the Palestinian residents.

The letter, written in Arabic and quoted below, focused on what Kollek had to offer Arafat. Kollek's request of Arafat was not put in writing, for fear the letter would be uncovered. Abu Khalid promised to pass it to Arafat verbally.

Dear Abu Khalid,
We met several days ago and you asked me about the possibility of setting up additional community councils in Arab neighborhoods. I have always supported increasing the number of community councils in Arab neighborhoods, on condition, of course, that this is what the residents want, and that they see co-operation with the municipality as a way to improve services in their neighborhoods. Today, I am still willing to give any new community council that is founded in a special geographic area the same conditions that we give the existing community councils.

There is in Jerusalem a single umbrella organization for all of the community councils, Jewish and Arab alike. The council representatives meet from time to time to discuss ways of improving municipal services. There is no doubt that this body helps us to improve our service to the residents. If in addition to this, the Arab community councils want to meet to discuss the special issues that the Arab neighborhoods and their populations face, I would not oppose it. We would look favorably upon such an initiative, because it would give us the opportunity to improve municipal services to residents.

I wish you well, and look forward to a fruitful cooperation between us.
Sincerely,
Teddy Kollek

Kollek's oral message carried by Abu Khalid was more straightforward: "If I am re-elected, you can be assured that I will push for granting limited autonomy to Palestinians in east Jerusalem. But it is important that I win, so the rights of Palestinian residents in the city can be assured." In Kollek's meetings with Husseini and other local Palestinian leaders, he was led to understand that the message was received by the PLO chairman. Arafat's answer: he would not come out in favor of participation, but he also would not vocally oppose it.

Kollek was satisfied. He believed that Arafat's position and what he viewed as the fear Palestinians had that Olmert would be elected would bring Arab residents to the polling stations in record numbers. Kollek later discovered how wrong that assessment was.

Aharon Sarig, the longtime city official and close associate of Kollek, anticipated what was to come. Kollek wanted Sarig to work for the campaign's east Jerusalem headquarters. In his three decades at city hall, Sarig had regularly helped raise support for Kollek in east Jerusalem. An Arabist by education, he served as the mayor's Arab affairs adviser in the 1970s. Sarig had excellent contacts in east Jerusalem. Kollek hoped Sarig, now retired from city hall, would be free to work full time on his campaign.

Sarig turned Kollek down, despite pressure from his former boss and the party.[6] Sarig was fed up with making promises to Arab residents that he knew would never be fulfilled. He had been involved in some capacity or another in all of Kollek's campaigns since 1967. In each, Sarig had watched, and sometimes even participated in, the workings of the rumor mill aimed at scaring Arab residents into voting. He had heard the promises made by Kollek's people of improvements for Arab east Jerusalem if only the mayor was elected to one more term. He had even made some of the promises himself, only to watch as nothing came of them.

Election day 1993 began quietly in east Jerusalem, and it stayed that way. Dozens of vans and buses hired by the Labor Party set out in the early morning from the parking area by Ammunition Hill, in north Jerusalem, where twenty-five years earlier, during the Six Day War, a famous battle was fought between Israel and Jordan. The Labor Party was prepared to literally bring Arab voters to the polls. But there were few riders. The polling station in A-Tur, on the Mount of Olives, was virtually empty most of the morning. So too were the polling stations in Shuafat, in Jabal Mukaber, and in other Arab neighborhoods of the city. Benvenisti was frantic, but he chose to believe that the Arab residents preferred to vote in the evening, under cover of darkness, when they could enter the polling stations without being seen. This was a commonly held view among Israeli political activists who operated in east Jerusalem. But when night came around, there were still few Arab voters. Out of approximately 85,000 eligible Arab voters in 1993, only about 5,000, or 5.8 percent, voted.[7]

Kollek ended the day the loser in east Jerusalem and in all Jerusalem. Party officials could not put the blame on Arab voters, because the mayor also was beaten by Olmert in the Jewish sector. An extremely high Arab turnout could have prevented the defeat, but Kollek had repeatedly failed to come through for Arab residents, so many, like Sarig, were not surprised that Arab residents did not come through for him.

6

The Eagle Has Landed

Enough can never be said about the importance of education in any society. Good schooling is traditionally considered the remedy for all ills. The economy is weak—improve the education system and children will grow up to be better workers. The nation's morale is low—turn to the schools to recharge the national vigor. A deadly disease is rampant—pump more into research and education. The examples may be exaggerated, but the principle remains. The education system is one of the bedrocks of any society.

It is no wonder that, right after the 1967 war, taking control of the east Jerusalem education system became a top priority of the Israeli government. Debates raged about many issues—what status Jerusalem Arabs would be given, where the city's borders should be drawn, which flag should fly on the Temple Mount, and a hundred and one other matters—but on the subject of education in east Jerusalem there was a consensus. Arab children must begin, immediately, to learn like any other Israeli child. And this meant doing away with the Jordanian system and replacing it with Israel's. East Jerusalem was now part of Israel, and so too were its schools; it was unthinkable that a foreign state should administer a part of the education system.

To understand this position more clearly, we must remember that just after the Six Day War, Jordan was, in Israel's view, an enemy state. Allowing east Jerusalem schools to be run by Jordanians was as unimaginable for Israelis as allowing New York City schools to be run by the Soviets would have been for Americans. No one in Israel would have even considered such a possibility. With this in mind, Israel brought the school system in east Jerusalem under its wing.

"One of the first decisions made by the government after the war was to make sure the schools in east Jerusalem opened as normal in the fall," recalls Aharon Sarig, who right after the war was put in charge of education in the Arab sector.[1] Sarig, a veteran municipal official, spoke fluent Arabic and over the years became known as one of the local government's leading experts on east Jerusalem. "We were desperate to open the schools at all costs," Sarig says. "We wanted to return life to normal as quickly as possible, and knew that as long as the schools remained closed this would not happen. All the schools didn't open at the beginning of the academic year. But after several months, most of them were opened." Rashidiya High School, the largest boys' public high school in east Jerusalem, opened in January 1968. The school's Jordanian principal, who resigned, was replaced by an Israeli hire, Rateb Ghabi. The largest girl's high school, Ma'amuniya, opened the next month. A new principal was also appointed there by the Israelis—a Christian Arab named Georgette Mabedi.

A number of teachers and principals fled east Jerusalem after the war and did not return. But of those who remained in the city, only a handful refused to work for the Israeli government. The Jordanian Education Ministry in Amman had promised to pay the salaries of Arab educators if they would stay out of the schools and help torpedo Israel's attempt to run them. But the salaries the Israelis offered were several times larger than the Jordanians'. Also, Arab educators in east Jerusalem were accepted into Israel's strong labor unions, which were well known for ensuring good working conditions for their members. In the end, most of the Arab teachers and principals who previously worked under Jordanian rule continued under the Israelis.

According to Sarig, the municipality had no problem finding candidates for the open slots that remained; a few of the new hires were Jews from west Jerusalem who knew Arabic. But in its drive to open the schools as quickly as possible, Israel dropped many of the usual requirements for new teachers and principals. Some of the new employees did not even have high school degrees. "We were set on opening the schools. It's true that all the teachers did not meet the normal standards. But we opened special enrichment classes and over the years all those teachers who originally weren't qualified received the training they needed," says Sarig.

Israeli administrators did not seriously consider that there would be opposition to the take-over of the schools—that Arabs would object, for example, to teaching the Zionist poet Haim Bialik in a third-grade classroom in Jabal Mukaber. Israel saw the education system as a tool it could use to try to influence Arab children in east Jerusalem to be supportive of the new Jewish state. But Israel was to discover quickly how unrealistic this goal was. On the other hand, when it came to schooling, Israel was understanding of the Arab residents' status as a minority. Even before the Six Day War, a large, heterogeneous Arab minority lived within Israel's borders. There were Christian Arabs, Muslim Arabs, Cherkassen, and Druze, and many of these groups had subgroups. Within the Jewish community itself, there were ultra-Orthodox, national religious, traditional, and secular Jews. Since the founding of the state, this ethnic and religious diversity had been reflected in the public school system as a whole. In reality, there was not one public school system but four systems for the four largest populations in the country: Arab, ultra-Orthodox, national religious, and secular Jewish. In addition, there were also many private schools that answered to various ethnic, religious, and vocational needs. All the systems fell under the ultimate control of Israel's Education Ministry.

Israeli policy-makers at first believed that an efficient way to integrate east Jerusalem schools into this complex picture was to fit them into two of the five existing categories. The public schools, which in 1967 numbered 68, were placed under the auspices of the Israeli-Arab school system, and the private schools were treated like other private schools in the country as a whole—independent but still answering to the Education Ministry.[2] Israeli policy-makers would soon find out, however, that this was not going to be an easy fit. Palestinian Jerusalemites resisted Israeli control of the public schools, and parents showed their dislike in two dramatic ways. Their first option was holding strikes and keeping their children out of school for days at a time. The protests and strikes began with the opening of the 1967 school year and did not let up. The other option was even more disruptive. They took their children out of the public system altogether and enrolled them in private schools.

East Jerusalem private schools have long been some of the best in the city. The most well-known include Frères College for Boys, near New Gate; Schmidt, near Damascus Gate; al-Wardiya in Beit Hanina; Antoniya in the Old City; St. Joseph for girls by Jaffa Gate; and Ibrahimiyya College in the Suwana neighborhood on the Mount of Olives. In addition to tuition paid by parents, many private schools received money from the foreign governments that originally founded them or at some point in their histories decided to take them under their wings, because of their location in Jerusalem. Various Christian groups and churches also supported, and ran, many of the private schools. This backing gave the private schools some financial independence.

It also gave them a large degree of political independence. Israel was hesitant to interfere with a school under the auspices of the Vatican, and for that matter with any of the Christian schools, out of concern for the international outcry it would likely provoke. Immediately after the Six Day War, Israel promised Christian leaders in Jerusalem—and sent the message abroad—that it would not interfere with their religious affairs and give them a great deal of autonomy. The promise was meant to relate to holy places, but after a short time church-run schools were also included.

Israel treated the Muslim religious schools similarly. There were 16 such schools in 1967, run by the Wakf, the Muslim religious authority in Jerusalem.[3] Israel allowed those schools to remain autonomous, making no attempts to influence curriculum or any other affairs of the Wakf schools. Instead, these schools continued to be supervised by the Jordanian Ministry of the Wakf, as were the Wakf schools in the West Bank.

There were also six schools in Jerusalem run by the United Nations Relief and Works Agency (UNRWA), in whose affairs Israel also did not interfere.[4] UNRWA had special status in Jerusalem because of its social and welfare initiatives. Israeli leaders knew that to hamper the work of UNRWA in Jerusalem would invite international criticism. Israel preferred to avoid this, and made no effort to incorporate the UNRWA schools into its education system. Overall, unlike in the rest of Israel, in east Jerusalem private schools functioned for the most part independently of the Israeli authorities.

Instead, despite their different sources of funding, all of these private schools fell under the academic supervision of Jordan after the war. Pupils at the private schools took Jordanian matriculation exams, and if they passed they received Jordanian graduation certificates. Husni al-Ashab, who had been responsible for Arab schools in the city before 1967 and who turned down Israel's offer to oversee Arab public schools in east Jerusalem, stayed on after 1967 as the chief administrator for the private schools. In reality, however, his job changed only a little. In the first years after the war, the public schools amounted to only 30 percent of the system.[5] Most east Jerusalem schools still fell under al-Ashab's authority. He continued to work out of an Old City office just outside the Haram al-Sharif. The office functioned as a branch of the Jordanian Education Ministry. Israel did not object, hoping that this concession would buy some peace in east Jerusalem.

The Jordanian-run private schools turned into a haven for Arab residents who did not want their children learning in Israeli schools. Rashidiya's enrollment dropped from nearly a thousand to twelve.[6] The mass exodus from the Israeli public school system continued year after year, until Israeli education officials realized that the system would collapse unless they took drastic action. Just before the school year in 1974, six years after Israel took control of east Jerusalem, the officials decided in favor of change rather than collapse. Then education minister Yigal Alon appointed a committee to investigate the problem. The committee recommended that the public schools be returned to the Jordanian curriculum that had been taught up to 1967. Alon accepted the recommendation.[7]

But the Israeli government did not take the decision easily. There were many officials, particularly in the Education Ministry, who did not want Israeli taxpayers to pay for Arab youngsters to learn the curriculum of an "enemy nation." Many Israel officials also saw the move as an affront to Israeli sovereignty in Jerusalem.

Much of the credit for the 1974 flip-flop that brought the Jordanian curriculum back to Jerusalem goes to Kollek. Kollek hounded the ministry on the issue. Kollek wanted quiet. He wanted to do away with as many of the points of friction as possible in the all-too-tense city. Kollek lobbied hard, and eventually the government officials above him, particularly in the Education Ministry, agreed. And from his perspective, the decision was a great success. After the change to the Jordanian curriculum, Arab pupils began enrolling in larger numbers in the public schools.[8] The protests ended, and relative normalcy returned to Arab east Jerusalem schools, as Kollek had hoped.

The condition Israel had set on the agreement to permit the Jordanian curriculum back in the schools was that Israel be allowed to review schoolbooks and other materials being sent from Amman.[9] Israeli education officials knew exactly what they were looking for when they read through the material: pages on Middle East geography and the history of the Arab-Israeli conflict. The Jordanian presentation of these and other issues was not exactly what Israel wanted taught to youngsters in east Jerusalem. The State of Israel was not even mentioned on maps in the textbooks, and when it was mentioned in the text, the Jewish state was depicted as an evil, imperialistic aggressor that brought only suffering to the region. Israel, in the first years after the Six Day War, still had visions of young Arabs in east Jerusalem accepting Israeli rule in the city. Keeping the anti-Israel curriculum away from them was a first step toward changing the next generation's view of Israel for the better, and so these pages were removed from textbooks, or altered.

The Israeli Education Ministry also added two subjects aimed at fostering identification with Israel. The first was the study of Hebrew. Arab youngsters had to begin lessons in Hebrew in the first years of elementary school and continue through high school. The second subject was civics. By adding it to the curriculum, Israel hoped to turn the Arab youngsters of east Jerusalem into good Israeli citizens.

It is one thing to hand down orders from above; it is quite another to make sure they are implemented on the ground. In ministry conferences and workshops, grand plans were drawn up for teaching Hebrew and civics in east Jerusalem's public schools. But most of those plans were never realized. There was simply no motivation on the part of Arab teachers and pupils to teach and learn Hebrew and Israeli civics. On the contrary, there was often outright opposition. "What could we do, put an Israeli supervisor by every Arab teacher to make sure that anti-Israeli material was not taught?" asks Sarig. "There is a reality, and you simply have to learn to live with it."

In some ways the Israeli take-over of the east Jerusalem education system was a success. Kollek managed to walk the fine line between calls by the national government to tighten control over the education system and his own desire to ease tensions in the city. By convincing the ministry to allow the public schools to return to the Jordanian curriculum, Kollek managed to revive the east Jerusalem school system as a whole. Public schools were again full, and private schools returned to their normal level of enrollment.

For the most part, Israeli education authorities steered clear of the Arab private schools in Jerusalem. They did not interfere with the curriculum, with hiring and firing of principals and teachers, or with any other aspect of operations. But some Israeli officials questioned this lack of supervision. Who was ensuring that a teacher was qualified, let alone the principal? Without any Israeli supervision, aren't the private schools bound to feel free to promote anti-Israeli sentiments among the pupils? What was to prevent the hiring of teachers who were active in Palestinian national movements or jailed in the past for security crimes? These questions remained in the back of the minds of Israeli education officials at both the national and local level throughout the 1970s and into the early 1980s. But nothing was done to answer them. The general feeling was that at all costs rocking the boat should be avoided.

But in the mid-1980s, Israel's educational and political concerns about the Arab schools were again hotly debated at city hall and in the Education Ministry. In the end, though, it was decided once again to leave well enough alone. The "don't rock the boat" mentality prevailed. Sensitive to the fact that any changes imposed by Israel on private schools in east Jerusalem would be interpreted by Arab residents as unnecessary interference and would have devastating effects on the system as a whole, Israeli administrators did nothing.

The semiquiet in the Arab schools came to an abrupt end in 1987, with the intifada. East Jerusalem schools were at the center of the uprisings. A major strategic component of the intifada was the participation of young Palestinians, including elementary school pupils, in the violent confrontations with Israeli security forces. Strikes to protest the Israeli occupation called by the intifada leaders did not just shut down Palestinian businesses; the east Jerusalem private schools were also closed by their administrators, who either identified with, or felt that they had to be seen as identifying with, the Palestinian protest against the Israeli occupation. In the public schools, Israeli administrators kept the doors open in defiance of the intifada leaders' call to strike, but the students stayed away just the same. Dozens of strike days were called by Palestinian leaders; some commemorated certain Palestinian national days and were known long in advance; others were announced just days or hours after some immediate event, such as the shooting of a Palestinian demonstrator by Israel soldiers. In the middle of the school day, masked youths would enter classrooms and call on the pupils to leave and take part in demonstrations against Israel. The teachers and principals were in no position to resist, and pupils walked out of school and joined the protests.

Even when the schools were open, they quickly became the sites of violent clashes between pupils and Israeli police and soldiers. The clashes normally occurred in the morning, as pupils made their way to school, and again in the afternoon, when classes let out. Unrest was most common at the Rashidiya Boys High School and Ma'amuniya Girls High School, both of which were centrally located and had large student bodies. But elementary schools were also involved. The youngsters would throw stones and bottles at a passing Israeli army jeep, and the soldiers would fire tear gas and some-times rubber bullets in response. More pupils would join in, and the soldiers would call in reinforcements. The clashes lasted from min-utes to hours. The pupils would run for cover inside the school, and depending on the severity of the incident, the soldiers would give chase. Tear gas in hallways and classrooms; broken windows from stones and rubber bullets; police on patrol by the school gate—this was the reality of east Jerusalem schools during the intifada. The municipality lost all control of the situation, and under these pres-sures the education system in east Jerusalem—public, private, Mus-lim, Christian—literally collapsed.

Mihtkal Natur, the Israeli-appointed head of the east Jerusalem public school system at the time, resigned. Natur, an Israeli Arab, felt there was nothing he could do to contain the unrest at the schools. He had headed the system for over a decade and had watched as it deteriorated from being Israel's great hope for promot-ing coexistence in Jerusalem to being the vortex of the Palestinian-Israeli struggle. By the time Natur left his post in March 1988, the police were calling all the shots in the schools. Natur would get a daily call from the Russian Compound police headquarters inform-ing him which schools were shut down and how many pupils had been detained. There was little education going on in Arab schools in east Jerusalem, and Natur believed that nothing he could do would make a difference.

One east Jerusalem educator who was able to keep the peace was Fouzi Abu Ghosh, the Arab-Israeli principal of a vocational high school in Ras al-Amud. One morning at the start of the intifada Abu Ghosh called the entire student body together. "The intifada is the only way to secure our freedom," Abu Ghosh began his address. "We must fight the occupation. I am too old to throw the stones like you, but I am still with you." Abu Ghosh quickly won over his pupils.

Let us consider together where is the best place to throw our stones. Here, from the schoolyard, the angle to the road is not very good. From just outside the school, the angle is much

better. But wait, let's consider this for a second. If we throw a
stone at a car from that point, it is likely to crash into the wadi
along the road, and the homes there. Fellow Palestinians live in
those homes. We don't want to hurt them. Come to think of it,
how do we know that the cars we are stoning are not being
driven by Palestinians? The road by our school is used by many
Palestinians. We must be careful not to injure fellow Palestinians . . . Maybe we should not throw stones from around the
school.

The pupils listened intently. They seemed convinced. There still were
several stoning incidents by the school after Abu Ghosh's speech,
but for the most part it was quiet. The vocational school remained
open even through the most heated periods of the intifada in Jerusalem, when, at other schools, studying and classes were the last things
on anyone's mind.

Israel might have learned something from Abu Ghosh. Instead,
the paramilitary border policemen it placed at the entrance to many
schools served largely as a provocation. Israel may have been right in
wanting to keep a presence near the schools, in the event of unrest,
and also as a symbolic reminder of who was in charge. But by plac-
ing policemen at the school gate, they were inviting unrest, and that
is what the police received, time and again. Opposition to this policy
at city hall did no good. Police chiefs in Israel are not answerable to
the local authority. Instead, they receive their orders from a national
police chief, who oversees the police force throughout the country.
The national police chief is under the authority of the police minister. The mayor has no say in police operations. The most a mayor
can do is appeal to the minister in hopes of having an influence on local police operations. When it came to the question of what to do
about the role of east Jerusalem schools during the intifada, city hall
was at the mercy of the police.

Kollek recognized that the schools were at times the center of unrest, but he preferred living with this situation for the sake of the little learning that was getting done. For Kollek, as always, it was an
issue of trying to keep life in the city as normal as possible, despite

the tensions and unrest. The sole concerns of the police, by contrast, were security and keeping the peace, and if that meant closing schools, they were set on doing so. The police preferred that teenagers protest and demonstrate in their own neighborhoods and villages rather than at school.

Rashidiya High School was shut down during most of the winter and spring of 1988. The school, located just outside Herod's Gate in the heart of east Jerusalem, had become the daily site of sharp clashes between pupils and police. The parents were informed of the decision, and despite their opposition the school was closed. Rashidiya was on a busy thoroughfare, which made protests there particularly disruptive. Most other major east Jerusalem schools were also located downtown or on central thoroughfares. It is one thing to detain a pupil; it is quite another to detain a rock-throwing teenager on the street. In the villages where the pupils lived, there was also less likelihood that the international media would be on hand when such incidents broke out. Thus, the police saw closing schools as being to their advantage.

Kollek was desperate to get Rashidiya, the largest high school in the east Jerusalem, reopened. He ordered Gal, the education department head, to find a solution. Gal's first attempt, however, failed. He had asked parents to sign statements that their children would not be involved in protests in or around the school, and they refused. But in a second initiative, Gal demonstrated that a little innovative thinking can solve some of the toughest problems in Jerusalem. The parents committee agreed that parents who were increasingly concerned that their children were losing out on their education because of the intifada would take turns standing guard at the entrance to the school in the morning when the pupils arrived and again in the afternoon when they left. The parents' presence was intended to keep the pupils from throwing objects at the police and other Israeli targets. And it worked. Rashidiya High School reopened and for the most part stayed open for the rest of the intifada. There were still sporadic stone-throwing incidents, but things were otherwise quiet.

With Natur's resignation in March, Kollek needed to find a new candidate to head the system, and quickly. He turned to the Israeli

Education Ministry, which "lent" him one of its experts on the Arab sector, Victor Gabai. Gabai was more assertive than his predecessor. With Kollek's backing, he forced the police to allow him to attend their daily "intifada meetings." At 2:30 each afternoon, senior police officers would meet at the Russian Compound to review the events of the day and plan for additional unrest. "When I first took over, it was as if the police were in control of the schools," Gabai recalls.[10] "I would get a call at the end of the day in which they would report what schools were closed down, and what problems there had been."

Gabai says the municipality did not oppose police being tough on pupils involved in stone throwing. But unlike the police, the municipality wanted to "use the carrot, and not just the stick," Gabai says. That meant working together with parents to keep schools open, trying to convince the police that it was sometimes better if they kept away from the schools so as not to provoke the pupils, and sending a clear message to the public in east Jerusalem that whatever their protest against the Israeli authorities, it should not come at the expense of the schools where their children learn.

> I would meet parents' group after parents' group and tell them one thing—that they and their children were the only ones that would be hurt when schools were closed down . . . I'd get a report of stone-throwing near Sheikh Abdallah School on Salah A-Din Street and run down there. That was one of the first things that I convinced Teddy, that I needed the municipality to provide me a car so I could move fast when needed . . . In front of Herod's Gate, border police would be firing rubber bullets and tear gas towards the crowd of pupils. I screamed, "Hold the fire, just for a few minutes. Give me a chance to talk to them." Then I would run towards the side of the pupils. My eyes were burning from the tear gas. Together with the teachers I convinced the pupils to stop throwing the stones and go back into the school.

Whether quiet was maintained at the schools, however, appeared to depend less on Gabai, the police, or other Israeli authorities than on the intifada leaders and pupils themselves. The total anarchy in the schools during the first months of the intifada was eventually brought under control, but the general atmosphere of revolt continued. Municipal officials would meet with parents to try to persuade them to help. The meetings would sometimes pay off, and sometimes not. Even when parents agreed to intervene, in hopes of keeping the schools open, their children would not always listen.

In one significant instance parents' intervention did help. In the spring of 1991 Israeli officials discovered rampant cheating on matriculation examinations at east Jerusalem high schools. At Ma'amuniya Girls School several teenagers stood outside the room where exams were being taken and passed answers through an open window. This was done in the full view of the exam monitors. There was little attempt to hide the cheating. The young people had become arrogant, believing the monitors would not dare turn them in. And they were right. The intifada leaders had decided that the struggle against Israel had made it impossible for the youths to learn and that they deserved a break on the exams. Neither the monitors nor teachers were in a position to question the decision. The Israeli education authorities, however, would not tolerate the action. Gabai announced that all examinations in the schools were being halted until the cheating ended. He then garnered an agreement from parents to monitor the exams. Only then were the exams resumed. And with the parents' help, they were successfully administered.

"Teddy was always saying that we need to know how to use both the carrot and the stick," Gabai says today. "Even during the most difficult times [of the intifada] he somehow would find extra money, even for the private schools. We would go down there in secret to small ceremonies in which a new classroom or program was inaugurated. The principals knew they faced being branded collaborators, but they still accepted the help, because they badly needed it." The municipality helped the private schools "because we also wanted them to be dependent on us," Gabai explains.

This was the crux of Israel's thinking toward the east Jerusalem education system, after the rosy-eyed days when it believed it could bring up Arab youngsters as Hebrew-speaking Zionists: the more dependent east Jerusalem schools were on Israel for support, the better. Dependence created numerous opportunities for promoting coexistence and understanding on the part of Arab residents. Arab teachers from east Jerusalem received enrichment courses in Tel Aviv or elsewhere in Israel and were thus brought into greater contact with Israeli society. Palestinian parents worked together with municipal authorities on improving school and after-school programs run by Israel. The school system offered many opportunities for such positive interaction between Israeli authorities and Arab residents of east Jerusalem. National leaders hoped that this positive contact would translate into at least some level of allegiance from Palestinian Jerusalemites with the Jewish state. But in the end, this hope was never realized. Gabai puts much of the blame on Israel.

Israel did succeed in attracting large numbers of Palestinian pupils to its school system. By 1992, 50 percent of Arab pupils, or about 26,000, attended public schools in east Jerusalem, compared to 30 percent and even fewer in the first years of Israeli rule.[11] The public schools had a good reputation, and the Arab parents wanted their children in the best schools. "At the height of the intifada, in Abu Tur and Shuafat [Arab] parents held demonstrations demanding their pupils be allowed into public schools," which had become overcrowded and had begun turning down Palestinian youngsters, recalls Gabai. For Israeli officials, the protests were a sign they were doing something right in east Jerusalem.

But Israel failed to follow through on its success. Instead of building more schools to accommodate Arab pupils, Israel turned the Arab youngsters away. (That the state should deny public elementary education to some of its residents never raised an eyebrow in Israel.) Neither the national nor municipal authorities could decide how to handle the situation. No comprehensive plan for expanding the Arab public school system in Jerusalem was ever developed. Kollek had general ideas about what he wanted, which he would pass on to Gabai, but there was never any coordinated effort. Long-range planning at the level of simply forecasting how many Arab pupils were expected to join the public school system in future years was never accomplished. Each year, school officials would merely react to the numbers they received from the field. "We never knew what would happen two or three days down the road, let alone in a couple of years," says Gabai. The vision of the education system becoming the bridge for better relations between Jews and Arabs in Jerusalem was never translated by Israel into a concrete plan. And because of this, for all the good intentions, the vision never became reality.

From Israel's perspective, the failure to devise and implement an effective plan for running Arab schools in east Jerusalem was particularly troubling, because it created a window of opportunity for its competitors to gain influence in the city. Between 1967 and 1994 Jordan played a central role in east Jerusalem public and private schools, through the curriculum and high school graduation exams. During this period, the PLO also tried to make inroads in the east Jerusalem private school system, primarily by transferring tens of thousands of dollars to Palestinian schools in east Jerusalem in the 1980s. But the group's funds dried up toward the end of the decade, and around the same time support from Jordan begin to drop off significantly.

In 1992, with the intifada still roaring, Israeli education officials began preparing for the worst. The officials reasoned that the Arab private education system was on the verge of collapse because funding from the PLO and Jordan was falling and that responsibility for the pupils in the private schools would fall upon the municipality. If the Jerusalem municipality meant what it said about being the local authority in not only west but also east Jerusalem, then it would have no choice but to care for the pupils from the private schools.

There were also other concerns. The continued unrest had put the Israeli police on edge. Police commanders were threatening to close down the entire east Jerusalem school system, private as well as public, hoping this would help them quell the uprisings. The Wakf schools were having trouble of another kind. Wakf school teachers were not being paid their salaries regularly, and for several months the teachers had received no salaries at all. Parents had had enough of the frequent strikes called by the teachers to protest not being paid and were threatening to enroll their children in the public school system, even though the system was overseen by Israeli authorities. All these developments signaled to Israeli officials that they had better ready themselves for major changes in the east Jerusalem schools.

In fall 1992, Gal, who had moved from head of the education department to the post of city manager—the senior unelected official at city hall—initiated a series of meetings to discuss the east Jerusalem school system. A central topic for discussion was on what basis to open a dialogue between the municipality and the city's private schools. The Israeli officials tried to foresee to what degree the private schools would be willing to cooperate with city hall. They even considered whether to offer some of the private schools the option of being completely absorbed into the public school system. A working paper was drawn up after the series of meetings was wrapped up in October.[12]

At the time, of the 40,000 Arab pupils in Jerusalem, 22,000 were in 36 private schools and 18,000 were in 35 public schools.[13] The municipality divided the Arab private schools into two categories, one largely Christian, the other all Muslim. City hall hoped that tight relations could be established with the former group, which included Schmidt, St. Joseph, Martin Luther, and Freres. There were also two Muslim schools in this category—Ibrahimiyya in Sawana and el-Vabala in the Old City. The latter group, consisting of the Muslim schools, was considered too hostile to Israel to agree to any kind of cooperation. These "hostile" schools included Nizamiyya in Beit Hanina; el-Umma in Dahiyat al-Barid; and Dar el-Aytam in Akbat al-Sariya. Israel viewed these school administrations as extremist, but officials expressed hope that limited relations could be established.

Indeed, the bottom line after the series of meetings and the working paper was that Israel saw the weakening financial situation of the private school system in east Jerusalem as a great opportunity to extend its influence and control. Israel was prepared to offer the private schools, even the so-called "hostile" Muslim schools, financial assistance, on the condition that Israel be given at least partial control of any school it supported.

What did the Israeli education authorities want? On the list included in the working paper were these items: teachers from the private school that received city assistance would be sent periodically to professional training courses organized by the municipality and Education Ministry; Hebrew would be added to the curriculum; anti-Israeli activity would be forbidden; Israeli government and municipal supervisors would periodically visit the school. The officials could not have thought of a more unrealistic set of conditions for cooperation with east Jerusalem private schools, which since 1967 had no official contact with the Israeli authorities. Previous attempts by Israel to extend its influence over these schools had failed. In 1992 Israel hoped it would do better, because the schools were hard up for financial support. But hardship was not enough to get the Arab private schools to agree to Hebrew classes and even limited Israeli supervision.

Some who were Israeli education officials at the time now say they might have been willing to give money to a school that met only a few of the demands, if the school had only asked.[14] One reason for Israel's willingness to bend their own rules was the lack of space in Arab public schools run by the Jewish state; these public schools would have had to absorb Arab pupils who found their private schools closed because of lack of funds. But no requests for funding were received from the private schools. The Arabs of east Jerusalem had survived the stick, and now they were rejecting the carrot.

The one private Arab school that did approach the municipality for assistance was not given the "easy treatment."[15] The municipality stuck by the book, demanding that all criteria be met, from Hebrew language instruction to Israeli supervisors. Not surprisingly, the school broke off negotiations with the municipality even before they really began.

Another incident the same year also speaks volumes about the approach of the Israeli government toward education in east Jerusalem. In the spring of 1992 the Education Ministry announced a new program it wanted adopted by schools nationwide. The program was titled "Our Town" and was aimed at teaching youngsters about the community in which they lived.[16] Youngsters from Tel Aviv would learn about Tel Aviv, those from Tiberias about Tiberias, and so on. Only the Israeli authorities forgot a small detail when it came to their capital—that there were also Arabs living in the city. The ministry, located in Jerusalem not far from the Old City, cannot claim it did not know better. A committee of "experts" put together an "Our Town" program for Jerusalem but apparently only for the city's Jewish schools. No one asked the Arab schools if they were interested. It was simply decided for them that their unique curriculum had no room for a project such as "Our Town," despite the potential of such a program for creating better understanding between Jews and Arabs in Jerusalem.

The experts worked for nearly a year. In the spring of 1993, the book on which the Jerusalem program was to be based was completed. It opened with a greeting by Mayor Teddy Kollek. "Now, as you begin to learn about Jerusalem . . . I wish you good luck. Learn about the city, tour the city, get to know the special characteristics from the human and social perspective of a city made up of different ethnic, religious, and cultural groups, that live in a fragile co-existence, that is slowly transforming into a co-existence of peace."[17] Kollek concluded the greeting, "Jerusalem was . . . a city of disputes, . . . but I am sure that you will be the ones to see Jerusalem become the city of peace that it should." Kollek's opening was moving. But a quick glance at the booklet's contents suggested that it could have been written before 1967.[18] Chapter One opens with the question, "Who is a Jerusalemite?" The answer: "Three friends, Yaron from the Morasha neighborhood, Yael who lives in Kiryat Hayovel, and Rami from Ramot, [who] state emphatically, 'We are Jerusalemites.'" There was no mention of the city's Arab population. Is the child reading the book supposed to understand that Mahmoud from Silwan, or Abdallah from Sheikh Jarrah, or Fatmah from Shuafat are not Jerusalemites? It would seem that way. It is as if everything Arab in the city is being hidden from view.

In the chapter "Majestic Jerusalem," there is a picture of Haram al-Sharif, the site of the al-Aksa and Dome of the Rock, which is held holy by Muslims around the world. Under the picture, it states matter-of-factly, "Mount Moriah (The Temple Mount), showing the Western Wall and on top mosques." There is nothing mentioned about the importance of the site to Muslims. Chapter Four gives details of eight Jerusalem neighborhoods. Not one of the neighborhoods described is Arab.

Kollek was furious when he was informed about the book's contents by aides. He angrily contacted the education minister and the deputy mayor in charge of education demanding changes. They promised Kollek the book would be revised. But it never was.

In a last-ditch effort to expand its influence to the east Jerusalem private schools, Israel offered the schools the status of "unofficially recognized school."[19] The idea was to allow the schools to continue to call themselves private—because of political and religious constraints—while they in fact would receive a large part of their funding from Israel. In return, the schools—again, unofficially—would permit Israeli supervision, but in a far less intensive manner than previously proposed. The new proposal was well received. Three private schools even became "unofficially recognized schools." Israel appeared to be on the verge of doing what it had set out to do in 1967: to spread its influence over the entire school system in east Jerusalem. Only again this time, Israel found itself outfoxed. Just when it seemed to have found the right formula, historic changes were in the making that would forever alter the relations between Arabs and Jews in Jerusalem.

The signing of the Oslo Accord in September 1993 on the White House lawn put the Palestinians on the map in Jericho and Gaza. It also gave them certain authority throughout the West Bank, including control over education. Publicly, the Israeli government reacted with surprise that the Oslo Accord appeared to give the Palestinians control over education in east Jerusalem as well. But privately, Israeli officials admitted they had not fully considered all the implications of the accord. One of these implications was that by permitting the Palestinian Authority (or PA, the Palestinian government in the new self-rule areas) to take over the entire education system in the West Bank, Israel was in effect also giving the PA control of Palestinian schools in east Jerusalem. The West Bank and east Jerusalem school systems had long been interlinked, starting with the fact that they both followed the Jordanian curriculum. This link could not be so easily severed.

The PA, for its part, wanted to make itself felt immediately. Its first move was to replace the traditional emblem of Jordan, an eagle, with that of the PLO, also an eagle but in a different design, on the front of textbooks given to pupils in the West Bank, Gaza, and east Jerusalem. It was only a symbolic act, but it caused a stir that was felt from the offices of the Jerusalem mayor to the prime minister of Israel. For the Israeli right wing, the sticker sparked a reaction that perhaps could only have been exceeded by the arrival in Jerusalem of PLO leader Yasser Arafat himself. For the Israeli government, the move appeared to be the first of many tests of just how authority might be shared in Jerusalem between Israel and the Palestinians. But instead of rising to the occasion, Israeli leaders reverted to old formulas of rejection and disapproval.

The textbook cover episode occurred just before the 1994–1995 school year. The previous year, the PA had announced its intention of implementing its own curriculum in east Jerusalem. With the announcement came rumors that better-qualified Palestinian teachers would be hired to replace existing teachers, many with only high school diplomas. New administrators were also to be brought in, according to the rumors. This made both the teachers and administrators employed at the time uneasy. But overall, there was a feeling of euphoria and pride among Palestinians at the prospect of having their own education system. Slowly, however, the realization of how difficult it is to develop and implement a new curriculum sank in. But still eager to make its presence felt, the PA decided that as an immediate first step it would replace the Jordanian symbol with the PA symbol on textbooks distributed in the West Bank, Gaza, and east Jerusalem.

The Israeli authorities were in a panic. They were unsure how to respond to what they perceived as a Palestinian threat to their rule in Jerusalem. Kollek had just been ousted as mayor, after nearly thirty years in office. The new mayor, Knesset member Ehud Olmert of the Likud Party, was strongly opposed to any PA presence in Jerusalem. At the same time, however, he appointed Jamil Abu Toumah to head the Arab east Jerusalem school system—the first time a Palestinian Jerusalemite had held the post under Israeli rule. Olmert was openly proud of his decision. He said it demonstrated his intentions of being even-handed with the Arab population—something he accused Kollek of not being. The move, however, in the long-run appeared to have been a grave mistake. An Israeli at the post would have had a difficult time fighting the rising influence of the PA. For a Palestinian Arab the fight was impossible. Just by taking on a post with the Jerusalem municipality, Abu Toumah was accused by many of his fellow Palestinians of collaboration with Israel. If he tried to work against the PA, his very life might be threatened.

Olmert's advisers warned about the PA's plans to take over the east Jerusalem school system. "It can be expected that the Palestinian curriculum that will replace the Jordanian curriculum in use today will also sooner or later make its way to Jerusalem," an adviser wrote in an internal memo to the new mayor.[20] "To try and prevent the process is impossible, and any attempt to stop it is likely to boomerang," the adviser warned.

Olmert read the adviser's report and decided to act.[21] He called an urgent meeting of senior city officials. The tone of the meeting was set by one of the deputy mayors, Meshulam Amit, a retired general and former commander of the border police. Amit held the security portfolio in the city government. This gave him little real power but allowed him to talk a tough game. He demanded that the municipality take forceful action to halt the infiltration of the PA into the east Jerusalem school system. The city, however, even if it wanted to use force, had no force to use. There was really little it could do. Not surprisingly, no concrete decisions were made at the meeting in Olmert's office.

Olmert himself took the path he normally did when dealing with politically hot topics: he blamed the Labor Party–led government coalition. The new mayor went public with the fact that the national government was allowing the PA to take over the education system in east Jerusalem. He hoped that what he lacked in practical power he could make up for by scoring political points. The mayor's thinking, which reflected that of his party, was that for the Israeli public, Jerusalem was a sacred issue. Israelis would accept compromise in the West Bank and Gaza but never in Jerusalem.

With this in mind, Olmert launched an all-out antigovernment publicity campaign around the issue of the PLO emblem on school textbooks. Inside, the books were the same as they had been when the Jordanian Hashemite Kingdom emblem was on the cover. The municipal government had discovered the PA move only days before the start of the academic year, when, as in the past, the textbooks arrived annually from Amman via Bethlehem and were distributed throughout the West Bank and east Jerusalem.

Olmert ordered the books collected from the public schools and taken to a city warehouse, where the PLO eagle was covered with a sticker of the municipality's symbol, the lion of Judea, and "Jerusalem Municipality" written in Hebrew and Arabic underneath. The covering took time, and many schools were without books until weeks into the academic year. With the private schools, there was nothing Olmert could do. Even a right-wing opposition-party mayor was not going to break a two-decade status quo by interfering in the affairs of east Jerusalem's Christian and Muslim private schools. The PLO eagle stayed.

The PA was soon to have more than just symbols in east Jerusalem schools. By the 1995 academic year, PA school supervisors were already making rounds in the private Arab schools in the city. The PA had completely usurped the authority of the Jordanians in the education system. In Bethlehem, to Jerusalem's south, there no longer sat a Jordanian Education Ministry representative but instead a Palestinian official responsible for education in the district—which included east Jerusalem. In Ramallah to the north, where the PA Education Ministry had its office. Palestinian educators were developing a Palestinian curriculum. It would take several years to implement, but it was only a matter of time before not only the cover but also the content of schoolbooks in the West Bank and east Jerusalem would be Palestinian. Israel could do little about it. It had already conceded to the PA control of the private Arab schools in east Jerusalem, and the public schools were probably not far behind.

In many ways, it appeared to be the natural course of things. If education is the bedrock of a society, there could be no denying the Palestinians control of their schools. Indeed, the Oslo agreement gave the Palestinians control of schools in the West Bank before virtually every other civil authority. The close ties between east Jerusalem and the West Bank also made it inevitable that the PA's control of schools would also extend to the city. Israel was left to watch as the instrument it hoped would strengthen its rule in east Jerusalem fell into the hands of its major rival.

7

The Forgotten Ones

Sewage. Water. Electricity. Trash. Most people in the West never think twice about these things, believing that it must be written in some Municipal Services Bill of Rights that people are entitled to have their feces flushed from their homes, clean tap water to drink, electricity to run the television, and a garbage truck to take away their empty pizza boxes. Israel likes to think of itself as a Western nation, and when it comes to the Municipal Services Bill of Rights, Israel meets the criteria.

In Tel Aviv, unless there is a strike—which can also occur in New York City—no one gets excited about the fact that the trash they put in canisters outside their homes is hauled away each week by city crews. It is just a fact of life in a normal city. But Jerusalem is no normal city. If you live in a Jewish neighborhood there, life may be close to normal, but it certainly is not if you live in an Arab neighborhood. Most Israelis would be surprised to know that in the city they call their capital, just a few dozen yards from the holiest spot for Jews worldwide, the Western Wall, there are Arab neighborhoods where human waste literally pours out into the streets. Some Arab neighborhoods do not have trash pick-up, and debris just piles up in abandoned lots. The streets in many Arab neighborhoods have not even been given names by the local authorities, because no one ever goes there to provide the services that are taken for granted in other areas of the city.

Why this disregard for the level of public services in east Jerusalem? The answer is a poorly kept secret: Arab east Jerusalem is simply at the bottom of the list of priorities of the Israeli authorities when it comes to funding public works. It has been that way under right-wing Israeli governments and left-wing Israeli governments, when Labor Party member Teddy Kollek was mayor and Likud Party member Ehud Olmert replaced him. Some would call it discrimination; others would point to mismanagement. Whatever the label, it does not change the picture of Arab east Jerusalem as largely undeveloped and unserviced for over three decades of Israeli rule.

In spring of 1986, city manager Aharon Sarig was working late, as was his habit. Meir Einsmiester, the ultra-Orthodox sanitation department director, sat across from Sarig, talking trash.[1] Garbage collection was not the most inspiring of topics, but somebody has to do it, and in this city of well over half a million residents, that "somebody" was these two officials.

Sarig and Einsmiester had a problem. A new neighborhood in north Jerusalem, Pisgat Ze'ev, had just been completed, and the first families were beginning to move into their homes. That meant a lot of things for city planners, among them the need to begin trash pick-up. The new residents did not expect anything less. The sanitation department, however, was low on manpower, and Sarig and Einsmiester were racking their brains trying to figure out how to clear trash out of this new neighborhood while continuing to operate in other neighborhoods, without having to hire dozens of additional sanitation workers.

They finally came up with a solution. Instead of purchasing canisters for the neighborhood and sending city trash trucks to empty them several times a week, residents would be asked to put their trash in plastic bags and at certain times during the week place them outside on the sidewalk. The city would hire a private contractor to pick up the bags. And to be extra fair to the residents, the city would provide them with the trash bags. Otherwise they would claim they were being discriminated against, because elsewhere in the city trash bags were not required.

Pisgat Ze'ev is a Jewish neighborhood. In many Arab neighborhoods of Jerusalem, to this day there is no trash pick-up. There are Arab areas of the city that no municipal trash truck has entered even once since 1967. For Jerusalem's sanitation department, places like Umm Tuba and Abadiya were for years not even on the map; there had been no evening meetings at city hall to figure out ways to provide Arab communities with this rudimentary service, no discussions about the pros and cons of trash bags versus canisters. For two decades after the 1967 war, no one at city hall thought twice about not providing trash service to many parts of east Jerusalem.

Then in the late 1980s, the city finally decided it was time to do something. The new city manager, Michael Gal, called Einsmiester, who was still in charge of the sanitation department, into his office.[2] Gal had learned that many Arabs were not being serviced by municipal trash trucks, and he demanded an explanation. Einsmiester went back to his office and then returned with a large map of east Jerusalem. The Arab neighborhoods were marked in three different colors: green, blue, and red. Einsmiester explained that "the neighborhoods colored in green receive regular trash pick-up, those colored in blue receive trash pick-up from time to time, and the red indicates neighborhoods that we do not serve at all." Gal could not believe what he was hearing. "How can you not provide service in some Arab neighborhoods, and in others just provide service from time to time or not at all? How can you justify such a policy?" Without missing a beat, Einsmiester replied that "my department simply doesn't have the money to do more than it is doing today. Do you want me to stop picking up the trash in Rehavia [a wealthy Jewish neighborhood]?"

Einsmiester's challenge worked. Gal called in the city treasurer and said that for the next fiscal year the sanitation department budget must be increased so trash could be picked up regularly in all Arab neighborhoods. In the years that followed, there were substantial improvements. But some Arab neighborhoods to this day continue to receive no trash pick-up and other sanitation services from the city. The department's priorities remain in the Jewish neighborhood of Rehavia, and not the Arab neighborhood of Umm Tuba.

If Arab residents in east Jerusalem have it tough when it comes to trash, the situation was much worse for those who moved to West Bank neighborhoods such as A-Ram, A-Zayim, Abu Dis, and Azariya. The Israeli army and its branch that deals with civilian Palestinian affairs, the Civil Administration, were in charge there. As new residents started pouring in, the Civil Administration's attitude was quite simple: if Palestinians want proper sanitation, they should organize those services for themselves.

The Jerusalem Arabs living in these neighborhood did not even consider pressing the Civil Administration about the matter. They never expected much from the Israeli authorities, and they knew that demanding improvements would get nowhere. Residents turned instead to Jerusalem city hall. They were still officially residents of the city. They held blue Israeli identification cards, issued by Israel, which stated that they were Jerusalem residents. On paper, at least, they were entitled to be treated like any other Israeli residents. They could move freely from their homes in the West Bank into the city—unlike their fellow Palestinians, whose orange identification cards formalized their second-class status. "Just because I had to move out of the city because there are no homes for Arabs inside the city limits doesn't mean I should stop receiving city services," the residents of the Arab suburbs argued. "Look, I even voted for Kollek in the last election," some would say.

For years, however, the city turned them down. City officials told them that as residents of areas outside the city limits they were no longer paying taxes to the municipality. Services, the city argued, go to taxpayers. Sounds fair, right? Maybe—if the fact that they were forced to leave the city limits because of Israeli housing policy is not taken into account. Or if the "only taxpayers are entitled to city services" policy is applied across the board. It is not, of course: Arabs with homes inside the city limits pay taxes but receive substandard municipal services, and in some areas no municipal services at all. The taxpayers-only argument given by city officials was not a policy but a deception.

The suburban Jerusalem Arabs found one handy solution to their trash problem. On their way to work in the big city each morning they would throw a couple of trash bags in the trunk of the car, drive through the army checkpoint that divided the occupied West Bank, where they lived, from the Jerusalem city limits, head up the road a little way, and then stop alongside a municipal trash canister. You could call it "deliver your own trash"—the next best thing to having it picked up for you.

Many suburban Jerusalem Arabs did not bother to look for empty canisters but just dumped their trash in the first empty lot they saw, whether inside or outside the city limits. Several favorite dumping spots grew to the size of municipal trash dumps, despite the fact that (or perhaps because of the fact that) they were right in the middle of a residential area or next to a main intersection. The Israeli authorities for a while tried to ignore the heaps. But eventually the stench became too strong for them to keep looking away, and trucks were periodically called in by the authorities to remove the refuse. This routine—residents created a dump, authorities eventually cleaned it up—quickly became the de facto sanitation policy in most of the suburban Arab neighborhoods.

In Sheikh Sa'ad, to the south of Jerusalem, residents had their own special way of dealing with the trash problem. This neighborhood of several hundred homes is situated on a low ridge that literally straddles the Jerusalem border. The single road leading out passes through the city limits, which makes it convenient for residents to give their trash to the city. They do not even need a car; a small child can carry a trash bag the two dozen yards to the road that marks the border with Jerusalem and then throw it into the gully below. The gully is on the Jerusalem side of the border.

Unfortunately for the cause of sanitation in Sheikh Sa'ad, residents there carry orange cards which identify them as residents of the occupied territories. Not only does the municipality refuse to pick up trash in the neighborhood but it also refuses to clean up the dump, even though it is within the city limits. There are no Jewish residents in this far-off corner of Jerusalem where only Arabs wander, so the municipality feels no urgency to clean up the mess.

So what about the Civil Administration? Its policy is that the Arabs should pay a private contractor for sanitation services. As for the health hazard posed by the makeshift dump, Civil Administration officials throw their hands up in despair. "We wish we could do something about it. But you have to remember that the dump is in Jerusalem, not the occupied territories, and we do not operate in Jerusalem."

As Gal and Einsmiester knew well, a little fresh thinking can make any trash problem go away. The municipality presented a plan to the Civil Administration: the city will pay for large trash containers for Sheikh Sa'ad, and the Civil Administration will pay for them to be emptied periodically. The Civil Administration turned the idea down. The municipality came up with another idea (the Pisgat Ze'ev solution). the city will provide large trash bags to Sheikh Sa'ad residents, and even pick up the bags. The Civil Administration's only job is to explain to the residents how the system works. The Civil Administration turned down that offer too.

As the ping-pong between the municipality and Civil Administration continued, the trash pile in Sheikh Sa'ad grew. It made for an unpleasant drive, to say the least, but this was east Jerusalem, after all, and not just any place in east Jerusalem but the edge of the edge, where east Jerusalem meets the occupied territories. It was a world where few Israelis ever ventured and where the cry by Arab residents for fair treatment is least heard. By contrast, the trash being dumped in Jerusalem by one of the city's largest Arab neighborhoods, Jabal Mukaber, should have been a different story. Yet, nothing was being done about that either.

Gal, who showed sympathy for the problems of east Jerusalem residents like few others at city hall, finally said stop. He ordered the municipal sanitation department to take full responsibility and to ignore the fact that Sheikh Sa'ad was in the West Bank and its residents did not hold Jerusalem identification cards. Large trash bins were placed near the neighborhood—on the Jerusalem side of the border—for the residents to dispose of their trash.

When Israeli officials made their first tour of east Jerusalem and its environs after the Six Day War, they found that many villages were without water. It was not really surprising. Most of the villages that

Israel included in its borders of Jerusalem were not within the city limits during Jordanian rule. The government in Amman saw no need to waste time and money with development of rural villages. So the villages had no running water. Instead, most homes had their own cisterns.

After the war, Israel decided that these villages, which it now included in the city limits, must be hooked up to the city's water system. The work on the new water lines was carried out briskly and effectively. To make the work go faster, crews put in lines that ran above ground, instead of underground ones that took much time to put in place. The lines were also small—reflecting the water needs of the time. Israel succeeded in bringing water to east Jerusalem, but in its quest to get the job done quickly it created much future trouble for itself.

After only a few years many lines were already broken, some by kids who had nothing better to do with their time than to damage the lines. The lines that still worked were so small that they could not carry enough water to meet the needs of the fast-growing population. To make matters worse, for years Israel paid little attention to development in east Jerusalem. When the funds were finally made available to improve the water lines in east Jerusalem, the lack of zoning plans for many Arab neighborhoods meant that no one knew exactly where to run new water pipes. That was enough reason for Israel to simply ignore east Jerusalem's water problem. Today, some east Jerusalem neighborhoods still do not have proper water lines.

The Shuafat refugee camp in north Jerusalem had a unique water problem. It was the only Palestinian refugee camp in Jerusalem, or for that matter in all of Israel. All the other camps were in the West Bank, Gaza, or neighboring Arab countries. Why Israel chose to keep the refugee camp inside the city limits remains a riddle. One theory is that Israel never intended for the camp to remain but rather for residents to be sent elsewhere to live and the camp torn down to make way for Jewish development. Shuafat, like other refugee camps, was run by the United Nations Relief and Works Agency (UNRWA). Immediately after the 1967 war, Israel agreed to continue to provide services, including water, that the camp had received from the Jordanian authorities from 1948 to 1967.[3] UNRWA had built water lines with public spigots at several points within the camps. Water from the spigots was free. But if a family ran a line from the public water system to their home, they would have to start to pay, according to the understanding reached between UNRWA and Israel.

Israel met its agreement with the U.N. An internal arrangement worked out between various Israeli authorities left it to the Jerusalem municipality to provide water to the Shuafat camp and then to turn the bill over to Civil Administration for payment. But that arrangement ran into problems at the start of the intifada. The uprisings cost the Civil Administration heavily in uncollected taxes from Palestinians in the occupied territories. Civil Administration officials began to look for ways to raise money and cut outlays. The budget cutters' search one day "discovered" that the Civil Administration was paying the Jerusalem municipality for water provided the Shuafat refugee camp and decided to put an end to the practice. In December 1988, a year into the intifada, the Civil Administration informed Jerusalem city hall of its decision. The reason given for the move: Shuafat camp is in Jerusalem, which is outside the authority of the Civil Administration.

Civil Administration officials suggested that city hall turn to the Defense Ministry for the funds. The Civil Administration officials had also gone back to the original agreement with the U.N. and noted the item that limited the free water to public taps. The Israeli officials discovered that most families at Shuafat had already hooked their homes up to the system, which meant they no longer qualified for free water under the U.N.'s own criteria. The hook-up was done without the Jerusalem municipality's knowledge. UNRWA had helped the camp form a water committee that organized the move from the public water system to a private one and had not told the Israeli authorities about the move. The municipality had never noticed that the camp residents suddenly had water in their homes, as it never really took note of anything that occurred in the camp, which had extraterritorial-like status.

City officials figured that UNRWA was taking care of affairs at

Shuafat, except for the water, which the Civil Administration had handled. Now that the Civil Administration was backing out, the municipality found itself in a bind. Providing the camp with free water was not cheap, and city officials frantically rushed to find a solution. They tried to contact the camp water committee but found that it had disbanded immediately after it succeeded in organizing the hook-up of all the homes in the camp to the water system. The city did not know where else to turn. One day, at a meeting with camp members organized by the border police to introduce a new commander to the residents, city officials took advantage of the opportunity to raise the water issue.

It was an odd scene. The Israeli police officers were used to chasing Palestinians at Shuafat, not sipping coffee with them at the small, run-down cafe in the middle of the camp. But in this region of the world, you have an obligation to offer even your bitter enemy a traditional cup of coffee and hospitality if he pays a visit. The border policemen came into the camp, on this occasion, not as policemen but as guests, and they had to be treated accordingly. The two sides exchanged greetings, and the new officer was introduced to the camp residents. That was the cue for the city officials to bring up the water issue.

Their presentation did not go over very well. In fact, the residents rejected outright the possibility they would now start to pay for water. It was bad enough that the municipality should all of a sudden abandon a policy of free water that has been in effect for decades, the residents said—having forgotten (or they simply might not have known) that the policy of free water applied only to the public spigots. But it is even worse that the change in policy should come at an economically tough period for residents, whose pocketbooks were already stretched to the limit.

The municipality tried to send letters to all the residents but could not find anyone willing to distribute such bad news within the camp, where the Israeli Postal Authority did not operate. The letter explaining why Shuafat refugee camp residents would have to start paying for their water was published by the municipality in several Arabic daily newspapers. Meetings were held between city and

UNRWA officials. But it was all to no avail. So the municipality got tough. It decided that if it cut off the water, even for just a couple of days, it would bring the residents to the bargaining table quickly. The spigots were closed. The municipality waited for a reaction from the camp. One day passed without a word of protest, then another, then another. Something was wrong. City officials began making inquiries. They quickly discovered that youths from the camp had found a way to turn the system back on.

The municipality was not giving up, however. This time the water was cut off from a point further from the camp, to make it more difficult for the youths to turn the system on again. But under the cover of night, the youths again succeeded in restoring water to the camp. A meeting was held at city hall and a decision made to try a third time to cut off the Shuafat refugee camp's water, in this instance by literally pulling up a section of the pipes leading into the camp. The camp's water was again halted. But residents managed to break a hole in a national water line near the camp and then queued up with pots and buckets to bring water for their homes. The line was long, but the residents were patient. In the end, they had more patience than the Israeli authorities. The national water company whose line had been tapped was angry with both the residents and the Jerusalem municipality. The hole was repaired, but the residents remained firm in their refusal to pay for water. They even refused to sit down and discuss the matter with the municipality.

The residents were succeeding in not only defying the Israeli authorities but also putting the U.N.'s back against the wall. U.N. officials were fully aware that the agreement signed with Israel stated that camp residents must pay for water in their homes. As a temporary measure, UNRWA trucks with large water tanks would daily bring a supply of water to the camp. The supply was not great, but it was enough for the camp's basic needs. Where was UNRWA getting the water it was trucking into the camp? Municipal officials made a few inquiries and discovered that UNRWA trucks were taking the water from fire hydrants in various parts of the city! The camp was still receiving free water from the municipality after all.

City officials had had enough. They decided it would be futile to protest to UNRWA about the water being taken from city fire hydrants, and even more futile to continue trying to press Shuafat refugees into paying for their water. The city reopened the water lines into the camp. The residents had beaten the Israeli authorities.

At about the same time, during the first year of the intifada, Israel was also involved in another battle over water in the Jerusalem area. The conditions were similar to those in the skirmish with the Shuafat refugee camp. In this case, however, the village, Azariya, was in the occupied territories. Still, the proximity of the village, just several kilometers east of the Old City on the slopes of the Mount of Olives, made connection to the city's water system practical, and Azariya had received its water from Jerusalem even during Jordanian rule.

Soon after the 1967 war, Israel placed a water clock in the line running into Azariya. The Israeli authorities did not want to deal with making sure village residents paid their individual bills. Instead, it put the responsibility on the village council to pay the city a lump sum and then collect from the residents. The arrangement worked for two decades. But with the outbreak of the intifada, it collapsed. Azariya residents quit paying their water bills to the village council, and the council in turn stopped paying the city.

The residents' action was part protest against Israeli rule, part taking advantage of the mess created by the intifada. Residents knew that while they were paying directly to the village council, the money eventually went to Israel. A major component of the intifada was rejection of everything Israeli, from products to, in this case, services, or at least to paying for those services. The residents' refusal to pay was also a challenge to Israeli authority. "We aren't going to pay, and what are you going to do about it?" Several months went by while the municipality weighed its options. It could cut off the water, as it had tried to do at the Shuafat refugee camp. After all, if a Jewish community in Israel was not paying its water bill, the national water company would cut off its water. It had happened before. It was not as though Israel would be singling out the Palestinians for some specially harsh treatment.

The city called Abu Mofeid, head of the Azariya village council, to a meeting at city hall. Several other council members joined Mofeid. The meeting was short but left city officials with a clear picture of what they were up against. The council itself had little authority. Even if the council wanted to, it could not press the residents to pay; the intifada leadership was too strongly against it. The city, for its part, had to be extra careful when dealing with Azariya. Though the village was in the occupied territories, many of its residents held Jerusalem identification cards. There was also a large population of foreigners in Azariya, including diplomats and U.N. officials. Cutting off their water could cause an international stir.

The municipality looked to other avenues. It appealed to the Civil Administration but found no willingness to cooperate, even though the village was officially under its authority. City officials contacted local leaders in an effort to reach some sort of compromise, but to no avail. The municipality initiated several articles in the Arabic press about the issue, but that also did not get results. Finally Kollek himself gave the word: "Cut off the water flow to Azariya." The mayor believed there was no choice.

As expected, the foreign residents in particular made a major fuss over the move. But they put pressure not just on Israel but on the village council. Some residents, particularly the foreigners, were paying their bills and they wanted to know what had become of their money. The pressure forced the village council back to the negotiating table with the municipality. A deal was reached under which the council was given easy terms to pay the money it owed Jerusalem, and the council agreed to start paying for water again. Everything was worked out to the satisfaction of both sides, or so it appeared, until the first payment by the council came due; it never arrived.

The water war continued. The municipality again cut off Azariya's water. The outcry from the residents was even more fierce this time. Kollek was fed up. He had too many problems in Jerusalem to be wasting his time with a village outside the city limits, even if many of its residents held Jerusalem identification cards. Kollek presented the Civil Administration with an ultimatum. Either it takes responsibility for Azariya's water supply or the village will simply receive no more water until it starts paying. Kollek won. The

Civil Administration took responsibility—and at times it too cut off the village's water supply until the council paid its bills. But for the most part the system ran normally. The city received a monthly check from the Civil Administration no matter whether residents paid their bills or not.

Water flowed back and forth between Jerusalem and the West Bank as if there was no border separating Israel from the occupied territories. This was nothing new. Even under Jordanian rule, the villages of north Jerusalem did not receive water from the city's system but from Ramallah. In the south, villages received water from Bethlehem. After the 1967 war, Israel hesitated to break these links, mostly out of concern that the companies providing the water in Ramallah and Bethlehem would appeal to the Israeli high court on the grounds they held the rights to supply water to the villages. Israel's national water authority was ultimately in charge of water distribution in both Israel and the occupied territories. But instead of doing away with the companies in the territories, it simply used them to literally funnel the water into the West Bank and Gaza. This may have given the Arabs a sense of national pride, but it also created problems for them.

In Beit Safafa, the south Jerusalem village split in two by the 1948 war, residents of the formerly Jordanian side who received their water from Bethlehem complained that the system broke down often. And they also paid much more than their fellow villagers who were hooked up to the Israeli system, even though the Bethlehem water system was more antiquated than its Israeli counterpart. The village mukhtars came to the Jerusalem municipality looking for a solution. They asked that the two-thirds of the village formerly under Jordanian rule and hooked up the Bethlehem company be transferred to the municipal water system.

The municipality jumped at the idea. Kollek was always uncomfortable with the fact that city residents were receiving water from an outside system. But he knew that it was a sensitive issue. The intifada was raging. Palestinian leaders would not be very happy about Israel expanding its "control," even over the water supply, in an Arab neighborhood of Jerusalem. Beit Safafa residents also received a not-too-pleasant surprise when they learned that while the city was willing to pay for the change-over, and the residents themselves would be paying much less on their monthly water bills, their building license fees would go up considerably because of the high "water hook-up" fee demanded by the municipality for new buildings, which was far greater than a similar fee asked for in Bethlehem. But it was too late to backtrack. The plan was already moving forward—with the overall support of the residents.

Only one thing was lacking: a way to approach the authorities in Bethlehem responsible for the water system. Kollek for years had been on good terms with Bethlehem Mayor Elias Freij. Both were veteran local leaders, well-respected in their communities and nationally. Kollek presented Freij with the plan to transfer Beit Safafa to Jerusalem's water system. The Bethlehem mayor heard Kollek out. Kollek stressed there was nothing political about the move. It was all being done simply in the best interest of the residents, he said. Freij was convinced and said he would not stand in the way of the move. He even promised to put in a good word with the Bethlehem water company and to recommend that it go along with the plan.

Both men, without even bringing it up, understood that they must proceed quietly. At all costs, the media should not get wind of the plan. There were Israelis and Palestinians who would try to politicize the move, and this would likely torpedo it. And so quietly and with little fanfare, Beit Safafa residents were cut off from the Bethlehem water system and hooked up to the Jerusalem water supply.

There may be no other company in the world with such a unique market definition. The charter of the Jerusalem District Electric Company (JDEC) is very specific. It declares that the company has exclusive rights in a 50-kilometer radius around the Church of the Holy Sepulcher, the site of Jesus' crucifixion. The area includes Jericho to the east, Ramallah and al-Bireh to the north, Bethlehem, Beit Sahur, and Beit Jala to the south, all of west Jerusalem, and the Jewish and Arab towns virtually all the way to Tel Aviv on the Mediterranean coast. Political realities put a little damper on the company's grand vision—the 1948 war cut off the company from its market in the west. But the other areas to the north, east, and south continued to be serviced by the company, which switched its name to be in synch with the new situation created by the division of Jerusalem.

After the 1967 war and Jerusalem's reunification, Mayor Kollek wanted the company closed down and electrical service brought under Israel's control. Kollek, however, was in the minority and was overruled by the Israeli government. The old diesel generators near Shuafat in north Jerusalem continued to spew out their black smoke and soot. Complaints by area residents about pollution were ignored by the Israeli leaders, as they had been ignored by the Jordanians before them.

In the first years after reunification, as Israel pressed ahead with plans to build Jewish neighborhoods in east Jerusalem, the old generators were pushed to capacity. The political realities that had left the JDEC supplying only Arab customers from 1948 to 1967 had changed. But the 50-kilometer rule was inclusive; it did not specify whether a community within the company's radius was Arab or Jewish. As Israeli rule brought an unprecedented flow of growth to east Jerusalem, the Israeli Housing Ministry, which oversaw the construction of new Jewish neighborhoods, paid vast sums of money to the JDEC, as did the new Jewish customers. The company soon found that business was better than it had ever been.

Although the JDEC was flourishing financially, it was heading toward disaster. Progress had come too easy and fast, and the JDEC soon found itself unable to meet demand. Thousands of new homes demanding electricity were being built, while the company was barely able to meet present needs. The old generators at Shuafat were tiring, yet directors failed to invest their newfound wealth back in the company. Seeing the writing on the wall, Kollek again pushed for the Israel Electric Corporation to be allowed to take over in east Jerusalem, but the proposal was rejected because of fear that it would cause an international ruckus. In the Arab world, an Israeli take-over of the JDEC would be viewed as another violation of U.N. declarations. But Israel still had to find a way to increase production by the JDEC, and fast. Israel's development plans in east Jerusalem were not going to be held up by the mismanagement of an Arab company.

Before long, a plan was worked out whereby the Israel Electric Corporation began selling electricity to the JDEC. This solution appeared to avoid the diplomatic problems that the Israelis feared. At about the same time, the JDEC also decided to buy new generators to replace the old ones at Shuafat and increase the company's production. A delegation of directors set out for Europe to see the possibilities first hand. The new generators were purchased and sent to Jerusalem, where they were inaugurated at a ceremony attended by Israeli and Arab notables. The nylon wrapping that helped protect the generators from the elements during their journey to the Holy Land was removed, and the machines were installed in a makeshift metal building put up by the JDEC.

The company had forgotten one important detail, however. It had not obtained a permit from the city for the building. A complaint was lodged in court against JDEC chief engineer Abed el-Rahman. Rahman was even arrested and held pending the start of the trial. Kollek himself had to intervene to get police to release Rahman on bail. Just when it appeared that things could not get any worse for the JDEC, the company discovered that building and planning codes would delay use of the generators for the foreseeable future.

It quickly became apparent to company heads that Israel had no intention of allowing them to employ the generators, that the machines would sit for years in their new homes in Shuafat, unused. Perhaps eventually permission would be given if the company decided to undertake a long legal battle, but the directors decided against a court fight. They realized that while Israel would not risk an international incident by shutting down the corporation outright, it would do its best to eliminate it through indirect means.

The company directors finally agreed to do what Israel wanted all along—to largely stop producing electricity themselves and to purchase most of the company's power from the Israel Electric Corporation. The JDEC held on to its exclusive rights in the 50-kilometer radius around the Church of the Holy Sepulcher. But the company that had served as a major national symbol for the Palestinians no longer produced anything, and instead functioned as a subsidiary to the stronger Israeli company.

These were tough times for Anwar Nusseiba, corporation director. Nusseiba had served as Jordan Defense Minister, and his family was among the most prominent in east Jerusalem. The Nusseiba family continued to maintain close ties with the Jordanians even after the 1967 war. But his family's wealth and connections provided little relief. His company was no longer producing electricity. Its main work now was maintaining lines and building infrastructure for new Jewish neighborhoods, and even these limited demands were proving too much for the JDEC.

Customer complaints were frequent, and Jewish customers took them straight to the government. They charged the JDEC with failing to provide adequate service, and they demanded to switch to the Israel Electric Corporation, like the rest of the country. Arab customers also complained about the JDEC, despite their national affection for the company. East Jerusalem Arabs made clear to municipal officials that they were fed up with the frequent winter blackouts from the rains and summer blackouts from overuse. Added to these complaints were those of the Israel Electric Corporation itself, which informed the Israeli government that the JDEC was far behind on its payments. The company's debt was growing fast, with no prospects in sight for meeting it.

The Israel Electric Corporation wanted to cut off the flow of power to Nusseiba's company, which is what it would have done to a normal customer. But the JDEC was no normal customer. It provided electricity to tens of thousands of families—Jewish and Arab alike. This put the Israel Electric Corporation—or more precisely the Israeli government, which would be held responsible for any decision to cut off electricity to the JDEC—in a serious bind. If the government had been up against only a possible outcry by Arab residents of east Jerusalem and occupied territories, it might have gone ahead with the cut-off proposal. But the government was not about to take a step that even for a short while would leave Israelis without power. The JDEC knew it, and hoped this would be its saving grace.

But time was running out for the JDEC. Its concession was set to end on January 1, 1988. As early as August 1985, Israeli energy minister Moshe Shahal began preparing for that date by ordering a study of the options.[4] He wanted to bring recommendations before the government as soon as possible. A committee formed by Shahal emphasized in its report that it was necessary once and for all to clear up the company's status, and that the upcoming deadline for renewal of the concession was the best opportunity. Two options were offered: the company could either be shut down and replaced completely by the Israel Electric Corporation, or Jewish communities could be taken out of the company's authority, leaving only Arab communities to be serviced by the JDEC. Shahal knew that the issue was too sensitive, with far-reaching international implications, to take a decision alone, and so he brought the matter before the cabinet.

Many reasonable voices in the government spoke in favor of eliminating the company. The company was indeed obsolete; Israel is a small country that does not need two separate electric companies, particularly when only one is really acting as a supplier; it was an economically unsound situation.[5] But in Jerusalem, there were other factors besides economic feasibility that had to be taken into account when making a decision, even about electricity. The JDEC was a symbol of pride for Palestinians. Israel could not expect to wipe out an important Palestinian national symbol without a reaction, possibly a severe reaction, from the Palestinian public. Mayor Kollek, who attended the cabinet meeting by invitation, surprised many of those present by recommending against disbanding the company. "You should have listened to me in 1967," Kollek told the ministers. "What we could have done in 1967 we can no longer do today. I'm not just referring to the JDEC, but to many things." Kollek said the company could have been shut down quietly right after the war. It was not yet a symbol of Palestinian pride. But now it is, and if Israel tries to close it will spark a sharp reaction from the Palestinians. "We can't close the JDEC today. It would be viewed as a provocation both by the Palestinians and to much of the international community," he said.

Kollek had no vote in the cabinet, but the mayor was going to do his best to make sure his opinion was not only heard but felt. He may not have been a minister, but he had a considerable amount of political weight to throw around. No decision was taken at the meeting, but Kollek sensed a decision in the works that would allow the JDEC to keep operating, but only in the Arab sector. The mayor also knew that Nusseiba, the corporation director, would consult with the Jordanians before he responded to any Israeli move. The corporation continued to see itself as an integral part of Jordan's national energy system, and Nusseiba was in close contact with the Jordanian Energy Ministry in Amman.

Kollek wanted to get a reading on the Jordanian position, and since there were no formal relations between Jordan and Israel at the time, he turned to the United States. At a meeting in his office with then U.S. Ambassador to Israel Thomas Pickering and U.S. Consul Morris Driefer, Kollek outlined the options Israel was considering and his own position.[6] Pickering presented the Jordanian position: King Hussein had indicated that Jordan was willing to provide the money the company needed to pay its debts to Israel, but on condition that Israel agree to extend the company's concession beyond 1988. Pickering also reinforced Kollek's concern over the international reaction to a unilateral Israeli decision on the company's future. Israel would come under sharp criticism if the company was closed, Pickering warned. The atmosphere at the meeting was good. The Americans and Israelis present were generally of the same mind on how to deal with the problem. Now it was only a question of convincing the parties who would make the final decision—the Israeli government, the JDEC, and Jordan—to follow their lead. Kollek promised Pickering that he would deliver King Hussein's proposal to the prime minister.

Kollek, however, never really needed to move ahead with the lobbying effort. It became apparent to all sides that only one solution would satisfy everyone: the continued operation of the JDEC but in a new format that would put all the Jewish communities within its service area under the Israel Electric Corporation's authority. The decision was taken in the early summer 1986. That left about 18 months to prepare for the transfer. The Israeli energy minister formed a team to be responsible for the technical logistics of the operation. In traditional Israeli style the operation was code-named "Light Unto the Nations."

A retired Israeli army general, Yona Efrat, was put at the head of the operation. Efrat had served as the West Bank Israel Defense Force commander. The planned transfer was indeed a quasi-military operation. The police and Shin Bet were on board to ensure the safety of the Israel Electric Corporation workers who were in the occupied territories and east Jerusalem preparing for the break with the JDEC. The operation was kept top secret. Both the Israelis and Palestinians involved wanted it this way. They were concerned that if the move was made public in advance, it would be scrapped. Palestinians would see it as an attack on one of their national institutions, while Israelis would be angry that the Palestinian company was being allowed to survive at all. Everything had to be prepared for the one evening in late 1987 when the systems would be switched—without either public finding out ahead of time.

Picking the exact date for the operation was also no easy task. There were Jewish holidays and Muslim holidays and Christian holidays to take into account. A visit to Israel by a senior American or European official was also reason to put off the transfer. Israel did not want to put a foreign guest on the spot. A date was finally set for mid-December, just before Christmas, which looked like it would be a quiet time. The Israeli officials, however, were in for a big surprise.

Operation Light Unto the Nations was ready to go. December arrived and all was on schedule. Then the unexpected happened. On December 9 a small incident in the Gaza district quickly turned into widespread rioting and unrest throughout the administered territories. Palestinian youths clashed with Israeli soldiers, and a few days later the intifada spread to east Jerusalem. Efrat, the retired general, in consultation with senior government officials, had to decide whether to go ahead with the operation. After several tense meetings, the operation got the green light. There appeared to be little choice. Everything was ready; the longer it was delayed, the greater the risk that the operation would become public, and January 1—the cut-off date—was fast approaching.

Heavy rain had been falling for hours when the work crews were given the go-ahead. From one Jewish community to the next, the electricity was cut off, disengaged from the east Jerusalem system, and started up again by the new Israeli provider. By dawn, all the Jewish communities in Jerusalem, including the Jewish Quarter of the Old City, and in the occupied territories were hooked up to the Israel Electric Corporation grid. It was a historic moment in a city where even such technical matters as electrical service are steeped in history and prejudice.

A sick man in the last years of his life, Anwar Nusseiba died shortly afterward. He had worked under heavy political pressure, from the Jordanians watching over him on one side and the Palestinians on the other. The workers' union, made up of persons aligned with the PLO, the rejectionist front groups, and those who supported Jordan, also dogged Nusseiba's every step, less concerned about the company from a business point of view than about political questions. Nusseiba helped turn the electric corporation into a national symbol for Palestinians at a time when Israel was doing its best to stomp out such nationalist expression.

For a short while Nusseiba was replaced by Hannah Nasser, deputy mayor of Bethlehem. He had a difficult time holding both posts, so he eventually left the company. Mohammed Ali el-Husseini, a member of one of Jerusalem's most prominent families, succeeded Nasser. For years Husseini had served quietly on the company's board of directors. This unexpected choice turned out to be an excellent one. Husseini was effective in putting political pressures aside and concentrating on getting the company back on the right economic footing.

Though the JDEC was a shadow of its former self, politically it remained a center of power for the Palestinians. The corporation was the largest single public employer in east Jerusalem. Even after the Israel Electric Corporation take-over, it still had about 400 workers. In the early 1990s, Israel watched with concern as leaders affiliated with Islamic fundamentalist groups seemed to be on their way to becoming the majority on the workers' union executive committee. On January 26, 1995, union elections were held. The campaign had been heated, and PLO activists knew that the results would be interpreted as a gauge of support for the organization's recent peace agreements with Israel. Hamas, the leading Islamic group, wanted a strong showing in the union election to show disapproval of the PLO's peace initiative. Nearly all of the 404 registered union members voted. The PLO took four seats, the Islamic fundamentalist parties took four seats, and the joint communist-democratic front list won a single seat. It was a virtual stand-off, reflecting to a degree the ambivalence in Palestinian society toward the recent peace accord. But regardless of the outcome, the election proved that the JDEC was still a force for Israel to contend with in Jerusalem.

There is a long-held belief in the Middle East that if the authorities are looking for you, it must be for something bad. From this belief stems the almost instinctual drive among citizens to hide their whereabouts from the ruling authorities. In Jerusalem, the Arab residents also held strongly to this view. Arab residents preferred that the authorities—whether they were Ottoman, British, Jordanian, or Israeli—not know their names and addresses. "Why would the authorities want you if it weren't for something bad? They want your address so they can force you to pay some new tax they have suddenly thought of, or maybe conscript your son into the army, or call you into some forced labor camp," the logic went. And this indeed had been the case for centuries under previous rulers.

When Israel took over east Jerusalem in 1967, it found that street names in the Old City were posted clearly in Arabic and English. Adding the names in Hebrew was a simple matter. The problem was in the villages. Even in Silwan, just meters from the Old City walls, street names did not exist. The situation was the same in the other villages. The lack of addresses made the job of postal and telephone workers particularly tough. Without street names, they could not provide proper service in east Jerusalem. The Israeli telephone company found itself time and again cutting off phone service to Arab residents because they did not pay their bills—often because the bills never made it to their homes. Israeli officials held endless meetings on the subject of east Jerusalem addresses. Their solution may not have been ingenious but it was historic. After centuries of anonymity, the streets of east Jerusalem would be named.

The Jerusalem municipality was given responsibility for the job. After delay upon delay, the project finally began in the mid-1980s, but even then the going was slow. The natural place to begin was the Arab neighborhoods that had strong local leadership. Beit Hanina was one of east Jerusalem's wealthier neighborhoods, where the population of Arab-Israeli and local Palestinian families were very interested in improving their community. The municipality contacted the director of Beit Hanina's neighborhood council, Ziyad Darwish. Darwish, an Arab-Israeli from the Galilee who had only recently moved to Jerusalem, was enthusiastic about the idea. He agreed, together with other council members and leading community members, to come up with a list of possible street names.

It was several weeks before the list was sent to city hall. As municipal officials reviewed the list, they slowly began to understand its significance. All the names were of Arab villages that had existed before 1948 but were destroyed by Israel during the war: Umm Rashrash, Banias, Majdal, Askalan, Yaffa, Pluga, and others. The municipality contacted Darwish, and he unabashedly explained the neighborhood council's idea: "We see the map of Beit Hanina as representing that of all Palestine," Darwish said. "In the north of Beit Hanina, we will give the streets names of the villages that once stood in northern Palestine, in the west of the neighborhood, the roads will have the names of the villages that once stood in the west of Palestine, and so on."

Darwish was told to try again. The municipality would not accept such an expression of Palestinian nationalism on the streets of the city. "You'd be better off choosing names of flowers and trees," Darwish was told. "You can also include great Arab figures, but stick to poets and writers, not conquerors. Do us a favor and include a short biography with each figure chosen. It would be good if you mentioned if he had any connection to Jerusalem." The municipality had a Names Committee that had final say on such matters as new street names. In those years, committee members were known to be on the whole from right-wing parties that were suspicious about any Arab name and would want to know details about a candidate's relation to the Jews. Darwish got the picture of what he was up against. He followed the new orders to the letter, and the second list of flowers and trees and Arab poets he presented to city hall was approved by the Names Committee with hardly a peep.

The names, however, were never posted on neighborhood streets. The municipality was not without excuses for the delays: "We can't send a work crew to put up the sign because it is too dangerous in the neighborhood"; "We can't go to east Jerusalem during the intifada"; "The border police unit that was supposed to accompany us canceled at the last minute." It was a shame. Israel had a chance to do something that would not cost much money and would symbolize that it took development in Arab neighborhoods seriously. But Israel could not seem to find the will to carry through the street-naming project. A decade after Darwish's list was approved, there are still no street signs in Beit Hanina. And to this day, many streets of east Jerusalem are not even named, let alone posted with street signs.

Israel learned the hard way that it could not unilaterally choose a name for a road in east Jerusalem without consulting the residents, or at least looking for a name that would appeal to them. For example, city hall decided that the road running where a fence once divided east and west Beit Safafa between 1948 and 1967 should be named Unification of the City Street. Residents, who rejected the "unification" of Jerusalem under Israeli authority, strongly opposed the street name. When the municipality put up a Unification of the City street sign, it was ripped down by residents. Not to be bullied, the city authorities reposted the sign, at which point demonstrations broke out in Beit Safafa and the sign was pulled down and set on fire.

At that point municipal officials decided to reconsider the name, and instead of doing it unilaterally, they consulted with village leaders. An agreement was reached. The road would be called Unification of the Village Street instead of Unification of the City. That Beit Safafa was no longer divided in two by a fence was a good thing, both the city authorities and residents agreed. A new street sign was put up, at a small ceremony attended by city officials and village leaders. The sign remains in place today.

Things did not go so well in the half-Arab, half-Jewish neighborhood of Abu Tur. As with many east Jerusalem development projects, the municipality was short on money for a new road, and so it made a deal with the neighborhood. The city would provide the materials for the road, and the work would be paid for by the residents. Most of the money came from the Zuaiter family, which was originally from Hebron and was among the most wealthy families in Abu Tur. Since several family members had homes along the new road, the municipality decided to show appreciation for the family's contribution by naming the new road after one of the deceased family heads. The Zuaiter family was overjoyed with this decision.

But the other major family that lived along the new road was not. Several members of the rival family went to city hall with their complaint. "Look, it is true that [the Zuaiters] are the largest family living along the new road, but it must not be forgotten that they are not a Jerusalem family. They are from Hebron," Rayisq family members said. "Our family is among the original families of the village. We have lived in Abu Tur for generations. As we were the first to arrive in Abu Tur, the road should be named after our family patron."

Not knowing how to contend with this argument, the city took the easy way out. It ruled that if both families continue to insist that their name go on the sign, then neither family will be chosen, and the road will be left unnamed. And so it has remained to this day.

The central welfare distributing organization in Israel is the National Insurance Institute (NII). Like any state-run organization that gives out benefits, the NII has strict criteria for its operation. In theory, NII officials work according to the book, with little room for guesswork or interpretation. And the book says that two types of residents are eligible for welfare benefits: those who hold Israeli citizenship and those who do not. After the 1967 war, nearly all east Jerusalem Arabs were residents of Israel though they were not citizens.

Under Israeli law, Arabs who moved to the occupied territories in the West Bank lost their residency and hence their social and welfare rights. But Israel knew well that if this law was enforced with respect to Jerusalem Arabs, many of them would not leave the city to find housing elsewhere. They would remain in crowded conditions within the city limits, and Israel did not want this.

So exceptions were made whereby Arab Jerusalemites could leave Jerusalem, move to the West Bank, and continue to receive welfare and social benefits from the state. Israeli leaders saw this as a good investment. In February 1973, for instance, the Ministerial Committee on Jerusalem decided to construct a housing project for Arab families from Jerusalem in the Azariya village, outside the city limits.[7] "The commander of Judea and Samaria [West Bank] will provide two sites in Azariya for the establishment of a housing project for Jerusalem families who are needy, or have been evicted from the Old City," the committee decided.[8] And to attract Jerusalem Arab families to the village, the committee promised that Jerusalem residents holding Israeli identity cards who keep up with their NII payments will continue to receive NII benefits even if they move to the West Bank.[9] The decision was precedent-setting. Israel hoped that it would encourage thousands of Arab families to leave Jerusalem and ensure a strong Jewish majority in the city.

How to encourage Arabs to leave Jerusalem was a major subject on the agenda of Israeli leaders framing policy in the city after the 1967 war. One such meeting when the issue was discussed occurred at the King David Hotel in December 1972.[10] Then Defense Minister Moshe Dayan and Mayor Kollek met to discuss a number of issues related to Jerusalem's future. Dayan strongly supported the idea of building housing projects in the West Bank for Arabs from Jerusalem. Dayan's major concern was that the work be done fast and cheap. An immediate solution was needed for Arab families that were being evicted to make way for a revitalized Jewish Quarter in the Old City. Large areas of land in the West Bank that were in the state's control could be used for the purpose, Dayan said. He singled out Abu Dis and Azariya, West Bank villages on the Mount of Olives, just outside the Jerusalem city limits, as the best possibilities for housing developments for Jerusalem Arabs. Dayan strongly opposed the suggestion that land would have to be expropriated for the development, saying that enough state land was available to make expropriations unnecessary.

El-Mashrua, or simply "The Project," was the name of the first housing development that went up under this policy of building for Arabs outside of Jerusalem. El-Mashrua was in Azariya. In some ways, Azariya and Abu Dis were natural places for Arab families from Jerusalem to move. The villages were closer to the business and shopping districts of east Jerusalem than neighborhoods within the city's borders to the north, such as Beit Hanina. Azariya and Abu Dis had been part of the Jerusalem District even under Jordanian rule, and residents identified themselves as Jerusalemites.

But Arab families were still hesitant. They knew well the laws pertaining to NII benefits and feared losing them if they moved out of the city. They did not trust the Israeli authorities. "Some people say that a government committee had decided they wouldn't lose their rights, but who knows for sure," was the general attitude. The apartments stood empty. The attractive mortgages they received were not enough to overcome the families' concerns. In an effort to quell their fears, the Israeli government released an official statement that Jerusalem Arab families who moved out of the city would not lose their Israeli residency papers.[11] "Whoever holds an Israeli identity card because of his residence in Jerusalem, and has made the proper payments to the NII, will continue to receive NII benefits even if he moves outside of the municipal boundaries of Jerusalem," the statement declared.[12] In addition, a public relations campaign was launched to remind Arab residents of the decision by the Ministerial Committee on Jerusalem.

But there was still concern among the Arab families. A special open house was held in Jerusalem's old Beit Agron theater. Representatives of the National Insurance Institute, the Bank of Jerusalem (which was financing the project), and Jerusalem municipality talked to several hundred Arab residents who were concerned that the move would strip them of their Israeli identification cards and NII benefits. The residents were finally convinced. The homes sold fast, making many Jerusalem Arab families happy—for a while at least.

It did not take long for the NII to backtrack on its earlier promises. It said it did not recognize anything but the laws it operated under—which stated clearly that if a resident left Jerusalem, he was no longer eligible for benefits. Verbal promises were worthless; so were the Ministerial Committee's decisions, at least in the eyes of the NII. The institute's position was that as long as the Israel Knesset did not change the welfare laws, there was no reason for it to change policy. Starting in about 1985, NII clerks began reviewing files to see which Arab Jerusalemites had moved out of the city, including to Azariya, and to stop their benefits. The Arab families, particularly those in Azariya, were up in arms. They petitioned the Israel High Court to intervene on their behalf.

The High Court ruled in the families' favor, but the court's decision needed to be translated into new regulations and laws for the NII. When this was all said and done, Arab families who has listened to Israel's promises and left Jerusalem came out the losers. "What do you want? That we change the law so that Jerusalem residents that move to the West Bank be still considered Jerusalem residents—This would be like annexing the West Bank, which we strongly oppose," was the position expressed by Ora Namir, at the time chairman of the Knesset Labor and Welfare Committee. Namir did not stop to think that Israel granted full welfare rights to Jewish residents of Jerusalem, or of anywhere in Israel, who moved to the West Bank, without making the area Israeli territory. Could Arab families from Jerusalem not expect equal treatment to Jewish settlers? Namir was from the left-leaning Labor Party, which the Arab families in Jerusalem thought might be somewhat sympathetic to their situation. They quickly discovered otherwise.

New regulations were eventually passed by the Knesset that allowed Jerusalem Arab families who moved to the West Bank to continue to receive NII benefits—but only at the level they received when they left the city.[13] That meant a young couple with a single child when they lived in the city would still receive the same amount in child benefits after they moved to Azariya and had four more children. It made no difference that the husband or wife paid the same amount in taxes as Israeli citizens.

If this seems a little unfair, it is nothing when compared with the different treatment given to noncitizen Arabs and Jews. The welfare regulation, adopted in 1987, reads, "The orders stated in the law [on welfare benefits] will be applied to a person who lives in [the territories], or works there, if he lives or works in Israel, if he is an Israeli citizen or has the right to immigrate to Israel under the Law of Return."[14] The only person who has the right to immigrate to Israel under the Law of Return is a Jew. Arabs who lived in east Jerusalem, of course, do not qualify, in this or any other category defined in the regulation.

How discrimination within the Israeli welfare system works in practice can be seen in the case of Fatmah Hamad, an Arab woman who was born in Jerusalem and held a blue Jerusalem identification card. Fatmah married a man from Nablus, in the West Bank, and moved there to live with him and his family—as is often the case in traditional Arab families. Late one night in the spring of 1991, Fatmah, her husband, and their young daughter were returning from a trip to a relative's through the center of Nablus. The family's car had yellow Israeli license plates, as it was registered in the name of Fatmah's brother, a Jerusalem Arab. Arabs in the West Bank drive blue-plated cars. Arab youths, believing Jews were inside the car, threw a bottle of acid that shattered the front window of the vehicle.

Fatmah and her daughter were seriously injured. But their nightmare had only begun. An Israeli army patrol that was nearby when the attack occurred took them to Rafidiya Hospital in Nablus, but that hospital did not have facilities to treat burn patients. An ambulance was called to rush the mother and daughter to Jerusalem, but every hospital they approached turned them away. One hospital said its emergency room was not on call. A second said it had no expertise in treating burns. A third, Hadassah University Hospital, demanded a guarantee of payment before it would treat them, since they did not live in Jerusalem.

The Office of the Adviser on Arab Affairs at the Jerusalem municipality was contacted by the ambulance company. The company director explained the situation. A call to the hospital confirmed what he reported. "We need a written guarantee of payment," the municipality was informed. Such a guarantee would have never been demanded of a Jew. But there was no time for argument. The municipality faxed a letter guaranteeing that it would pay for treatment, if the NII did not meet its obligations. Fatmah and her daughter were accepted into the hospital's emergency ward nearly ten hours after they were wounded.

Eventually, the Civil Administration agreed to pay for the daughter's treatment, since she was a resident of the territories. The mother, however, was a Jerusalem resident, and the NII should pay, the Civil Administration concluded. The NII saw things differently, however. It recognized that Fatmah had a Jerusalem identification card, but she in fact was no longer a Jerusalem resident and therefore was not eligible for Israeli benefits. The municipality appealed to the Civil Administration, contacting Col. David Shahaf, at the time the deputy director of the organization. Shahaf, who would later become Civil Administration head, acknowledged that his office had a special budget for such emergency cases—but Fatmah did not qualify.

The hospital all the while continued to press for payment. The municipality was left with little choice. It had guaranteed payment, so it now had to come up with the money. The city turned to the Jerusalem Foundation, a fund-raising organization for projects in Jerusalem founded by Kollek in 1966. The foundation, whose criteria are set by humanitarian and not political considerations, within a week had sent a check to Hadassah University Hospital to pay for Fatmah's treatment.

Jerusalem Mayor Teddy Kollek promised time and again to bring municipal services in east Jerusalem up to par with those in west Jerusalem. He said it to all who would listen—foreign diplomats, visiting groups of American Jews, Arab notables from the city. Kollek made the promise so many times that it eventually lost its meaning. Advisers told Kollek that perhaps he should refrain from continuing to make the promise, or change it somewhat to make it more realistic, so he would not be accused of trying to deceive. Instead of saying you will bring services and conditions in east Jerusalem up to par with those in west Jerusalem, they would advise him, simply say you will work to substantially improve things in east Jerusalem. But Kollek did not listen. He continued to plug away with his promise for equality and to search for some sort of miracle solution—one that would satisfy Arab residents but not consume too much of the municipal or national budget.

In August 1986, the mayor turned to Efriam Shilo, who served for many years as the coordinator of the government's Ministerial Committee on Jerusalem, for ideas. Shilo was no longer with the government committee but was working instead as chairman of the Religious Affairs Ministry Office for the Establishment of Religious Buildings. "I would be grateful for your helping the municipality in its plan for the development for the Arab sector, most importantly the villages that are within the city limits," Kollek told Shilo.[15] "I am certain that you will know how to put the emphasis on the small, immediate needs, things that are lacking, and which it is easier to deal with in the short term, while at the same time working on larger plans that are scheduled to be carried out in the more distant future," the mayor said.[16]

Shilo did not reply immediately to the mayor. He took his time—two months to be exact—to study the issue at hand and to speak with city officials. But mainly, he relied on his own first-hand knowledge of the situation in east Jerusalem, which came from the years he had with the Ministerial Committee on Jerusalem. When Shilo finally responded, his words were eerily prophetic. "I myself look with great concern on the rise in tensions between the two parts of the city," Shilo told Kollek.[17] "The physical conditions in which east Jerusalem residents live is not the reason, or perhaps not even a major reason for the increasing tensions, but it still surely helps create the hostile atmosphere." Shilo made his comments exactly a year before the outbreak of the intifada.

Kollek at the time was disappointed. He had hoped that his old friend would help find a quick and easy solution to his growing problems in east Jerusalem. Instead, the friend only added to Kollek's worries. Shilo's concern that the poor conditions and services were endangering the already sensitive situation in east Jerusalem did not translate into action, however. These warnings and those of others that improvements were urgently needed, if for nothing else than to calm tensions, were ignored. Kollek continued to promise help, but the promises were never followed through.

When the tensions in east Jerusalem—as well as in the West Bank and Gaza—finally broke out, the mayor renewed his calls for a concise plan of action in east Jerusalem. Kollek turned to the Jerusalem Institute of Israel Studies, a local think-tank affiliated with the municipality, and asked institute researchers to put together a report on municipal services in east Jerusalem. In early 1989 they began their work. The researchers went directly to city hall, met with municipal department heads, reviewed the budget books, and even met with Arab municipal workers to find out what they had to say about the situation. The researchers came up with an in-depth study that detailed the wide range of services that were deficient or nonexistent in the Arab sector. But nothing ever came of the study. Policy did not change. Services in Arab east Jerusalem were not improved. Even worse than that, the study never even received an in-depth analysis on the part of Kollek, his aides, or senior municipal officials.

Two years later, in 1991, the Office of the Mayor's Adviser on Arab Affairs presented its own plan for improving services in Arab east Jerusalem. The proposal was to form independent units in various city departments that would be responsible for dealing with Arab neighborhoods. The units would receive annual budget allocations, with which they would have to provide the necessary services to the Arab sector. The idea was that by having a special unit in each department dealing with Arab east Jerusalem, with its own budget, it would be more difficult for department heads to take money away from Arab neighborhoods and put it into Jewish ones.

Gal, the city manager, called a meeting to discuss the proposal. Department heads were asked to attend. After a short presentation of the proposal at the start of the meeting, the department heads—one after another—gave their opinions. They were all in agreement: they wanted nothing to do with this plan. Their stated reason was that having separate units dealing with east Jerusalem would imply that there was still a division at city hall between east and west Jerusalem. The proposal, the department heads said, would only endanger Israel's claims to east Jerusalem.

But the officials were not really concerned about the political implications of establishing east Jerusalem units in their departments. A similar argument was given for many of the reforms suggested for improving services and infrastructure in east Jerusalem. But the argument does not stand up to close analysis. Why was it all right to set up neighborhood councils in Jewish neighborhoods as a way to improve communication between local residents and city hall, but such as move was considered problematic in Arab neighborhoods on grounds it would be construed as the first step toward autonomy? Similarly, separate units already existed in the education department, as well as several social affairs and welfare-related departments. The concept that Jerusalem was a heterogeneous city in which the municipality can sometimes set up special departments to better serve specific populations was already long accepted when it came to subgroups within the Jewish population. The ultra-Orthodox and national religious Jews had their own units in the education department. This was considered the best way of ensuring that the special needs of these populations were met. But the same logic was not applied to the Palestinian community.

The department heads were against separate Arab units because they feared a loss of authority and funding. Each year the sanitation department, for example, drew up its budget request as if it were servicing the whole city and then proceeded to spend nearly all the money on Jewish neighborhoods. That decision was made solely by the department head. It should come as no surprise that the department heads' solution to the problems in east Jerusalem was that the city manager should approve additional funds to their departments. In theory, these new funds would then go to service the Arab neighborhoods. Gal knew better than to believe them. But he also did not have the power at city hall to make them change, so the meeting ended with no results.

Kollek was in a bind. He knew that if his hopes for coexistence in Jerusalem were to be realized, the level of services to Arab residents needed to be improved considerably. But the mayor also knew that investment in improving services in Arab east Jerusalem meant taking funds away from Jewish neighborhoods. For Kollek, that spelled disaster, so he desperately looked for a solution that would provide improved services without costing the city considerably more money. Many would say Kollek was looking for the impossible, and a few people even told him that. The mayor, however, ignored the critics and continued to promise a better future for the city's Palestinian residents, despite having nothing on which to base his promise.

8

Security Breach

On an early Saturday morning, December 19, 1987, the wave of violence that started in a refugee camp in the Gaza Strip hit the Israeli capital, spreading like fire through the Arab neighborhoods of the city. Outbursts were reported first in Jabal Mukaber, Wadi Kadoum, and then Silwan. Hundreds of Palestinian youths in those neighborhoods on the outer reaches of the city took to the streets. They blocked roads with burning tires and waved flags of the outlawed Palestine Liberation Organization. The unrest moved north to the Mount of Olives, picking up speed and strength on the windswept hillside holy to Christians, Jews, and Muslims around the world. A-Tur and Asana were soon encompassed in the flames of unrest.

At that point, even if Israel had been ready—which it was not—there was no stopping the course of the unrest. Downtown east Jerusalem, the heart of the Arab business district, was hit next, and the Old City soon followed. Roads were blocked with burning tires and debris. Any Israeli vehicle that by chance entered the area was the target of stones and bottles. For that matter, anything identified with the Israeli authorities was considered fair game. On Salah A-Din and Azara streets, the windows of three Israeli banks were smashed and the banks were looted.

Yosef Yehudai, the Jerusalem police chief, together with an entourage of police brass and senior municipal officials, rushed to Lions Gate. They set up a Forward Command Post (FCP), from which they hoped to oversee the squashing of the mini-rebellion. The Israelis were well aware of the irony of their position. At the same spot two decades earlier, on the third day of the Six Day War, Israeli paratroopers began their historic push to take the Old City and Temple Mount. The battle has since taken on legendary proportions for Israelis and Jews worldwide, who for thousands of years prayed for the moment when Jerusalem would be theirs.

But the days of the glorious Six Day War offensive had long passed. The Israeli force at the Lions Gate FCP was on the defensive. A flurry of stones rained down from inside the Old City on the Israeli officers, who moved in close to the walls to avoid injury. Yehudai radioed for reinforcements, but extra manpower was hard to come by. His men already had their hands full containing the unrest that had broken out all over east Jerusalem.

One of the immediate issues on the police commander's agenda was the planned visit to the Old City of the Italian foreign minister. Yehudai considered contacting the Foreign Ministry and canceling the visit. But he decided against this. Police and municipal officials knew it was important to keep up pretenses to the world that everything was normal in Jerusalem. In the early days of the intifada Israel was obsessed with demonstrating that it was in total control of east Jerusalem. Yehudai gave the green light for the visit. But he made clear to the policemen escorting the Italian minister that the visit should be quick and should keep to the quieter streets of the Christian Quarter. The VIP entourage drove in Jaffa Gate and was hurriedly taken by foot to the Church of the Holy Sepulcher, and then as quickly taken out of the Old City and returned to west Jerusalem.

The Israeli police and municipal officials at the Lions Gate FCP, ducking stones as they listened on their short-wave radios to reports of unrest in much of east Jerusalem, did not really understand the scope of the events that were unfolding. Unrest was nothing new to them. Neither were riots. Israel may not have liked to admit it, but since 1967 it had developed a seasoned occupying authority in the West Bank, Gaza, and east Jerusalem. Palestinian residents had periodically turned to stones and terror to protest the occupation, but in general Israel was militarily and emotionally prepared for this.

Terror and unrest were also nothing new to Jerusalem. They had existed during the British Mandate, then under Jordanian rule, and after the 1967 war. In 1968 a car bomb placed by Palestinian nationalists in the heart of the Jewish market at Mahane Yehuda killed 12 persons and injured 67.[1] The following year three Jews were blown up in an explosion perpetrated again by Palestinian nationalists.[2] A year has not passed since 1967 in which there were not casualties as a result of Palestinian terrorism. The worst attack occurred in 1975, when a PLO-backed bombing at Tzion Square, one of the busiest intersections in Jerusalem, killed 23 people and injured over 100.[3] Between 1967 and the end of 1987, when the intifada began, 75 persons were killed and 880 were wounded in Palestinian terror attacks in Jerusalem.[4] Most of the victims were Jews. A handful were tourists. There were also several Palestinians who accidentally wandered into the death traps laid by fellow Palestinians fighting against Israel.

The intifada, however, was different. Before, rioting was generally localized and involved relatively small groups of Palestinian protesters. During the intifada, it spread over a wide area, ranging from the refugee camps in the Gaza Strip to the neighborhoods of West Bank cities and east Jerusalem, and involved the mass of Palestinian people, particularly young people. Before the intifada, the unrest lasted at worst a day or two and then died down. Intifada violence never let up.

The Israeli authorities, so confident in their control of the occupied territories, including east Jerusalem, at first did not notice these differences. They continued to believe that they were witnessing just another passing spate of violence with the Palestinians that would quickly die down. Jerusalem Mayor Teddy Kollek is one of a handful of leaders who can say they warned that it was coming. Kollek was well-enough connected to what was going on in his city to realize that the quiet, or more accurately the relative quiet, would not last. In retrospect, a senior Israeli security official noted that "the infrastructure was already in place in Jerusalem well before it started. The Palestinian youth were organized. Everything was ready. It was like a bomb waiting to explode, with no one knowing exactly when it would go off."[5] Kollek did not have access to this kind of intelligence information on the activities of the PLO or other Palestinian nationalist groups in Jerusalem. He just had an excellent feel for what was happening in the city.

"I am concerned about the situation in Jerusalem," Kollek told Prime Minister Shimon Peres a year and a half before the outbreak of the intifada.[6] "There is no guarantee that the quiet and calm will continue much longer," he said. "We live each day on miracles, that neither the public, or even you, ever hear about." Peres had just paid an official visit to Jerusalem. As was customary on such visits, the mayor took his guest around the city, showed him the new Jewish neighborhoods in east Jerusalem, revitalization projects in west Jerusalem, and even a token city project in an Arab neighborhood. Peres was only shown the positive side. "Perhaps, the visit you just had, in which you saw only the beautiful things in the city, worked against us, as it is likely we didn't succeed in transmitting to you the serious concerns and fears that exist," Kollek told Peres.[7]

Several months later, Kollek raised similar concerns with police minister Haim Bar-Lev.[8] The mayor called for measures to improve police operations in Jerusalem in order to avoid a further deterioration of the situation.[9] "There is one point that I simply don't seem to be able to get across to you and convince you of—and for that matter with all the governments of Israel. That is, Jerusalem is the city with the most complicated problems in the world," Kollek told the minister. "In order to keep the peace, and strengthen our authority, coordination and cooperation are needed [between local and national agencies] on many subjects," the mayor added. He then went on to outline the various religious and geopolitical tensions in Jerusalem, and warned that without better cooperation between the various branches of the government, Jerusalem faced serious troubles. "To my sorrow, I fear that the day will come when the government, and as a result also the residents of the city, will pay a high price for this failure to act." A year after those words were written, the intifada was roaring, and Kollek and Bar-Lev, two elderly Israeli statesmen, would again confront each other, wondering where they had gone wrong.

Once the intifada began, Israel's security establishment predicted a quick end to the violence, particularly in Jerusalem. Instead, the city's Arab sector became the daily scene of clashes between Israeli security forces and Palestinian youths, and the intifada dragged on for months, and then years. Israeli vehicles were the targets of stones, bottles, and firebombs, when they ventured into Arab neighborhoods of east Jerusalem. Even Arab drivers were hit, when they were mistaken for Jews. Public buses were considered "Israeli targets," even though their passengers were both Arab and Jewish. Israelis' cars parked in Arab neighborhoods were torched and stoned; so were rental cars, as intifada leaders hoped to scare tourists away from Jerusalem. Palestinian youths quickly became experts at setting cars on fire, despite the watchful eyes of the Israeli security forces. In a matter of seconds, the youths would break the car window with a stone, pour various forms of highly flammable liquid inside, and then set the vehicle ablaze.

The east Jerusalem office of the Interior Ministry was set on fire on several occasions, as was the headquarters of the city sanitation department. Indeed, city property, ranging, from lamp posts to sewage lines, were badly damaged, as the Palestinians took out their anger against anything remotely connected with Israel. In the village of Silwan, residents dropped an old washing machine into a sewage manhole, clogging up the system. When city workers arrived to remove the machine, they were stoned by residents. This became the norm throughout Arab east Jerusalem, so much so that the city simply stopped carrying out repairs in Arab neighborhoods because municipal workers were being attacked. In Silwan, one of the hot spots of the intifada, even Israeli ambulances on their way to help sick residents were stoned.

The intifada was ripping apart Jerusalem. The old border between east and west Jerusalem was being reestablished by the unrest. Israelis from west Jerusalem and throughout the country stopped going to east Jerusalem. Residents of the new Jewish neighborhoods in east Jerusalem found alternate routes between work and home to avoid passing through Arab neighborhoods. Jewish residents who lived near Arab neighborhoods would wake up each morning and look outside to see if their cars had been smashed or, worse, torched. Arab youths from Jabal Mukaber did not even have to leave their own neighborhood to stone the Jewish homes on Meir Nakar Street in East Talpiot, the two neighborhoods were so close. Some Jewish residents covered their windows with metal shutters to prevent them from being broken.

The Old City was perhaps the major center of unrest. From a political perspective, intifada activists understood that any type of protest they organized would draw the greatest international attention if it took place in the ancient walled city. Strategically, the narrow alleyways, rooftop paths, and generally crowded conditions were ideal for the activists. The area quickly acquired a reputation as a dangerous place, and foreign tourists responded by keeping away, as did Israelis. The Old City, home of holy places for the three great monotheistic religions, turned into a virtual ghost town that few visitors dared enter.

Kollek—who perhaps more than anyone else wanted to continue to believe in a united Jerusalem—had his first awakening to the new world created by the intifada just several days after it hit the city. It was a cold and rainy December afternoon. The mayor, in his fourth floor city hall office, was dictating a letter. He still had about thirty minutes before his five o'clock meeting, and the slight lull in the usual rush of municipal business, particularly in the days since the start of the uprisings, was a relief. What Kollek did not know at the time was that in a nearby office an aide had just received a telephone call that would alter his schedule and return him to the tense new reality in Jerusalem. Sheikh Ali Taziz, chairman of the East Jerusalem Chamber of Commerce, was on the line. He said he and other chamber of commerce members would not be able to make their meeting with Kollek at five o'clock.

The cancellation was unprecedented. The East Jerusalem Chamber of Commerce was comprised of the leading Arab business figures in the city. They had a reputation for being moderate. Business dealings had put them in close contact and even on friendly terms with Israelis. Kollek had hoped economic ties between Arabs and Jews in the city would be a first step toward improved relations. Taziz and Fayik Barakat, the group's director, met frequently with the mayor. Kollek was a guest on several occasions at the chamber of commerce's headquarters, and the Arab businessmen were Kollek's guests at city hall. But with the intifada, circumstances had changed. Taziz had called to say they would not meet with the mayor. Taziz knew that Kollek wanted the meeting to demand an end to the commercial strike called by intifada leaders. He also knew that intifada leaders would be watching the chamber of commerce closely to see how they dealt with the Israeli authorities, and that to be branded a collaborator with Israel meant possible death.

The police and municipality had been pressing the businessmen to open their stores. Israel saw breaking the strike as an important step toward returning the city to normal. The mayor's adviser subtly inquired of Taziz what the problem was with the meeting. Taziz hinted that if the businessmen went to city hall of their own free will, that would look bad for them. If the police, however, asked for them to come in, they would have to oblige, and the intifada leaders would understand this. Taziz was asked to hold. On another line, the adviser contacted Yehudai, the police chief. He was scheduled to come to Kollek's office for the meeting with the chamber of commerce. He readily agreed to hold the meeting at his office at the Russian Compound Police Station. Taziz, Barakat, and about a dozen members were soon in his office, as was Kollek, who had come to expect surprises at any time in Jerusalem.

Kollek was in for another surprise when he arrived at the Russian Compound—a cluster of old buildings that served as the Jerusalem police headquarters and jail. Middle Eastern custom dictated a clearcut code of behavior at such meetings, no matter who the participants were. The guest would always allow the host to speak first; there would be a long exchange of greetings and inquiries about health and family; coffee would be served; and only then would a real discussion begin. Israeli officials who dealt with Arabs had grown accustomed to this protocol, and Kollek and Yehudai were among the officials who knew the codes best and felt most comfortable with them. That is why they were shocked when Taziz, Barak, and company entered the meeting room, sat down, and did not wait for Yehudai to speak or for the traditional introductions.

"We understand you have invited us here to talk about the commercial strike," Taziz began. "We want you to know that we did not initiate the strike, but we identify with it, and wouldn't, even if we could, put an end to it and open up our stores and businesses. That's all we have come here to say." With that Taziz and the others stood up to leave. Kollek could not believe his eyes. The affront to Yehudai was that much more forceful because it was taking place at Israeli police headquarters. The police commander jumped to his feet and motioned for the Palestinian businessmen to sit back down. "Coffee is on its way. Please, sit down. There is no reason to rush off," he pleaded with the businessmen, who themselves appeared uncomfortable with the scene that was unfolding. It did not take much on Yehudai's part get them seated again.

Yehudai tried to get the businessmen to consider a plan to break the strike by having a few major stores and businesses in different areas of the city open first, in an effort to pave the way for others to follow suit. The police department had already mapped out the city and pin-pointed several businessmen and storeowners it hoped to convince not to honor the strike. Taziz sat and listened quietly. He allowed Yehudai to present his position, knowing that it would only be bad for him to interrupt the police chief in the middle in order to reject the argument. But Taziz made clear afterward that the East Jerusalem Chamber of Commerce was no longer in a position, even if it wanted, to meet the Israelis' demands.

Two months later, however, Taziz had changed his mind. The frequent commercial strikes continued, and while that may have shown a strong Palestinian national will, they were bad for business. The owners of larger businesses who ran the chamber of commerce were not the only ones being hurt. Dozens of small Arab vendors in Jerusalem were devastated by the strikes and violence, which scared away shoppers. Taziz and several other Palestinian businessmen indicated to municipal officials that now there was something to talk about. But by this time the Israelis were no longer willing to listen.

The municipality arranged a meeting but sent only a few low-level city officials and police officers. The meeting was held at the Kishleh Old City police station and not at the main headquarters at the Russian Compound. This time the Palestinian businessmen suggested that the strike could be broken if a few stores in different areas opened first—perhaps with the appearance they were being forced to by police—and then other storeowners would also open. But the police and city were not interested. They had already decided that there had been enough talk, and it was time to crack down on the intifada in Jerusalem.

For people who had decided to get tough, the Israeli security establishment officials gathered on the third floor of the Police Ministry appeared oddly unsure of themselves. The atmosphere was tense. Around a table sat the senior members of Israel's security establishment.[10] Police minister Haim Bar-Lev, a former Israeli army chief of staff, sat at the head. He was joined by Ya'acov Pery, chief of Israel's renowned Shin Bet internal security service. Pery was a veteran; he had joined as a field agent just after the Six Day War and had worked his way up quickly. He had headed the Jerusalem Office of the Shin Bet before taking charge of the service.

Pery's identity was a closely guarded secret at the time, as were the identities of other Shin Bet officers. It was forbidden to publish his picture or even his name. To most Israelis, and for that matter, most of the world, he was known simple by his first initial, "Y." Israel did not take chances with allowing internal security force officers to become targets for attack by Palestinian nationalistic groups or other hostile organizations. Gidon Ezra, Pery's deputy, was also present. Known as "G," Ezra was a quiet-mannered chain smoker who would later become a Knesset member with the right-wing Likud Party. He had also worked his way up through the service and was already eyeing his boss's position. At the time, he held his boss's old job as head of Shin Bet operations in Jerusalem. The Israel police inspector-general, David Krauss, and Yehudai, Jerusalem police chief, were the senior officers present. Commander Meshulam Amit, National Police Operations Division head, also attended. Several months afterward, Amit was appointed head of Israel's paramilitary border police, whose central task was intifada containment.

Due to the sensitivity of the matter being discussed, Kollek and a senior aide were the only nonsecurity figures allowed to attend. Kollek had no official standing at the meeting. In Israel, internal security is exclusively in the hands of the national government. The local authority has no official say, even with regard to police operations within its jurisdiction. Still, Bar-Lev believed it wise to have Kollek present. For Bar-Lev, Kollek was a fellow Labor Party member with close ties to the government. The minister knew it would be best to have the mayor's backing for any steps taken by the police and the Shin Bet in Jerusalem.

The intifada had been raging for two months, and Israeli security officials were desperate to put an end to it, particularly in Jerusalem. The question for the officials at the table was how this was to be done. But instead of coming up with concrete plans, they exchanged accusations. The Shin Bet accused the police of not doing enough. The police said they were doing the best they could given a shortage of manpower, which resulted from a lack of state funding. Kollek all the while sat quietly, only making a few not particularly relevant comments about the effects of the intifada on life in Jerusalem. Everyone left with a feeling that things were getting out of hand.

Pery, the Shin Bet chief, was given the floor at the start of the meeting.[11] "Things have quieted down somewhat in recent weeks," he began. "But we shouldn't get the wrong idea. Things are only quieter because of the additional men we and the police have brought into east Jerusalem. The minute we pull those forces out, or even cut manpower in any significant way, the unrest will intensify." Pery's analysis was not exactly what Bar-Lev wanted to hear. Since the start of the intifada the entire Israeli police force was working twelve-hour shifts, and all vacations had been canceled. Bar-Lev knew that if he tried to keep this type of work schedule up it would surely have an ill effect on his men. But for the moment, he did not interrupt the Shin Bet chief, and only jotted down a note to himself.

Pery continued, "The police manpower that is out in the field is not being properly utilized. We know the identities of many Palestinians we suspect of involvement in unrest, including a number of the leaders, but the police aren't providing us the support needed to arrest them. We see the main problem being with the police investigations division failing to do its job."[12] The Shin Bet chief did not hide his criticism of the police and legal authorities for, in his eyes, not doing enough to contain the Palestinian uprisings in the city. "The police allow the Palestinian store-keepers to open and close when they please," Pery said.[13] "In that way, the store-keepers are able to maintain a strike for most of the day, and then open up for only a few hours and do all their business then." As for those Palestinians being arrested for their involvement in the unrest, many are being released soon after the detention because of foul-ups by police investigators and the district attorney's office, Pery told the forum. "We must also set our priorities. Our major goal must be to deal with the business strike, and only afterwards should we move on to the matter of the strikes at the schools," he said.[14] "We have intelligence information showing that the Democratic Front for the Liberation of Palestine is trying to take advantage of the large concentrations of young persons at schools to spark unrest, but we must be careful in how we deal with the issue."

Next, Krauss, the national police chief, stated his position. He began with a laundry list of police anti-intifada operations in Jerusalem: "Since December 19 some 603 suspects have been arrested in east Jerusalem, including 269 minors. Some 152 legal files have been opened pertaining to nearly half of the suspects. Of those files, 32 involving 51 suspects have been transferred to the district attorney's office. Another ten files dealing with 33 suspects were transferred to the Military Prosecutor's Office."[15] His comments were meant to counter the arguments of Pery that the police were not making enough arrests. Krauss confirmed, however, that there were problems in the investigations division. He said police could not handle the caseload, given the manpower shortage. "We received an extra 100 investigators in Jerusalem, but not on a regular basis," Krauss complained. "Just about every week they are returned to their normal posts elsewhere in the country and are replaced by new investigators. This creates problems. The new investigators have to re-learn much of the material, which wastes a lot of time. But at this stage, I don't see any other way to deal with the issue."

Krauss noted that police intelligence assessments predicted a hot

Land Day, at the end of March, when Palestinian Arabs annually hold demonstrations to protest the expropriation of their lands by Israel. The first weeks of April will also demand additional manpower in Jerusalem, because of the large numbers of visitors to the Old City for Passover and Easter, he noted. "Until then, we will continue to cancel leaves and work 12-hour days. But soon after Easter, I hope we will be able to begin cutting back and slowly returning to normal," he said.

Kollek was then given a turn to speak.[16] He knew quite well that on security matters he was not only out of his league but also out of his jurisdiction. Kollek began by noting that despite calls for the municipality's 1,500 Arab workers to join the strikes against the Israeli occupation, nearly all of them continued to do their jobs. He then emphasized that city services to east Jerusalem were hurt by the uprisings. Trash was no longer being collected in many neighborhoods, and street lights, sewage lines, and other municipal infrastructure had been severely damaged. The mayor also mentioned that Jewish residents of the north Jerusalem neighborhood of Neveh Ya'acov complained of the repeated stoning they endure when riding public buses to the city center that drive through the Arab neighborhoods of Beit Hanina and Shuafat and that the residents want the buses to use alternate routes.

The security officials at the meeting were not interested in the local issues raised by Kollek, however. The mayor was advocating coexistence. They were concerned with security, and wanted other considerations to be put aside until quiet was restored. The security officials were also less than pleased with Kollek when, just as he appeared to be finished, he said he had one more issue to bring up, police brutality. The mayor said that Arab residents complained they were "ill-treated" by the police. That was a nice way of saying that they reported being kicked, clubbed, or worse by Israeli policemen. Kollek had finished his presentation. The room fell silent.

Bar-Lev had the last word. Not surprisingly, he took the side of the police officers under his command, defending them against the criticism of the Shin Bet and Kollek.[17] "The steps taken by the police so far have given results," Bar-Lev said. He then predicted a quick end to the intifada, at least in Jerusalem. "The present level of forces [in Jerusalem] will remain until Land Day on March 30. Toward the end of March, a plan involving the gradual cutting back of forces in Jerusalem will begin to be implemented, although extra forces will still remain on the job in the city," the police minister said. He appointed Ezra, Amit, and city manager Aharon Sarig to "by this weekend study the alternatives for dealing with the commercial strike and offer some solutions." As for the east Jerusalem schools, Bar-Lev said they should be allowed to reopen on condition they return immediately to a normal schedule, and do not open and close on the orders of intifada leaders. Any school reopened that becomes a center of unrest must immediately be shut down, Bar-Lev added. He then turned to Kollek. "If there are any concrete complaints concerning humiliating treatment by border policemen of the local Arab population, they will be dealt with appropriately." With that comment the meeting was officially adjourned. The optimistic assessment that the intifada was on the verge of ending prevailed. But not for long.

Just two weeks later, Bar-Lev decided that enough was enough and reconvened the same forum of security officers.[18] The intifada had intensified, rather than let up. The Palestinians continued to pound away at the Jewish state, and not just in far-off refugee camps and villages but in the capital itself. The Israel security establishment was desperate for answers. Bar-Lev wanted concrete decisions taken on containing the unrest. It was time for Israel to get tough with the intifada in east Jerusalem.

What Bar-Lev and company had in mind was "To show the [Arab] population that Israel has control of the unrest and that they [the Arabs] are more troubled by the situation than we are."[19] To do this, "pressure must be put on the entire population of all the areas and villages that are the centers of unrest." The Israeli security officers wanted to make sure they kept control. "The pressure must be placed with care in order that it will not cause a boomerang effect," they concluded. "The pressure must be such that it is understood [by the Palestinians] that Israel is still in control."

The Israeli officials decided on a series of measures to crack down on Palestinian unrest in east Jerusalem. The measures included "curfews, municipal actions, such as cutting of water supply, halting trash pick up, etc., holding up payments of social benefits."[20] The Israeli security establishment wanted to beat the intifada in Jerusalem by showing the Palestinians that they had a lot to lose if they continued with their protests, and it was willing to go to great lengths to do this, even if it meant bringing thousands of policemen and soldiers to the city. The security officials decided on "massive police presence in villages where unrest is centered."[21] They also devised some novel ways to get the extra manpower needed. Soldiers would be transferred to the service of the police, retired policemen would be called back on the job; policemen in office jobs would be brought into the field; and civilians would be encouraged to join the civil guard, the volunteer corps that works together with police. All the troops were being called out. Israel was declaring war on the intifada in Jerusalem.

Yehudai, the Jerusalem police chief, was one of the biggest "get tough" proponents in the security establishment. Even before the intifada he was well known in east Jerusalem for his attempt to physically break commercial strikes against the Israeli occupation. It became known as "the crowbar method." Yehudai ordered his men to break open the locks on Arab stores on strike. Most Arab stores had metal shutters, and policemen found that a crowbar worked best to force them open. Israeli police would go from store to store on Salah A-Din and Sultan Suleiman streets, in the heart of the east Jerusalem shopping district, breaking the shutter locks and letting the owners decide whether they wanted to leave their stores unattended or open for business. In those days, the tough tactics worked. The owners were just looking for an excuse to reopen, and the police provided it.

The intifada changed that. In the first days of the uprisings police applied their crowbars to east Jerusalem stores, and the owners would come to work. But the owners would also turn away customers, explaining that it was a strike day and they were at work only because the police had broken open their stores. The owners would not do any business, and Jerusalem police eventually put down their crowbars.

Israeli security officials then came up with a new method to break the commercial strike—the military order. Normally only used in the West Bank and Gaza, military orders calling for shopkeepers to open or face criminal charges were issued in east Jerusalem. But there was a slight catch. Regulations required that the military order be for a specific date and time. The problem was with half-day strikes. If, for instance, the intifada leadership called for a morning strike, a military order would be issued saying stores must remain open in the morning. If the leaflet called for an afternoon strike, the order would demand an afternoon opening. The intifada leadership would release a leaflet defining the strike days and half days, and Israel would respond accordingly with military orders.

This quickly turned into a cat and mouse game. The intifada leadership at the last minute would switch a strike day, or move it from the afternoon to the morning, in an effort to free the shopkeepers from the military order. But the game was short-lived. Eventually, police chief Yehudai outsmarted the intifada leaders: he began to keep a stack of pre-signed military orders (they needed the signature of a senior army officer) on hand in his office. All he had to do was fill in the date and time. But even when the police chief got the time of the strike correct, the orders proved ineffective. Palestinian businessmen simply ignored them. Several Palestinian businessmen were detained and then soon released, pending a court ruling. It took the court nearly a year to find them guilty of a misdemeanor and fine them the equivalent of approximately $100 each. That was not enough to make anyone break the strike, particularly when intifada leaders were threatening physical violence to shopkeepers opened on strike days.

Yehudai decided that if he hit the shopowners in their pocketbooks, he would get better results. So he ordered police to stop enforcing antivending laws, and as a result Salah A-Din and Sultan Suleiman streets became crowded with street concessions. Yehudai hoped the storeowners, seeing that others were taking away their business, would open. But the owners out-foxed him. Instead of opening, they joined the vendors on the sidewalk, selling their wares at stalls. Not to be outdone, Yehudai shut down Salah A-Din Street to traffic altogether and allowed hundreds of vendors to crowd not only the sidewalks but also the street itself. But this move, too, did not work. Yehudai may have hurt the storeowners, but he failed to break the commercial strike. The intifada prevailed.

Desperate to contain the uprising, Israel police began detaining Palestinian suspects without trial and imposing curfews on Arab neighborhoods that were centers of unrest. But there was a high cost to Israel for imposing these stringent emergency measures. Israel had been trying to distinguish east Jerusalem from the occupied territories since 1967; the imposition of military law in east Jerusalem in order to put down the intifada was again blurring this distinction. This outcome was exactly the opposite of what Israel wanted. Intifada leaders were winning the war of nerves with the Israeli security authorities, who were beginning to appear incompetent rather than in control.

Kollek looked on in despair as east Jerusalem grew closer in character to the military-ruled West Bank and further from west Jerusalem, which like the rest of Israel was governed by democratic means. Publicly, Kollek opposed the use of military law in east Jerusalem, whether in breaking a strike or demolishing the home of a terrorist. But for all his public pronouncements against these measures, the mayor for the most part sat quietly when the police and Shin Bet planned and implemented them. Kollek was present at most of the meetings when concrete decisions were made to take these harsh measures, and he barely expressed a word of protest. Bar-Lev approved punishing Arab residents by cutting off city services, and Kollek did not raise a word of protest. Police closed schools in east Jerusalem, and the mayor was not even consulted. When curfews were imposed on east Jerusalem, the municipality (along with private debt collection agencies) took advantage of the police presence to confront Arab residents in their homes and try to force them to pay outstanding bills.

Debt collection during curfews by municipal tax collectors was eventually stopped by the mayor. He also stood in the way of the security establishment's plan to cut off city services in Arab neighborhoods where the unrest was the most intense. He said little in Bar-

Lev's office when plans were discussed to halt garbage collection or turn off the water in unruly neighborhoods, knowing that in such a forum he had little authority. But the city controlled the services, and Kollek very diplomatically ignored any request he received from police to curtail them.

Kollek was opposed to cutting off services because he saw it as collective punishment. Punish the criminal, he said, not the community. The mayor also viewed the demolition of the home of a terrorist—a punishment endorsed by the Israeli security establishment—as an unfair collective punishment because innocent family members were hurt. But the mayor's view was overruled by those who believed that threatening the family home might discourage future terrorists. Kollek had little recourse in this instance. He may have had control of the city's water spigots but not its bulldozers.

Kollek did, in one case, give approval for a water line to be temporarily shut down in the Arab neighborhood of Abu Tur, where in his view intifada violence had gotten out of hand. The mayor viewed it as a special case. Municipal repair crews were stoned repeatedly when they came to Abu Tur to fix a ruptured water line. Kollek decided that if the residents were not going to allow the line to be fixed, then they would simply have to learn to live without running water. The neighborhood remained without water for three days before the city decided that while it still was not going to turn the line back on, it would provide a fire truck to bring in drinking water. Hundreds of residents lined up beside the truck with pails and pots. There was no stone throwing, but the Israeli driver still refused to get out of the truck, for fear of being attacked by the residents.

Neighborhood leaders decided they had seen enough when residents began pushing and shoving for a place in line. They contacted the municipality and promised that if the city would again sent a repair crew, there would be no problems with stone throwing. The crew came the next day and fixed the line. Residents brought them coffee and cakes, and the municipality never again cut off water or stopped any other service to an Arab neighborhood. On this point, despite pressure from the police and Shin Bet, Kollek remained firm.

Before the intifada, police rarely ventured to the outlying Arab neighborhoods and did not normally patrol even more central areas of the Arab sector. The intifada brought the Israeli security forces and the local Arab population in day-to-day contact to a degree they had never known before. The experience was largely negative. The complaints of police brutality were widespread, but there were even more visible signs of the tendency of police to treat Arab residents like second-class citizens. For example, police were much quicker to use force to quell a demonstration of Palestinians in Issawiya than a demonstration by ultra-Orthodox Jews in Mea Shearim, even though both protests had the same characteristics: throwing stones and bottles, burning tires, attacking property and persons considered outsiders. Judge Khalil Silwani, head of the Jordanian-affiliated High Court of Appeals in east Jerusalem, recalled once being stopped by a policemen and verbally abused because he did not speak Hebrew. In another incident, an Arab bus was stopped at a police roadblock and passengers were forced to get off, because the policemen decided the bus was not mechanically fit to be on the road. The driver's attempts to show the police that only two days earlier the bus had passed inspection were ignored.

For Arab residents, the police roadblocks were one of the most annoying steps Israel took to show it was "in control." Before dawn, several jeep-loads of border policemen would lay metal spikes and a barrier at the entrance of an Arab neighborhood and begin stopping all vehicles going out. Driver registrations were checked, and then Transport Ministry mechanics would determine whether the car was mechanically sound. All these inspections would, of course, take a long time. The line of cars would grow. Arab residents on their way to work or school would have to wait, and all the while their anger at Israel would grow. Neighborhoods that were the center of intifada unrest were singled out for this treatment. Police wanted to send a clear message to the residents: as long as your community remains a center of unrest, we will make your life miserable.

The Israeli police have faced charges of brutality and mistreatment not just from Arabs but also Jews. But there is little comparison in degree. For instance, the police would never dream of using a Jewish neighborhood as a firing range. But that is just what they did in Silwan, the Arab neighborhood just southeast of the Old City. Police brass knew that a police patrol through Silwan was sure to be met with stones and bottles during the height of the intifada. New weapons aimed at dealing with intifada unrest, mainly antiriot equipment, were constantly being experimented with by the police, and Silwan was the testing ground. Police knew they could always find a target there. Whether it was new type of rubber bullet or tear gas, police would go to Silwan first to see how it worked. The local youths always cooperated.

The intifada gave the security establishment an opportunity to limit the travel rights of the city's Arab residents. East Jerusalem Arabs were free to travel to Jordan, as were Arab residents of the West Bank. Israel was proud of its liberal travel policy to Jordan after the 1967 war. The Hashemite Kingdom was an enemy nation, but Israel was aware that many Arabs in the occupied territories had families, friends, and business concerns on the eastern side of the Jordan River. So Israel allowed them to travel with relative freedom over the border, at the Allenby Bridge crossing. The only limitation was that men between the ages of 16 and 36 who went to Jordan had to stay there for at least nine months before being allowed to return to Israel. Security officials reasoned that this policy would deter some smuggling by West Bank Arabs, including weapons, across the border. East Jerusalem Arabs, however, had been exempt from this regulation. This was one of the privileges they were awarded, in Israel's effort to create a distinction between east Jerusalem and the West Bank. But after the outbreak of the intifada, the government heeded the demands of the security establishment and put the nine-month limit on Arab residents of Jerusalem. Here again, east Jerusalem residents were being brought closer to their brethren in the West Bank, with the help of the Israeli government.

What was even more worrisome for Israel, east Jerusalem quickly became the political center of the intifada. The intifada leadership was headquartered in east Jerusalem, and all the major Palestinian national groups had their main offices in the city. The violence of the uprisings may have been worse elsewhere, but Jerusalem was still the center of the action. From the perspective of the Israeli security establishment, this situation was totally unacceptable. The government could not tolerate the intifada in its "united capital," and security officials were under great pressure to shut it down. But the intifada continued to roar in Jerusalem, and Jewish-Arab tensions there grew.

In August 1990 two Jewish teenagers from the Ramot neighborhood went missing. Police suspected they were kidnapped by terrorists. For days, emotions in Jerusalem were on edge. Israeli security officials were not optimistic, but the public continued to hope they would turn on the radio and hear that the teenagers, Ronan Karmani and Leor Tobol, were safely back home. Unfortunately, Karmani and Tobol were found murdered, and all the signs pointed to Palestinian terrorists being responsible.

The double murder sparked an unprecedented outpouring of anger against the Arab population. Jewish youths took to the streets and stoned any vehicle that looked like it had an Arab driver. The youths entered Arab neighborhoods, breaking the windows of homes and cars and setting fire to trash bins and pulling them into the road to block traffic. Arab bystanders accidentally caught up in the wave of riots and not quick enough to flee were beaten. On Hebron Road, Jewish youths forced a truck carrying hundreds of bottles of soda pop to halt, pulled out the Arab driver and beat him, and then began pulling off the bottles and breaking them on the street. The police were nowhere to be seen.

Leor Tobol had lived in one of the Jewish neighborhoods adjoining Beit Safafa, an Arab village surrounded by Jewish neighborhoods in south Jerusalem. During good times, Arab and Jewish children in the area played together, went to the same parks, and even in some cases attended the same schools. But the ties that came with living as neighbors were forgotten by the Jewish residents after the murder of the two teenagers. Traffic on the Patt-Gilo Road, which bordered Beit Safafa, was forced to a halt as Jewish protesters by the hundreds began a rampage in the direction of the village. There was shouting and screaming of "Death to Arabs, Death to Arabs." A vehicle parked along the road was lifted by the mob and thrown into the wadi below. In the village itself, Jews were throwing stones at Arab cars and homes. Many of the villagers ran inside for cover, but dozens of the village youth climbed to the roofs of their homes, taking armloads of stones with them. When the Jews approached, the Arabs rained stones down on them.

An Arab woman holding an infant ran frantically down a village street but was suddenly stopped at a police checkpoint. "No one is allowed through," one of the young policemen told her, in Hebrew. But the woman simply looked at him dumbfounded and tried to keep running. The policemen, who had been ordered to let no one through the checkpoint as part of the police's futile effort to return calm to the village, prevented her from passing. She screamed to them that she was only trying to get to her home with her young child. The Jews were coming after her. But the policemen did not understand a word the woman was saying, and she did not understand them. The woman was screaming in Arabic, and the policemen spoke Hebrew.

Most of the Arab policemen on the Israeli force in Jerusalem had quit long before the Beit Safafa riot. To remain an Israeli policeman during the intifada was to be labeled a collaborator and risk assassination. Some Israeli policemen spoke Arabic, including the many Druze border policemen. But there was still a shortage of Arabic speakers, and police patrols of Arab neighborhoods were often made up of men who spoke only Hebrew. This was particularly true during large operations such as the Beit Safafa riot, when much of the police manpower being used had to be brought in from outside the Jerusalem district. The policemen from outside usually did not know Arabic, and on top of that were not sensitive to the delicacy in Arab-Jewish relations in Jerusalem. The Arab mother and infant, however, were lucky. As the mother and policemen attempted to carry on a conversation that neither side could understand, a municipal official who spoke Arabic passed by and explained the situation to the policemen, who then let the woman and her child pass.

Riots like the one in Beit Safafa occurred simultaneously in other spots in the city and only got worse as darkness fell. Not until well after midnight were police able to restore quiet. Hundreds of paramilitary border policemen cleared the Jewish rioters out of Beit Safafa and forced them back in the direction of the Jewish neighborhoods. The policemen—more used to fighting riots by Arabs than by their fellow Jews—at first did not know how to handle the disturbances. Israeli police traditionally allowed for a certain level of violence on the part of Jewish protesters in order to allow them to "vent their anger," particularly after terror attacks. But the situation in Beit Safafa got totally out of hand. The lenient policy of police was seen by the protesters as a go-ahead to wreak havoc on the village. No one in Jerusalem had doubted that news of the two murders would spark unrest, but police failed to prepare adequately for this inevitability.

Kollek and a his aides drove into Beit Safafa early the next morning. The streets were empty, but the mayor, who had long refused having a driver, had to dodge stones and debris in the streets as he drove. He saw for himself the broken windows of the cars and homes and other damage caused by the rioters. Kollek parked the car and walked up a short path to the home of Abu Tarek, the village mukhtar. The home was quiet but crowded. About two dozen villagers called together by the mukhtar were sitting in a large circle. They left several chairs open for the mayor and his aides. The villagers looked as if they had been up all night. Abu Tarek opened with the traditional Arabic greetings. Coffee was brought in for the guests from city hall. Then Abu Tarek began to speak about the matter for which Kollek had come.

"I am sure that you have seen as you drove here what was done to our village. There was no reason for it. We did nothing. We condemn the killing of the two Jewish boys. Why do they have to attack us in return?" Abu Tarek began. Villagers were particularly infuriated that the police had refrained from firing rubber bullets at the Jewish rioters, which they often did to break up Palestinian demonstrators. Instead, they said, the policemen fired at Arab youths in an effort to force them back into their homes. Several of the youths were wounded and hospitalized. "My own son was shot, and is in the hospital right now," Abu Tarek said. The mayor promised he would bring the matter up with the police chief. He called for restraint by the villagers and said he hoped that within days life would be back to "normal." Kollek also publicly condemned the Jewish rioters. He said there was no justification for their actions, even given their anger over the murder of the two Jewish teenagers.

Life in Jerusalem, as Kollek predicted, did after several days return to normal; that is, to normal for intifada Jerusalem. But Jewish-Arab relations in the city remained a powder keg ready to blow up again at any moment. That the first explosion had occurred in the one place in Jerusalem where coexistence always really seemed possible made the situation all the more disturbing. Beit Safafa had been torn in two by the 1948 war, but between 1948 and 1967 residents of the western half of the village lived on good terms with their Israeli neighbors. The village prospered. Residents were even absorbed into the Israeli establishment, taking positions in both local and state offices. The good relations continued after the city and village were reunited in 1967. Jewish neighborhoods were built around Beit Safafa, and the physical closeness of their homes created a closeness in relations between Jews and Arabs. Even during the intifada, Beit Safafa was known as a "quite village," which Israelis continued to enter unafraid. There were incidents, including the shooting of a resident by police during an intifada demonstration. And many buildings and homes in Beit Safafa were scrawled with intifada slogans, as elsewhere in east Jerusalem. But overall, relations between Arab villagers and Israelis remained good. Thus the brunt of the Jewish mob's anger was being vented against not just any random Arab village but the very one that embodied Israel's hopes of coexistence in Jerusalem.

But Israeli policy-makers appeared to learn nothing from the rioting. There was no shake-up in the city's police brass. The police knew they were not properly prepared for the riot, and minor operational changes were made in hopes that they would not be caught off guard again. But beyond that there was no overall re-evaluation that such a serious incident demands. Indeed, the police position was that they were there only to "put out the fires." It was the local and national Israeli leaders that needed to take the steps to bring about a lessening of tensions in Jerusalem. The police—and for that matter also the Shin Bet—felt they were responsible only for public order. The problem of making peace between Jews and Arabs in Jerusalem, the security establishment reasoned, was the job of others.

During the over five years that the intifada raged, Israel never managed to develop a comprehensive plan to deal with it. Rather, one arm of Israeli authority would work against another. Kollek would meet with Arab notables to assure them that Israel understood their concerns and might even be willing to grant them more authority in east Jerusalem. At the same time, the national government would be pushing measures to squash any form of Palestinian nationalism in the city.

This was the case with a cross-party parliamentary proclamation adopted in the Knesset toward the end of the first year of the intifada. The proclamation was proposed by Labor Party Knesset member Shlomo Hillel. It had the strong backing of all the Jewish political parties, except the far-left Meretz Party. Kollek, however, scoffed at the proposal, calling it an empty proclamation that only hurts Israel's claim to Jerusalem. "The Knesset reiterates and maintains that unified Jerusalem, the capital of Israel, is not and will never be a subject for negotiation," article one of the proclamation stated. "The Knesset maintains that every effort must be taken to maintain security in Jerusalem, including east Jerusalem and the Old City, and calls on [Jewish] residents to volunteer for the Civil Guard and help the police . . . The Knesset calls upon the municipality and government to do everything possible to ensure normal business activity in east Jerusalem, and to consider the possibility of setting up stands to fill in for the stores that are closed down [due to strikes]."

In Palestinian eyes, this was an Israeli government call to arms to the Jewish public. Kollek agreed, and this was one of the main reasons he opposed it. The proclamation went on to deplore any action "that disturbs the peace and does injury to co-existence of all parts of the city's population." The statement was meant as an additional warning to Palestinian residents that the authorities would take tough action against disturbances. The proclamation ended with a call to expand the Jewish population in "all parts of the city." Palestinians could understand this as nothing less than a challenge.

One attempt, on the local level, to come up with a new approach to security in east Jerusalem came from Michael Gal, the ex-Israeli army general who was Jerusalem city manager during the intifada. Gal called a handful of senior municipal officials to his office on the third floor of the old city hall building several days after the Beit Safafa riots. The old office building was a fitting place for the meeting. The outside walls were covered with gunshot holes from the 1967 war. The building was on Jaffa Street, just outside the Old City. After the war, Kollek ordered the gunshot holes left in place. He wanted them to be a reminder that city hall sat on the border of the once-divided city, between east and west Jerusalem.

Gal's office was on the third floor, just below Kollek's. The city manager's office windows looked out onto a spectacular view of the walled city. As in a romantic novel, the view reflected well the character of the hero. Gal was not your typical ex-army officer. He was more the philosopher type. He liked to analyze issues, to think about them and then think about them again, and then discuss them, before coming to a decision. Everything was done in a controlled and slow manner. Detailed minutes were taken at meetings; if problems arose participants were broken into working groups to solve them; nothing was left to chance.

But when it came to dealing with the intifada, Gal could not keep up with events. Like other Israeli officials, for the first few months he had preferred to sit back and wait it out, believing the unrest would subside on its own. He felt pressed to act, however, after the Beit Safafa riots. "The new reality created by the intifada has left us with a situation in which our city, and I mean the entire city, east and west, Jewish and Arab, is running at a constant high potential of explosion," Gal told those gathered in his office.[22] "In my view, the potential for explosion—I mean that a crisis-situation will develop—is not confined to areas where there is a normally high amount of contact between Jews and Arabs, such as in the Old City, the border neighborhoods, the major arteries that cross the city from north to south along the old border, such as Route 1, Ramallah Road, and Hebron Road. Rather, even areas that are far from these points of friction have the potential of exploding at any time."

Gal went on to tell his fellow city officials that they must also be aware of the effects of events outside of Jerusalem on the tense atmosphere within the city. An attack by Palestinian guerrillas launched from south Lebanon on an Israeli community in the north could provoke protests by Jewish residents of Jerusalem and conflict with Arab residents, according to Gal. "The fact the government offices are in Jerusalem often brings instigators from outside the city," Gal added. For the city manager, this tense atmosphere created by the intifada posed two major questions: How has the city prepared itself to prevent unrest from erupting? And what will its response be when it does erupt?

He posed the questions to his colleagues. After a lengthy discussion, the following plan was adopted: (1) define potential dates when tensions are particularly high, such as intifada anniversary days, or Jewish holidays when large numbers of Jewish worshipers go to the Old City and Western Wall; (2) identify major points of friction; and (3) take advantage of municipal channels of communication with the Palestinian population of the city to conduct nonpolitical dialogue aimed at keeping the peace. As to the city's response in the event of a crisis, the officials emphasized that security proper was in the hands of the police and Shin Bet, not the city. But the city still had a role to play, they concluded, by promptly providing the material support needed in the wake of a crisis—including everything from food to welfare aid.

Gal was satisfied. Nearly three years after the Palestinian uprising first began, he finally felt as though he was ready to go out and try to take whatever the intifada might deal him. A code name was even given to the municipality's intifada emergency procedures: *Havatselet* or "Lily." In line with his pedantic style, Gal had specific orders sent out to various city departments on how to deal with a long list of intifada-related emergencies. "War games" of a kind were carried out several times to make sure the departments were prepared. Gal got his first chance to try out Havatselet in real life soon after the plan was formulated, and in a big way.

Tensions were particularly high in Jerusalem in early October 1990. A Jewish extremist group that openly called for the removal of the Dome of the Rock and al-Aksa mosques to make way for a re-built Jewish Temple was preparing to hold a demonstration at the site on the Jewish holiday of Sukkot. The group, the Temple Mount Faithful, and its head, Gershon Solomon, represented for Jerusalem's Muslim leaders the threat of Israel trying to oust them from Haram al-Sharif, the Arabic name for the walled complex the Jews call the Temple Mount. Jewish extremists in the past had tried to destroy al-Aksa and the Dome of the Rock. Muslim leaders were on constant watch for another attempt. Police were well aware of the violent consequences likely if Solomon and his followers were allowed onto the Temple Mount, so the group was forbidden from holding the protest. Israel's Supreme Court upheld the police decision.

The Temple Mount Faithful wanted to enter the Temple Mount on Monday, October 8, the second day of the Sukkot holiday. On Sunday, Kollek held his annual reception for the public at The Tower of David Museum, next to Jaffa Gate. The gathering was held outside, in the pleasant fall weather. City councilors and senior municipal officials were present. So were many notable figures in the city, as well as many plain folk who came to shake hands with the popular mayor. The atmosphere was festive and the setting, as always, glorious. The museum itself is situated along a section of the Old City wall. The verandah outside overlooks the red tiled roofs of the Mishkenot Sha'ananim neighborhood and Hinnom Valley. It is perhaps no wonder that a worrisome report that was being discussed at the reception failed to catch anyone's serious attention.

Several senior municipal officials had heard rumors going around in the Arab sector of the city about plans by hundreds and maybe even thousands of Palestinian youths from the West Bank to converge on the Haram later in the evening, in an effort to protect the holy site from the Temple Mount Faithful. Several senior advisers to the mayor had also heard of the report. Inquiries were made with Adnan Husseini, the director of the Haram, late Sunday night. Husseini confirmed that young people were believed to be coming and were encouraged to do so by Palestinian leaders. A senior municipal official reminded him that there was no need for the Palestinian youths to converge on the holy site, as the Supreme Court had already forbidden the Temple Mount Faithful from entering and that the youths' presence might lead to unnecessary tension. Husseini said there was no reason to worry. The municipality took his word. There were no more inquiries. The police were not notified by the city officials looking into the issue—although they probably knew what was happening already.

What exactly transpired later in the night and the next day remains unclear. Each side accuses the other of being the instigator. But no matter who threw the first stone or fired the first shot, what cannot be argued is the results of the clashes at the Haram al-Sharif between hundreds of Palestinian Muslims and the Israeli police on Friday, October 8, 1990. Seventeen Palestinians were shot dead by police. Several Jewish worshipers were hit and injured by stones thrown from inside the compound as they were praying at the Western Wall. It was an incident that would rock Palestinian-Israeli relations for years to come.

International criticism for Israel was harsh and brought back into question Israel's claims of authority in east Jerusalem. The United Nations decided to send a team of investigators to find out what had happened. Israel, however, flatly rejected the idea, and made it clear it would not allow the U.N. investigators into the country. The U.N. eventually backed off from the idea. But the damage to Israel's image remained. The Palestinians, meanwhile, tried to use the killings to gain momentum for their effort to end Israeli rule in east Jerusalem. Under heavy international pressure, the Israeli government set up a commission of inquiry. The commission put the blame on the Muslims at Haram al-Sharif for instigating rioting and throwing stones on Jewish worshipers at the Western Wall. But the commission also took the police to task for ignoring intelligence reports warning of possible unrest and, when it occurred, not taking the proper steps to contain it.

Overall, the commission revealed nothing new. Its report could have been written about any one of dozens of incidents during the intifada before the Temple Mount clashes. The findings did force some changes in Israeli police operations, but only pertaining to the Temple Mount, and even those changes took years to implement. Meanwhile, the unrest and clashes continued in east Jerusalem, but no one in Israel's security establishment seemed eager to see if maybe they were doing things incorrectly. Instead, the old policies were continued. They had not worked in the past, and they continued not to work.

The afternoon after the Temple Mount unrest, senior municipal officials held an emergency meeting in Gal's office at city hall. Kollek entered about halfway through the meeting. He looked pale and upset. His dream of coexistence and peace in Jerusalem had taken another blow, and the loss in human life was heavy. He wanted to visit Muslim religious leaders in the city to pay his condolences and speak to them about ways to lessen tensions. His advisers told him the time for such a visit had not yet arrived. He would be poorly received, with the Palestinian anger over the clashes still intense. The mayor took the advice, and stayed away from east Jerusalem. For Kollek, the man who perhaps more than any other worked for a united Jerusalem, the intifada had literally redivided the city.

9

Damage Control

Kollek's dreams of Jerusalem being a "normal city" had slowly crumbled before his eyes. The mayor had worked hard since 1967 to present Jerusalem to the world as a unified city. But already at the start of the intifada, just a couple of weeks of violence and unrest in the city had done much to obliterate that image. Damage control, for Kollek, meant in large part "image control," or restoring the view of Jerusalem as a united and mostly quiet city. The mayor sent off hundreds of letters to supporters of Israeli rule in Jerusalem, in an effort to restore their confidence. Many of those letters went to persons affiliated with the Jerusalem Foundation, the fund-raising organization for the city founded by Kollek in 1966, and the Jerusalem Committee, a group of leading intellectuals and businesspersons from around the world who had agreed to use their influence to ensure that Jerusalem remained united under Israeli rule. This is what Kollek had to say to the members of the Jerusalem Committee,[1]

Dear Friend,
Seeing the local events of the past two months in the international media, you may have asked yourself: "How widespread is this violence? What does it do to the daily life of Jerusalem? Where did the violence originate? What is its impact for the future of Jerusalem?" This letter, is meant to try and answer these questions, and if there are new developments I shall continue to keep you informed.
What did actually happen in the past two months?

In the villages within our municipal borders and on the roads leading to the West Bank—Azariya, A-Tur, Shuafat, Abu Tur, Jabal Mukaber, Sur Baher, Arab teenagers in some 20 incidents threw rocks at cars and buses and burned tires.

In central Jerusalem there were several demonstrations by Arab high school students, and a PLO flag unfurled near Herod's Gate.

The adults did not take part in any of this, and in some instances even tried, albeit unsuccessfully, to stop the youngsters. There has been a commercial strike in East Jerusalem, and at least one shop owner had his shop burned down for opening it on a strike day.

On Friday, in front of the al-Aksa Mosque on the Temple Mount, Muslim youths burned Israeli and U.S. flags; during the ensuing violence one policeman was dragged into the mosque and grievously injured and the police were forced to use tear gas to disperse the mob and save their comrade.

Since then, there have been isolated incidents, mostly at night, of rocks and sometimes Molotov cocktails being thrown at cars and buses, mostly on the main road leading out of Jerusalem to the West Bank, as well as rocks thrown at Jewish homes.

How has daily life in Jerusalem been affected?

Everything goes on almost as usual. Of the 1,500 Arab employees of the municipality, some 1,450 or more come to work daily; municipal services are maintained as usual, although at times there are short interruptions necessitated by technical obstacles.

. . . There were times during the nice weather in December when the police were dispersing some 50–60 teenage demonstrators just 200 yards away from tourists walking along the walls of the Old City or through its gates.

. . . There has been an increase in the number of Arabs shopping in Jewish neighborhoods; those with cars visit the supermarkets and department stores in the city center, others shop in the smaller stores adjoining Arab neighborhoods.

Kollek presented here and elsewhere a rosy picture of the intifada. A few stones here, a few Molotov cocktails there, all the result of some teenagers who were disobeying their parents. The mayor tried to downplay the intifada violence, so he could in turn argue there was still a chance for his "united Jerusalem" under Israeli rule.

Kollek, like most Israeli policy-makers, misread the intifada. There is little argument over the central role played by young Palestinians, teenagers and younger, in the intifada. They daily threw stones and clashed with the Israeli authorities and carried out terror attacks against Israeli targets. But most of their parents were far from being sympathizers with Israeli demands for quiet. The parents had seen their children killed in clashes with Israeli security forces, and viewed them as martyrs for a cause in which they too believed. In the first months of the intifada, a mother from the Gaza refugee camp who was interviewed for Israel Television had this to say: "If my son comes home with rocks in his pocket, I send him to bed without his dinner." She then explains that she is not mad at her son for throwing rocks, but for not throwing all of them. This should have been an early lesson for Israel not only in Gaza but also in east Jerusalem.

In the same letter, Kollek goes on outline a possible "solution" to the intifada:

For 20 years I have been saying that it may take a Muslim minority a hundred years to accept as a fact that they must share Jerusalem with the Jews and the Christians, and for coexistence to become an established fact in Jerusalem but, meanwhile, it was imperative that we improve the quality of life in the Arab communities. Many people took it for rhetoric, but now no one can claim that there is no need to do anything because Jerusalem's Arabs are happy with the situation. Housing, education, and most of all, employment must be improved; the rights, privileges, and duties of the Muslim community must be anchored in law and guaranteed by the government before the Muslims can feel secure in Jerusalem . . .

There is no alternative but there is hope. Jerusalem must re-

main one, undivided and indivisible, a Jewish city with a large
Muslim and a small Christian minority. The details of combin-
ing Israeli sovereignty with Muslim and Christian autonomy,
privileges, citizenship etc. can be worked out. If the standard of
living of Jerusalem's Arabs keeps improving and the regional
political question is resolved, we can look forward to a more
peaceful future.

I hope you and other members of the Jerusalem Committee
will be able to spread this word in the world, individually for
now and collectively when we next shall all meet in Jerusalem
. . . In the meantime, let us all pray for the peace of Jerusalem.
Yours Sincerely,
Teddy Kollek

Kollek could not help but say "I told you so" to Israel's national
leaders. According to the mayor's thinking, the uprisings that broke
out in Jerusalem as part of the intifada were the direct result of the
failure of the government to invest more money in improving living
conditions in east Jerusalem. If residents had better schools, bigger
homes, and more jobs, the conflict could have been avoided, or at
least toned down considerably. "For 20 years I have been saying that
. . . it was imperative that we improve the quality of life in the Arab
communities," he wrote to the Jerusalem Committee members. This
is classic Kollek. He had been saying that for years, and continued
saying it even after the intifada. It is not surprising that when the unrest first broke out at the end of 1987 and continued to rage in the
first months of 1988, Kollek stuck to his old formula—hoping to appease the Palestinian population, through development projects and
improving services.

Kollek believed he could buy peace and quiet in east Jerusalem by
improving services and carrying out public works projects to make
the Arab residents feel they are being treated fairly. Publicity was a
central part of Kollek's policy. He repeatedly told aides that no matter how small the project they were carrying out in east Jerusalem,
they should try to get big media attention. If a new road was built in
east Jerusalem whose opening was not publicized, it was a waste to

even build it, according to Kollek. Publicity meant letting the Arab residents know the city was taking action to improve their living conditions. Publicity was also aimed at showing the world Israel was a fair ruler.

If there is any bottom line from which it is possible to judge Kollek on east Jerusalem at any time, but especially during the intifada, it is the budget line. The numbers, however, do not look good for the mayor. The city was forever putting together reports showing the great amount of work that needed to be done in east Jerusalem, but little of the money needed to carry out the work was allocated. East Jerusalem was neglected by Israel before the intifada, and things only got worse during the uprising. Kollek and many other Israeli leaders—the mayor was far from being alone on the issue—may have believed they could buy quiet in east Jerusalem, but they must also have thought they could buy it cheap.

Kollek did not find the funds he needed for east Jerusalem in municipal coffers, and he had no luck convincing the national government to put up money for the city's Arab sector. The mayor was left with only one resource: supporters from outside of Israel, Jews and non-Jews alike. Just days after Kollek sent off the letter explaining the intifada to Jerusalem Committee members, he sent a similar letter to Jerusalem Foundation contributors.[2] The main addition was a detailed explanation of where improvements were desperately needed in east Jerusalem. The message was clear. Send money; you can help buy peace for Jerusalem.

Dear Friends,
I am writing you today because I am sure that your thoughts have been with us during these difficult days. We are still filled with anguish at the seeming impossibility of finding a resolution to the problems which have beset Arab-Jewish relations in our region. The recent disturbances in and around Jerusalem have been our ongoing concern, and I suspect you share this concern with us.
... We must try and substantially increase our effort [to bring a better life to both Jews and Arabs in Jerusalem]. Accordingly,

we have set ourselves a detailed course of action in response to the situation.

What are the objectives?

1. To augment our efforts to provide equal services and opportunities for the Jewish and Arab sectors (insofar as we can under present conditions) and to be prepared, once the situation has stabilized, to initiate major programs for the Arab community and offer a further helping hand. We again concluded that it will take far more than nineteen years to bridge the differences in language, values and political conceptions and to make up for the nineteen years of Jordanian neglect.

2. To strengthen the morale of the Jewish population in the city, especially the communities which are adjacent to Arab neighborhoods and which feel threatened, for example Abu Tur, East Talpiot, Gilo, French Hill, Ramot Alon, Pisgat Ze'ev, and Neveh Ya'acov. This is where we must create new programs in the schools and community centers while augmenting existing ones.

3. To intensify every program of joint activities for Jewish and Arab youngsters—be it through art, music, film, sports, handicrafts, or other activities sponsored by the Municipality and by the Jerusalem Foundation. Such programs have always been financed on a shoestring budget. The present situation demands a dramatic increase.

We have to strengthen activities in those facilities which serve as a meeting ground for Jewish and Arab families, such as the Liberty Bell Garden, the Biblical Zoo, the Jerusalem National Park around the Old City Wall, the Haas Promenade, the Israel Museum, the Alpert Music Center for Youth, and the Jerusalem Film Center.

While we have little say in influencing the regional situation, we are determined to respond to our responsibilities to preserve Jerusalem as an exceptional city. We can do this in the assurance that while there may be wide differences in opinion throughout our country as to the political future of the West Bank and Gaza, the one national, and to a large extent international, consensus which exists is the agreement that Jerusalem must remain undivided, the Capital of Israel, and that we can give Muslim Arabs and the various Christian denominations (many clearly defined national churches) full self-expression to an extent they never experienced before.

The responsibility we bear is a heavy one. And if we needed your helping hand throughout the past twenty years, we shall need it now even more so. For this reason, I am calling on you today to put Jerusalem at the top of your list of priorities.

I have asked my colleagues at city hall and at the Jerusalem Foundation to prepare together a list of the most urgently needed projects. We would be deeply grateful if you would consider helping us in one of these vital undertakings.

I offer you the opportunity to do something tangible, not to allow our dreams of a Jerusalem in which all can live together in peace and harmony vanish. Our thoughts go beyond the boundaries of our city and even our country, for Jerusalem as a place for peace is the symbol for the hopes and aspirations of many. Please join us in helping keep this symbol a reality.

With every good wish,
Yours,
Teddy Kollek

This letter, in a nutshell, outlines Kollek's response to the intifada. It was intended for donors living far away from Jerusalem, and therefore did not go into the details and fine points Kollek's aides considered when dealing with the daily problems that cropped up during the intifada. But the principle remained the same for city hall: "to augment efforts to provide equal services and opportunities for the Jewish and Arab sectors."

The policy of trying to improve services as a means of appeasing the Palestinians had failed between 1967 and 1987. Why would it work now? Kollek did not like that question at all. He was fully aware of Israel's failures in east Jerusalem and believed it was unfair to now demand of him an explanation for the outbreak of the intifada. It was the national government, and not city hall, according to

Kollek, that had failed Jerusalem. During one interview in the first months of the uprising, he verbally pounced on a reporter who asked him if there was anything that he could do to stop Jerusalem from being redivided. "Why didn't you ask this question during all these years when I said that if we don't provide services that are truly comparable, we won't hold our ground here?" the mayor angrily replied. Kollek was well-known for his feisty outbreaks when he heard things he would rather not, but in this case he quickly calmed down, taking a short pause to consider his remarks before adding, "I'm not sure we could have held our ground, now that all this has happened. But we never gave it a fair chance."[3]

Kollek believed it was important that he serve as an example of how Jewish and Arab residents could live together, how east and west Jerusalem were united under Israeli rule. Before the intifada, he roamed Arab neighborhoods of the city unprotected. During sensitive periods, when police feared a possible attack on the mayor, they offered him protection, but he always refused. Kollek argued it would be absurd for him to be seen walking around east Jerusalem with a platoon of policemen tagging along, or even a bodyguard, in light of his claims that the city was united and for the most part peaceful. He wanted Jewish residents of west Jerusalem to feel comfortable about coming to east Jerusalem. That is much of what being a united city was supposed to mean—that residents were free to move from one part to another, that there were no barriers between the two sides. If Kollek was to allow himself special protection in east Jerusalem, then how could he expect other Jews to feel safe there?

Before the outbreak of the intifada, police allowed Kollek to have his way most of the time. The mayor went unaccompanied everywhere, from Shuafat refugee camp to the markets of the Old City. There were several exceptions when the Shin Bet, which is responsible in Israel for the safety of government officials, insisted that its men accompany Kollek, out of concern for his safety. Kollek greatly resented the presence of a bodyguard at his side. Most of the time he simply ignored the guard. Other times, however, he would outwardly express his anger at being "followed" and even refuse to go to events because of the guard by his side. About two years before the outbreak of the intifada, the Shin Bet received intelligence information on plans by Palestinian terrorists to attack the mayor, and a guard was assigned to him. Kollek reacted in his usual manner of simply ignoring the bodyguard's presence. But at one point, he angrily refused to proceed with his schedule. The mayor was expected at a giant *hafla* or party being given in his honor by Arab residents of Sur Baher. "What are you doing here?" Kollek snapped at the Shin Bet bodyguard who got in beside him in the car about to leave city hall for the hafla. The bodyguard had been briefed on the mayor's disdain for being protected and answered simply that it was his job to follow him wherever he went. "Well, if you're going, then I'm not going," Kollek said, and got out of the car, slamming the door behind him.

Aides tried to convince the mayor to go, on grounds that the whole affair was planned on his behalf, and it was important for Arab-Jewish relations in the city. But to no avail. Kollek refused to go. In another incident, Kollek refused to accompany the then-minister for Arab affairs, Moshe Arens, to the Old City because of the security measures the Shin Bet demanded. It insisted on a bodyguard for Arens, because he was a government minister. Kollek sent Arens on the tour accompanied by several city officials and waited for him back in his office. He was not going to be seen as needing special security precautions in east Jerusalem.

The outbreak of the intifada put Kollek even more at odds with the Shin Bet. In the security establishment's eyes, there was no question that Kollek needed protection every time he went to the Arab sector of east Jerusalem. The police and Shin Bet decided to avoid confrontation with the mayor by keeping his protection secret. They provided him protection—everything from bodyguards to police escorts to sharpshooters—but undercover so that the mayor himself would be oblivious to their presence. Uniformed policemen and border policemen kept their distance when, for instance, Kollek sat in a cafe at Damascus Gate in one of his many efforts to mingle with the Arab population. Nearby, however, were several undercover policemen and Shin Bet bodyguards. Kollek never realized that one of his major trademarks as Mr. Jerusalem—that he could travel anywhere in the city without special protection—was in fact a sham.

In the summer of 1991, Kollek sat at one of the Damascus Gate cafes he often frequented with Mike Wallace of the popular U.S. television news magazine *Sixty Minutes*. Kollek would often take well-known journalists and other guests to a Damascus Gate cafe in an effort to demonstrate that everything was generally normal in Jerusalem. He also wanted to show that he did not require any special protection in east Jerusalem—believing himself he was not getting any. The intifada was still roaring. Wallace was in the country to do a "Jerusalem in the intifada" story. He asked for an interview with Kollek as part of the show and jumped at the mayor's suggestion that it be done in the Old City.

Damascus Gate is one of the most colorful scenes in Jerusalem. The Old City gate lies just beyond Sultan Suleiman Street. To reach the street from the gate, you have to walk down a steep amphitheater-shaped staircase. The steps are filled with vendors selling everything from Jordan Valley grapes and oranges to imitation Levi jeans from who-knows-where. The scene of scattered vendors turns into a full-fledged bazaar at the bottom of the steps, so crowded you have to push your way between the salesmen, fruits, vegetables, wares, and groups of tourists, in order to make it through Damascus Gate and inside the Old City. Kollek chose the spot for the interview well. He wanted to give the impression that he, and Israel, were in control of the city, despite the tensions between Jews and Arabs.

Kollek did not notice the paramilitary border policemen watching from rooftops and the nearby undercover police, on duty to make sure tensions did not erupt, and if they did to contain the explosion. As expected, the interview quickly turned to the tough issues of life in Jerusalem during the intifada. Kollek began to outline his already well-known position on the matter—admitting there was tension and sometimes violence but always ending up by reminding the interviewer, no matter who he or she was, that Jerusalem is a safe city. You did not have to look further than the fact that the Jewish mayor of Jerusalem was sitting undisturbed in the heart of the Arab *shuk*, and even exchanging casual hellos with Arabs in the vicinity.

Kollek and Wallace were so caught up in their discussion they failed to notice what was beginning to transpire around them. First, the border policemen were making their way quickly down the rooftops, in hot pursuit through an adjoining alleyway. A few shoppers noticed the border policemen's movement and, knowing that it indicated trouble, started to clear out of the area. The movement turned to a fleeing mass as more and more people realized that an "incident" was in the making. By that time, Kollek and Wallace also noticed that something was wrong. But it was too late. The tear gas had already been fired, and there was nowhere for them to turn for cover. A cloud of smoke overtook the outdoor cafe.

For those unaccustomed to the experience, tear gas comes as a surprise because its name is so deceiving. The gas makes you cry, yes, but what the name does not tell you is why you cry—because of the burning in your eyes. It is temporarily blinding. Your eyes squeeze shut in a desperate attempt to stop the pain, but it does no good. Your nostrils and throat burn from the fumes. Many people react by throwing up or going into a spitting fit, as their bodies desperately try to cleanse themselves. Kollek, who in 1991 was 80 years old, and Wallace, also an elderly man, made their way inside the cafe, coughing and crying. A local Arab man gave the two visitors rags soaked in vinegar to put over their mouths and noses. It was a homemade remedy for tear gas, and it worked. What set off the firing of the tear gas was never clear. Apparently some Palestinian youths had thrown stones and bottles at the border policemen, and they had responded accordingly.

There was nothing unique about what had happened. It was part of life in intifada Jerusalem. Just as quickly as it had happened, it ended. The shuk was crowded again with shoppers and vendors, as if nothing unusual had transpired since they fled and returned. Kollek and Wallace, however, decided to call it quits for the day.

10

A First Friendship

Israel's de facto annexation of east Jerusalem following the Six Day War created a new reality for city residents. The walls and barbed wire fences that divided the city were torn down. Jews and Arabs who had lived on opposite sides of the old border between 1948 and 1967 had in fact lived in two different cities, even two different worlds. Now they were neighbors, living in a single city. The massive construction of new Jewish neighborhoods in east Jerusalem initiated by Israel in the postwar years created even more points of contact between Jews and Arabs in Jerusalem. Still, the two groups continued to live apart. They had some limited contact in business and commerce, but on the community level there was little connection. Indeed, the hostility and tension between them appeared only to increase with the years.

An incident in the neighborhood of Abu Tur, just south of the Old City, demonstrates the complexities involved when two communities in conflict live side by side. Between 1948 and 1967 Abu-Tur was divided into two parts—one Jewish, under Israeli rule, and another Arab, under Jordanian rule. The 1967 war reunited the neighborhood, and today a narrow road more or less divides the Jewish and Arab communities. But relations between the two groups remained poor. In the mid-1980s, after the city completed renovations on Nahamia House, a community center named for a fallen Israeli soldier, the Jewish residents assumed that the renovated building was for the use of their children only. When Arab children from Abu Tur also began using the facilities, Jewish residents became angry, and the Jewish neighborhood council informed city hall that it was going to prevent Arabs from using the center.

The city would not allow it. The municipality threatened to close the center if the Jewish council tried to prevent Arabs from entering, and the council backed down. But officials at city hall concluded that having Jews and Arabs use the center together would create an explosive situation, and the only answer was to find a space exclusively for the Arab children. A bomb shelter was eventually located and renovated to accommodate them. Thus, Abu Tur was provided with separate Jewish and Arab recreation facilities. No one ever imagined that the Jewish and Arab children of Abu Tur might be able to play together in the same space.

A similar playground conflict broke out about the same time in East Talpiot, which borders the Arab neighborhood of Jabal Mukaber in southern Jerusalem. Arab children from Jabal Mukaber wanted to play on one of the school grounds in the Jewish neighborhood, since their own schools were without playing fields. The Arab children cut a hole in the school fence to gain access, and the grounds quickly became the site of confrontations between the Jewish and Arab children. In this instance, the leaders of the two communities were able to sit down and work out the problem. Again, there was no discussion of the possibility the children might play together. That remained unthinkable to both sides. But it was agreed that the Arab children would be allowed to use the grounds by themselves once a week, on Fridays, when the school was closed. The school principal, as a gesture of good will, also agreed to turn the hole in the fence into a new entrance.

City officials were pleasantly surprised by the dialogue the incident opened between residents of the two neighborhoods and tried to make the connection more formal. A meeting was arranged between leaders of the two communities, but it failed to produce any immediate results. Several years later, however, Jabal Mukaber and East Talpiot took part in an experiment in Arab-Jewish coexistence that would demonstrate the limitations, and possibilities, of improving relations between the two peoples of Jerusalem.[1]

The experiment officially began in early June 1994 at the west Jerusalem YMCA on King David Street. The outdoor cafe on the patio in front of the hotel was crowded with tourists and locals who were enjoying the pleasant weather and majestic surroundings of the historic YMCA complex. No one noticed the two dozen men and women who made their way to a back room, just off the lobby. The YMCA was one of the few places in west Jerusalem were the presence of Arabs did not stand out.

On one side of the meeting room table sat representatives of East Talpiot. Across from them sat the mukhtars and village notables of Jabal Mukaber. Dr. Jay Rothman, a young American researcher from George Mason University, who specialized in intercommunity conflicts, sat at the head. Next to him was Robin Twite, a retired British diplomat who made his home in Jerusalem and was now affiliated with the Hebrew University's Truman Institute, and Danny Daniel of the Jerusalem Fund and the Eindenhaur Fund of Germany. The municipality's adviser on Arab affairs and his deputy took their places at the head of the table.

Around that table officially began perhaps the most important project since the Six Day War aimed at improving Jewish-Arab relations in Jerusalem. Just a year earlier, in the midst of the tensions and violence of the intifada, the idea for Project Jabal Mukaber–East Talpiot was first raised by the municipality's Arab Affairs Office. The concept itself was simple: to try to open a dialogue between the neighboring communities, with the aim of easing the tensions and hostilities between their respective residents. The goal was to create an atmosphere and framework for the Jews of East Talpiot and the Arabs of Jabal Mukaber to put aside their political and ethnic differences and work together on local issues of common concern.

The intifada had taken a serious toll on Jewish-Arab relations in Jerusalem. Lives were lost on both sides in terror attacks and clashes with police. The former border between east and west Jerusalem, which ran between East Talpiot and Jabal Mukaber and which divided other Jewish and Arab communities as well, was particularly tense. Arab youths from Jabal Mukaber would frequently throw stones and bottles at the homes of their Jewish neighbors in East Talpiot. The Israeli police would respond with force, sending patrols into the village and harassing residents. The mistrust and hostility felt in both communities seemed only to be growing with time.

East Talpiot was also bordered by another Arab village, Sur Baher, with which relations were also not good. But Sur Baher was several hundred meters from East Talpiot. The homes of Jabal Mukaber were just a few feet from those of the Jewish neighborhood. The confrontations between the Jewish and Arab residents occurred daily. The municipality's experiment in coexistence was an attempt to prevent a bad situation from deteriorating further. There was also another important factor in the choice of East Talpiot and Jabal Mukaber for the project: the two communities had strong local leaders who were respected by their residents. For the dialogue and cooperation envisioned by project initiators in city hall, strong leaders were essential.

Between the summers of 1993 and 1994 a series of secret meetings were held between representatives of the two communities, under the auspices of the municipality and Twite. The Arab community leaders were the most apprehensive about the project and feared that if news of the meetings leaked out, they would be branded collaborators. The municipality tried to emphasize that the project was local, but like nearly everything else that involves Israelis and Palestinians in the city, there was no way of hiding its larger political implications.

Jabal Mukaber was originally settled by Bedouins of the Sawarha tribe just after the turn of the century. The village to this day is also known as Sawarha. After the Six Day War, most of the village land was expropriated by Israel to build East Talpiot. The Palestinians of Jabal Mukaber were being asked to sit down and talk with Jewish leaders who were living on their confiscated land. The local leaders knew they would face serious criticism for such a move and might even endanger their own lives. They would not have been the first

Palestinians killed by their brethren for allegedly acting against Palestinian national interests.

Community leaders in Jabal Mukaber also failed initially to see the potential benefit that might be drawn from meeting with their Jewish neighbors. They had heard promises before from the municipality about steps that would be taken to improve conditions in the village, but throughout Arab east Jerusalem such promises were broken so many times by Israel that few Arabs still believed them. And if nothing ever came from a meeting with the mayor or senior municipal official, what good would it do to sit down with the lowest level of municipal leadership, at the neighborhood level, the Jabal Mukaber leaders wondered.

On the Jewish side, there was also great skepticism about the project's chances of success. The initial meetings began soon after an East Talpiot resident was stabbed to death by a Palestinian terrorist at a bus stop near his home. The terrorist was never apprehended, but Israeli security officials believed he was either a resident of Jabal Mukaber or had hid in the village with the help of residents before carrying out the attack. East Talpiot had suffered much during the intifada. Homes had been stoned by Arab youths from Jabal Mukaber. Vehicles in the neighborhood had been torched. This latest terror attack sparked a wave of anti-Arab sentiment, and Jews from East Talpiot threw stones at Arab vehicles and homes in Jabal Mukaber. Hundreds of Jewish residents participated in a noisy demonstration at the site of the attack on the evening that it occurred. When Kollek and Jerusalem police chief Rafi Peled arrived, they were met with angry catcalls. Kollek tried to engage the residents in a dialogue, but the atmosphere was too heated for anything other than shouts and demands.

Kollek was not intimidated. In fact, he was in his element. During his long tenure as mayor, he had arrived at many a similar scene after a terrorist attack, and he knew that residents must be allowed to vent some of their rage. But he also stood his ground amidst the jostling and shouting, and when he began to sense that the situation might get out of control, Kollek called a meeting for later that evening between city officials, police, and neighborhood leaders. At the meeting, the neighborhood representatives demanded that police take immediate action to improve security in East Talpiot. Kollek and Peled expected this and promised to beef up police presence in the neighborhood. But the neighborhood leaders made an additional demand: the construction of a fence between East Talpiot and Jabal Mukaber to prevent Arabs from entering the neighborhood except along the main roads connecting the two communities.

The demand touched on Kollek's worse nightmare: a de facto redivision of the city. For Kollek, fences dividing Jewish and Arab communities were a symbol of the divided Jerusalem of 1948–1967. He had fought the idea in the past and had given in only once before, when he agreed that a high fence could be built on the northern side of the Neveh Ya'acov neighborhood, along its border with several Arab neighborhoods. In that instance, he felt compelled by intifada violence to capitulate to residents' demands. But he had hoped it would be an isolated instance. Now, circumstances were forcing his hand again.

Kollek agreed to the fence. Perhaps to ease his conscience, the actual fence he eventually approved was not the high metal kind that had been put up in Neveh Ya'acov but a lower, more decorative model. It divided only an approximately 300-meter stretch between the Jewish and Arab neighborhoods where the most recent attack had occurred. Elsewhere between the neighborhoods, passage remained unhindered. Security officials agreed that the fence, easily climbed over, would do little to prevent a future attack. But for Kollek and Jerusalem residents, both Arab and Jewish, the fence became another important symbol of where the city was headed.

It was in such an atmosphere of tension and mistrust that Project Jabal Mukaber–East Talpiot was launched. The East Talpiot neighborhood leaders needed to be convinced that the project would be worthwhile. A few leaders strongly opposed the idea. The neighborhood's security officer—a civilian who receives a salary from the neighborhood council to, among other things, present the residents' security concerns before the police—was among the opponents. "We don't want the Arabs of Jabal Mukaber in our neighborhood, whether they mean good or bad," he remarked at one of the late-night gatherings of community leaders held to discuss the project. Even the proponents of coexistence argued that the time was not right, given the continued attacks on the community from the direction of Jabal Mukaber.

Dozens of preliminary meetings were held separately with each side, in order to persuade community leaders to give coexistence a try. Given their apprehension, it is not surprising that both the Arabs and Jews agreed to take a chance on the project only on condition that it be kept a secret. The media were not to know about the meetings. Nor were most officials and councilors at city hall. Only the mayor (first Kollek and later Ehud Olmert), Yossi Cohen, a senior adviser on community affairs, and the municipality's director-general were in the know during the early months of preliminary work that culminated in the joint YMCA meeting.

Hassin Issat, a Jabal Mukaber mukhtar, was given the honor of being the first to speak before the forum. As expected, Issat read from a prepared speech, in which he presented the traditional Palestinian demands in Jerusalem. Issat, a handsome and stately figure, was among the outstanding community leaders in Jabal Mukaber. His father had also been a prominent local leader. Issat conditioned his participation in the project on the Arab representatives being free to raise the official position of the Palestinians in Jerusalem. And this he did at the opening meeting and the meeting which followed, emphasizing the sensitive issue of Jewish neighborhoods, such as East Talpiot, built on Arab land confiscated by Israel.

Issat's words were primarily aimed at his fellow Arab representatives at the table. Issat knew well that the Palestinian leadership in Jerusalem was aware of the Jabal Mukaber–East Talpiot project and that every word said at the meeting, particularly by the Arab participants, would be reported to the leadership. The last thing Issat wanted was to say something politically unwise and be summoned by Faisal Husseini, the senior PLO official in Jerusalem, or worse, a Palestinian intifada committee that had less than diplomatic methods for obtaining explanations from transgressors.

Despite the fact that the Jewish participants had been prepared in advance by city officials for what to expect from Issat, the Arab community leader's aggressive words created a tense atmosphere in the room. Only at the end of his statement did Issat even refer to the project. He expressed hope that it would lead to positive results, both in improving relations between the communities and convincing the authorities to invest more funds in Jabal Mukaber.

Yossi Harel, chairman of the East Talpiot community council, spoke first for the Jewish side. Harel reviewed the Jewish residents' relations with their Arab neighbors over the years, and in particular during the tense intifada days. As with Issat, Harel's opening speech was aimed not at the persons who were to be his partners in dialogue but to his fellow community representatives. Harel was religious and was known to be politically affiliated with the right. For Harel, participation in the meeting was a political and personal gamble. He knew that he risked losing the backing of many of his supporters on the right who were less than anxious to get involved in such coexistence initiatives and would be extremely critical of his decision to go ahead with the project if it failed.

The major issue for Harel—and in this he apparently stood for most East Talpiot residents—was security. In his opening remarks and in many subsequent meetings, Harel demanded again and again that Jabal Mukaber representatives restrain the extremist elements who threatened to harm Jewish residents. In closing, Harel praised the initiative and the willingness of the Arab representatives to participate, thus acknowledging the great pressure the Arab representatives were under not to take part. Throughout the project, though his major goal was to improve security in East Talpiot, Harel also saw the importance of taking steps to ease the Arab residents' anger at being treated as second-class citizens.

The speeches by Issat and Harel summed up the respective sides' motivations for agreeing to participate in the project. The Arab representatives hoped their contact with East Talpiot would help push the municipality to improve city services in their neighborhood. The Jewish representatives hoped the Arab representatives would restrain extremist elements in Jabal Mukaber that were targeting the Jewish neighborhood.

Between June and December 1994 six meetings were held, all at the YMCA. Despite ups and downs, it was clear after several meetings that both sides were sincere in their desire to begin looking for ways to improve relations between the neighborhoods. An important sign of just how far the project had moved ahead came in early 1995, when the Arab representatives agreed to meet at the Jewish neighborhood's community center. Just six months earlier, the neutral grounds of the YMCA had been the only acceptable meeting site. The Arab local leaders' entrance into the Jewish neighborhood's community center was a major step, and it was taken with apprehension—the meeting was held late in the evening, in hopes it would remain a secret. Soon, however, the veil of secrecy was to be lifted, and Project Jabal Mukaber–East Talpiot was to truly bring together residents of the Jewish and Arab neighborhoods.

The breakthrough came just several months later. On a Friday afternoon in spring 1995, hundreds of children gathered at a new East Talpiot playground. In addition to Jewish children and their parents, there were dozens of Arab children from Jabal Mukaber and their mothers and fathers. The Arab residents were invited to attend the opening by their Jewish neighbors as a gesture of good will, as if to formally say that the playground was meant for all area residents. It was hard for many of those involved, both Jews and Arabs, to hide their excitement as the playful voices of Arab and Jewish children filled the air. At least for that one April day, good will on both sides had triumphed, and through a joint effort of local leaders the wall of hatred and fear between the two communities had been pulled down.

Local Arab and Jewish leaders acted quickly to further the newfound relations between East Talpiot and Jabal Mukaber. Excited over the success of the playground gathering, they organized a joint health day. Residents of the two neighborhoods participated in a wide range of health-related activities, including free check-ups by doctors and informational seminars about health services. The Israeli deputy health minister, Walik Tsadik, a Druze, was invited to attend, and his presence gave the occasion a semiofficial status. But the climax of the project came just a month later, in mid-May, in the auditorium of the East Talpiot community center, where a Jewish-Arab music and dance festival was held for residents of the two communities. Jewish and Arab artists performed side by side, and neighbors who had been divided by a deep hatred sang and danced together. An outsider would never have imagined that just two years earlier relations between the two neighborhoods were explosive.

Later that summer, the Jewish community's representatives showed their newfound trust in their Arab neighbors by meeting with the Arab community representatives in Jabal Mukaber itself. City officials joined the East Talpiot representatives as they drove a chartered bus into the village, where Jews since the start of the intifada had rarely traveled for fear of attack. "I can't believe that I'm doing this," an East Talpiot school principal on the bus muttered to herself, summing up the feelings of the other Jewish participants.

The Arab representatives came onto the bus and gave the Jewish visitors a tour of their community. The Arab leaders had asked their Jewish project partners and municipal officials to come to the village to see first-hand the substandard conditions in which Arab residents lived, just meters from the well-groomed Jewish neighborhood. For many of the Jewish participants, it was their first visit to an Arab neighborhood anywhere in Jerusalem, and they were shocked to find unpaved roads, sewage flowing freely from houses, and children playing in the streets because they had nowhere else to go.

The tour marked an important turning point for Project Jabal Mukaber–East Talpiot. It strengthened the East Talpiot participants' commitment to helping their Arab neighbors secure improved services from the municipality. The tour also provided a concrete show of the growing trust between the Arab and Jewish participants—the Arab side in its willingness to openly receive the East Talpiot representatives into their village and the Jewish side in their confidence that the visit would be safe.

The visit in August to Jabal Mukaber had dramatically demonstrated to the Jewish project participants that state investment in improving conditions in the Arab village was desperately needed. The East Talpiot representatives told their Arab counterparts they would try to lobby the municipality to do more in the village. And they indeed tried, but to no avail. Yossi Cohen, Mayor Olmert's senior adviser and a permanent member of the project team, attended all the meetings and seemed to honestly try to move things at city hall. But in the end, nothing changed, when it came to the basic demand of the Arab residents—that they be treated the same as their Jewish neighbors.

Both the Jewish and Arab local representatives were greatly disappointed by the lack of response from the authorities to their calls for improving conditions in Jabal Mukaber. The Arab representatives were particularly hurt. For them, the major reason for taking part in the coexistence project was the hope that it would advance their demands for equal services. Over and over again, the Arab representatives made clear that without substantial improvements in their neighborhood, they would not be able to continue to participate. They emphasized that the mandate they received from their constituency, the residents of Jabal Mukaber, to be part of the project was tied to getting services improved. There had been a few minor changes: the elementary schools in the two neighborhoods had joined together in several activities and outings, which the Arab children would likely not have experienced otherwise. But these small items were a far cry from what Jabal Mukaber wanted. By the spring of 1996, when it became clear to all involved that no major plans were taking shape to improve conditions in the village, the project was disbanded.

No one involved in Project Jabal Mukaber–East Talpiot ever believed the going would be easy. So many factors were beyond the control of the participants. The issue of equal services was just one example. More dramatic was the peace process itself, whose ups and downs constantly influenced the ways Jews and Arabs in Jerusalem felt about one another. The signing of the first Oslo Accord in September 1993 left project participants upbeat. The agreement seemed to show they were on the right track by trying to improve Jewish-Arab relations in Jerusalem, just as their respective national leaders were now working together to improve their ties. That optimism, however, gave way to a period of distrust and hostility, when in February and March 1996 dozens of Israelis were killed in a series of suicide bombings by the extremist Palestinian group Hamas. Jewish participants expressed willingness to continue with the project, but the Palestinian side preferred to suspend the cooperative work at least until the atmosphere improved.

Why did the municipality wait until 1993 to launch a serious effort to improve Arab-Jewish relations in the city? This is the real question that Israeli leaders, who paid much lip service to the idea of coexistence in Jerusalem, must ask themselves. Jerusalem is a complex city. The relations between the different ethnic and religious groups are equally complex. There are not just Jews and Arabs in Jerusalem; other dynamics are also at work—Christian-Muslim, Jewish-Christian, intra-Muslim, and so on. As far back as the rosy-eyed days just after the 1967 war, Israeli policy-makers failed to fully grasp the importance of trying to improve relations between the different groups that made Jerusalem their home. A sustained local effort to ease the tensions created by the political and religious conflict in which Jerusalem was immersed might have gone a long way.

Today, we can look back upon Project Jabal Mukaber–East Talpiot and see that much progress can be made toward improving Jewish-Arab relations, if Israeli authorities make it a high priority. The project left much undone in the two neighborhoods, but who would have believed just a few years previously that a bridge of understanding and mutual purpose could be built where before there was only a wall of hostility? A generation of Arab children who lived in that mountainside east Jerusalem village grew up learning how to throw stones and firebombs at the Jews from the adjoining neighborhood. A generation of Jewish children grew up, in the new homes of East Talpiot, learning to hate and fear the Arabs who lived nearby. Even in such an atmosphere there arose persons, Jews and Arabs, whom fate had brought together as neighbors and who wanted to foster improved relations between their respective communities. They did it for themselves, their children, and the city as a whole. The project participants, Jews and Arabs, men and women, were not politicians or statesmen. They were simple people who refused to allow those who spread hatred, fear, and suffering decide their own and their children's future, and instead tried to live together as tolerant and respectful neighbors.

Project Jabal Mukaber–East Talpiot may have collapsed, but it still left much hope. It demonstrated that coexistence is possible in Jerusalem and that reason and humanity can one day win out in the war-torn city. It also gives a glimpse of what might have been if Israeli leaders had opened their eyes to the importance of promoting good relations between residents of all faiths and nationalities in the city.

11

No Judenrein in Jerusalem

Mussa Abassi was awakened by a rumbling outside his home in Silwan. It was a rainy and cold December evening in 1992. Abassi peered out his window to see a group of armed Israelis climbing over the stone wall that surrounded his family's courtyard. The Israelis then entered the empty apartments that adjoined Abassi's home in the 150-year-old complex. They carried with them sleeping bags and basic supplies. But they had not come for a short stay. And they were not the only armed Israelis who were moving into the village that night. Several other Arab homes in Silwan were also occupied in what was later revealed to have been a well-planned operation by one of the Jewish settlement groups working in east Jerusalem.

Even more significantly, however, the entire operation had the strong backing of the government. The move by Jewish settlers into Silwan—home to the ruins of the ancient City of David, where King David founded Jerusalem 3,000 years ago—was no rogue operation. It had been planned for years, spearheaded by the Elad (the Hebrew acronym for "To the City of David") settlement group, but with the support of the government. Elad was headed by a retired Israeli army fighter pilot, David Be'eri. Be'eri viewed the City of David as Jewish property. He wanted the Arabs evicted. Be'eri knew, however, that a call by his group to expel Arabs from the village would make trouble, so publicly he used a different argument to justify the Jewish settlers' move into the village: "In Jerusalem, of all places in the world, Jews must have the right to live anywhere. No part of Israel, of all places, can be declared Judenrein." It was a difficult argument to oppose in Israel. Just the use of the term Judenrein—the German word the Nazis had used to forbid entry to Jews—conjured up strong feelings.

Ideologically, the work of Elad and other settlement groups can be seen as a natural offshoot of Israel's push after 1967 to expropriate as much land in east Jerusalem as possible and to settle it with Jewish neighborhoods. In the first decade after the Six Day War, Israel's settlement effort in east Jerusalem centered on building new Jewish neighborhoods. One after another, Jewish communities cropped up on the formerly barren hillsides of east Jerusalem. But by the latter part of the 1970s, a new target was found for Jewish expansion—the Arab neighborhoods themselves. One reason for this sudden shift was practical: there was simply little land in east Jerusalem left for expropriation by the Israeli government. The settlement effort in east Jerusalem was also influenced by similar efforts that were just getting under way at the time in the West Bank and Gaza. Many of the same government officials and activists involved in establishing those settlements were also behind the push to move Jewish families into Jerusalem's Arab neighborhoods.

The right-wing Likud Party's 1977 election victory had a profound effect on Israeli policy in east Jerusalem. The Likud was ideologically closer to the settlement activists than Labor. Some of the settlement activists were Likud Party members. Prime minister Menachem Begin, the Likud Party leader, made the building of settlements and the acquisition of Arab homes in east Jerusalem a top priority. It would be incorrect, however, to present the settlement drive in Arab neighborhoods solely as a movement spurred by Likud and the Israeli right-wing. The Labor Party also provided financial and administrative support. The Abassi family of Silwan, rudely awakened on a cold December night by Be'eri and company, were soon to find this out for themselves.

The next morning, Abassi and his new Jewish neighbors discovered that the eyes of the world were upon them. Hundreds of Israeli policemen and paramilitary border guards converged on the village, one of the poorest and most run-down in Jerusalem. A handful of right-wing Israeli Knesset members (MKs) came to show their support for the settlers. News cameras broadcast pictures of MK Guela

Cohen of the right-wing Tehiya Party, a large, outspoken woman, precariously climbing over a wall into a courtyard of a home taken over by the settlers and then tumbling down on the other side, breaking her leg. The news of the settlers' takeover of village homes was already out. The meticulously planned operation was no longer a secret.

The mayor heard about it before dawn. Kollek opposed Jewish families moving into Arab neighborhoods. He wanted coexistence between Jews and Arabs in Jerusalem, but in separate neighborhoods. Jews and Muslims would do best living with their own, in the mayor's view. He did not deny that Jews had the right to live everywhere in Jerusalem, including in Arab neighborhoods. He simply thought that it was unwise. For Kollek, Jews and Arabs living in the same neighborhood was a formula for tension and conflict.

Outraged at what had transpired in Silwan, Kollek appealed to the Likud government to halt the settlers. He called on Prime Minister Yitzhak Shamir to order the police to evict the settlers from the village. But his demand fell on deaf ears. The cabinet met and passed a motion supporting the settlers. Even before the operation, Shamir publicly supported settlers' efforts to take over Arab homes in east Jerusalem.

Kollek responded with an urgent memo to the prime minister, charging the settlers were damaging both Israeli-Palestinian relations in Jerusalem and Israel's standing in the international community. "I don't have and never did have differences with those who believe that Jews have the right to live in all parts of Jerusalem," Kollek wrote in the memo.[1] "I believe there is a national consensus on this point," he added. "The argument is over the lack of intelligence in which this right has been realized [in Silwan]."[2] The settlers' move into the village and the government's support for it "does not foster quiet and co-existence between the different peoples of the city," Kollek wrote. "The settlement of Silwan is not a lone act, but rather just one more in the long line of provocations that have included the takeover of the building [St. John's Hospice] next to the Church of the Holy Sepulcher in the Christian Quarter, and the settlement of the Muslim Quarter, to name a few."[3]

Shamir ignored Kollek. So for the first time in his three-decade tenure as mayor, Kollek literally took to the street to protest against the government. It was a one-man vigil on a cold winter afternoon about a week after the settlers had move into Silwan. Kollek stood near one of the homes taken over by the settlers, with a protest sign in hand. He was 81 years old at the time and nearing the end of a long and illustrious political carrier. Indeed, that is what made the entire Silwan episode so tragic. It had brought one of Israel's most renowned leaders to his wits' end because no one in government would listen to his protests. Kollek was left with nothing else to do but stand alone with a placard and hope someone would take notice.

Things never got better for Kollek—at least when it came to the Israeli government and east Jerusalem. Summer brought high hopes, with Rabin's election to prime minister. Kollek approached Rabin with a long list of demands for Jerusalem, the first of which was halting Jewish settlement in Arab neighborhoods.[4] "Reforming the state's housing policy in Jerusalem must be a top priority, and must be treated with as much sensitivity as the policy of settlement in Judea and Samaria," Kollek wrote Rabin.[5] "Poor planning in Jerusalem is seriously detrimental to the future of the city and peace in the region." Kollek challenged Rabin to show he was as tough on containing settlement in east Jerusalem as in the West Bank and Gaza. Rabin, however, failed to meet the challenge. Kollek again found himself politically isolated on a crucial Jerusalem policy issue.

Kollek did manage to convince Rabin to establish a commission of inquiry into allegations that the previous Likud government had illegally transferred state funds to the east Jerusalem settlers.[6] Setting up the commission was politically expedient for the new Rabin government. The prime minister saw the commission as providing an opportunity to further push the defeated Likud Party into a political corner. Haim Klugman, a well-respected official, was chosen to head the commission, which began its work in August 1993. In just over a month, the inquiry was completed.

The findings startled the Israeli public. The Klugman Report revealed that the previous Likud government secretly funneled funds to the east Jerusalem settlers, at times using what appeared to be illegal means.[7] The Israeli public, for the first time, was shown how the government worked behind the scenes to support the settlers in east Jerusalem. From Silwan and the Old City to the Mount of Olives and Wadi Joz, millions of dollars of state funds had been used by the settlers to aquire Arab homes, according to the report. In other cases, the settlement activists, with the support of state officials, took advantage of outdated legislation—the Absentee Property Law of 1950—to take over Arab homes and evict their Arab residents.

One point uncovered in the report was particularly startling, and for the mayor was most significant: state support for the east Jerusalem settlers had come at the expense of helping needy Israeli families purchase homes. "Some of the funds for purchasing properties were taken from the budgets that were earmarked for new immigrants and families in financial distress," the report stated.[8] Kollek had long argued it was not only morally wrong to move Jewish families into Arab neighborhoods, it was also financially unwise. The state's money could be most effectively spent building homes in undeveloped areas of east Jerusalem, Kollek believed.

Just how much money was spent by Israel to move Jewish families into Arab neighborhoods of Jerusalem? It is impossible to say exactly, because money was being transferred from so many different state sources. The Klugman Committee traced NIS 23 million ($8.2 million) in state funds going to the east Jerusalem settlement movement.[9] That figure was based on records obtained by the commission showing the purchase, rent, and lease prices the settlers and government had paid for Arab homes. For the Abassi home in Silwan, for instance, the commission of inquiry found the state paid NIS 98,630 ($35,000) to fix up the settlers' apartments.[10] But that was only a small project compared with others carried out at the Israeli government's expense for settlers in east Jerusalem. In 1985 Israel spent some NIS 15 million ($12 million) repairing Arab homes taken over by settlers.[11] In 1987 the Israeli Housing Ministry paid some NIS 1.229 million ($800,000) to fix up buildings occupied by Ateret Cohanim in the Old City.[12]

That was not the only money Ateret Cohanim was getting from the authorities, the commission found. The state-owned Jewish Quarter Redevelopment Company transferred NIS 4.215 million

($1.7 million) to the major settlement groups—Ateret Cohanim, Atara L'Yoshna, Magaleh Orot, and Elad.[13] The money was taken from a Housing Ministry fund, totaling some NIS 7.5 million ($3 million), earmarked for acquiring Arab homes in east Jerusalem.[14]

The purchase by Ateret Cohanim of the St. John's Hospice in the Christian Quarter—one of the moves by Jewish settlers in Jerusalem that drew the greatest international attention—was also heavily financed by the Israeli government, the commission found. On April 8, 1990, the Housing Ministry approved an allocation of NIS 2.2 million ($1.1 million) specifically for the purchase of the building, and the sum was transferred to Ateret Cohanim to carry out the purchase.[15] The involvement of the Israeli authorities in the purchase, however, was kept secret, to allow the Israeli government to distance itself from the move, in light of international criticism.

Without Israeli government support, the acquisition of Arab homes in east Jerusalem would have been difficult if not impossible. The settlers could not take hold of Arab properties with ideology alone. They needed the money and support of the authorities, and they got both. In 1982 the government set up a special committee to locate Arab properties in Jerusalem that could be purchased by the state or acquired under the Absentee Property Law (1950) and then transferred to settlement groups, such as Ateret Cohanim.[16] Arab residents were under pressure from their brethren not to sell to Jews. Both Jordan and the PLO threatened to kill any Arab who sold to a Jew. But some sales were still made. In many cases, the Arab landowner would be helped by the settlers to flee with his family to Europe or the United States. In others, the settlers worked through shell companies that hid their identities, as was the case with St. John's Hospice.

The settlers were more keen, however, on the second avenue for obtaining Arab properties, which cost neither them nor the government a cent. Under the Absentee Property Law, the state is allowed to take control of all properties whose owners have left Israel for "Lebanon, Egypt, Syria, Saudi Arabia, Trans-Jordan, Iraq, or the Yemen."[17] Palestinians who have left Israel for the occupied territories are similarly designated as absentees, and the state has the right to take their property. The law made sense in the immediate aftermath of Israel's War of Independence in 1948. Tens of thousands of Arabs fled or were forced to leave their homes during the fighting, and entire villages were vacated in the newly created Jewish state. At the same time, tens of thousands of Jews fled, or were forced to leave, their homes in Arab countries, and the authorities in Israel were desperate to find them homes. The Absentee Property Law, when it was passed, represented an important tool for a young state trying to survive. In the post-1967 era, however, the Absentee Property Law became a ruthless weapon to strip Arabs in east Jerusalem of their homes. The law became a tool not for finding homes in Jerusalem for displaced Jews but for driving Arabs out of the city.

The settlers and Israeli government worked together to locate "absentee" properties. That was one of the major jobs of the government committee established in 1982. Ariel Sharon—agriculture minister at the time—was behind the establishment of the committee. Sharon's name for the next decade would remain linked with the settlement of the Old City and other Arab sections of the city. The method was simple: representatives of Mordot Moria and Even Rosh—companies formed by settler-activists—would try to locate Arab homes whose owners, they believed, had fled the country in the 1967 war. The settlers, now given official positions by the government, would register the homes with the custodian for absentee properties.[18] By law, the custodian was supposed to determine if the owners indeed fled the country, and if so put the property up for sale. Instead, the custodian took the settlers—who did not hide their goal of taking over as many Arab homes as they could—at their word and then turned the properties over to them.[19]

The cooperation between the settlers and state (the custodian was a state official) reached its height in the late 1980s and early 1990s. With Sharon as head of the powerful Housing Ministry, east Jerusalem settlement activists literally became operatives for the government. Matti Dan, head of the Ateret Cohanim settlement group, and Be'eri of Elad were themselves personally allocated ministry funds.[20] Ministry documents show that between September 1991 and August 1992, Sharon's ministry paid NIS 813,277.98 (approximately

$300,000) to Be'eri and NIS 727,263.42 (approximately $280,000) to Dan.[21]

In October 1990 Sharon met in his office with Dan and Meir Davidson, who worked closely with Dan at Ateret Cohanim, and mapped out a comprehensive plan for obtaining Arab properties in east Jerusalem.[22] Sharon ordered Arab homes and lands under the authority of the custodian of absentee properties to be "sold" to Ateret Cohanim, Elad, and a third settlement group, Atara L'Yoshna. In fact, however, the settlers put up little money of their own.[23] Instead, the custodian was ordered to mark down prices, and the ministry transferred money to the settlement groups to purchase the properties.[24] The settlers were "charged only token rents. For example, a two-story building on one of the busiest streets of the Old City was rented for NIS 33 [or $10.50 per month]," the Klugman Commission found.[25]

The next year Sharon went a step further in institutionalizing the east Jerusalem settlement movement. In July 1991 the minister established a special committee to oversee the acquisition of Arab properties in east Jerusalem, and their transfer to the settlement groups.[26] The settlers were now operating with the complete backing and support of the Israeli government. Even the Israeli security forces helped the east Jerusalem settlers during the Sharon period. Paramilitary border policemen accompanied Be'eri and company on their midnight operation in Silwan, ostensibly to provide the settlers protection. It did not hurt Be'eri's cause that he was a close friend of inspector-general Ya'acov Terner, Israel's police chief at the time who also was an ex-fighter pilot.

Be'eri, Dan, and other settlement activists were at the height of their power. In Silwan, Be'eri wanted to build a 200-unit project literally on top of the ancient artifacts of the City of David. (An architect hired by Elad proposed building the units on stilts so as not to damage the artifacts.) In the Muslim Quarter, Dan wanted to build a high-rise building with underground parking for yeshiva students and their families.

Dan also wanted to construct a large Jewish housing project in Wadi Joz, in the heart of Arab east Jerusalem. The proposal called for the Ma'amuniya Arab girls school under construction at the site to become part of the Jewish neighborhood instead. The settlers also hoped to build new Jewish neighborhoods on the Mount of Olives, adjoining the Beit Orot Yeshiva, and in the heart of the Ras al-Amud village, just outside the Old City. There were many other plans for moving Jews into Arab sections of the city. And all had the backing of Sharon and many others in the Likud government.

Sharon and company—believing strongly in their cause—pushed the boundaries of the law, perhaps even breaking them. Sharon eventually lost the ministry when his party was ousted in the 1992 election, and the new government eagerly uncovered the misconduct of the Likud in east Jerusalem. But the new government took virtually no steps to put an end to the wrongdoing and to discipline or prosecute those involved. Labor MK Binyamin Ben-Eliezer, who replaced Sharon as housing minister, ordered state funding for the purchase of Arab homes in east Jerusalem halted.[27] That was all the government did. None of the recommendations of the committee was implemented. Danny Seidman, a Jerusalem attorney who has led the fight against the settlers in east Jerusalem, appealed to the High Court to force the government to take action. A left-wing Knesset Member, Haim Oron of the Meretz Party, joined Seidman in the appeal. But in the end it was to no avail. The petition was rejected by the court. The government, the court found, could not be forced to take action against the alleged wrongdoing in east Jerusalem.[28]

Because of the Rabin government's lack of decisive action, the settlers were slowed but not stopped. For instance, in 1992 Ateret Cohanim's Muslim Quarter high-rise plan was rejected on grounds it would damage the architectural and historical integrity of the Old City.[29] But in May 1998, under the Netanyahu government, the plan was again raised in the Jerusalem municipality and Housing Ministry, in reaction to the recent murder by a Palestinian terrorist of an Ateret Cohanim student in the Muslim Quarter.[30] Ateret Cohanim agreed to fund archeological excavations in hopes of finding a way to build a Jewish housing project at the Muslim Quarter site.[31]

The plan to build a Jewish neighborhood in Wadi Joz remains under discussion. In the meantime, construction is frozen on the Arab school, and settlers and their supporters count this as a success. The Beit Orot project also remains under discussion, and the Jerusalem municipality, under Likud Mayor Ehud Olmert, has given its backing.[32] Approval was recently granted for construction of the Jewish housing project in Ras al-Amud, but international criticism has held up the start of work.

Kollek had tried to use his influence in the Labor Party to force the Rabin government to stronger action to halt the settlers, but also to no avail. He knew why: Sharon had not acted alone. Labor had also helped the settlers. Like other aspects of Israel's policy toward east Jerusalem, the overall line followed by the two major political parties was similar. As wrong as it is to characterize the efforts to take Arab homes in the Old City as the rogue doings of a small number of settlers, so too is it mistaken to speak of the settlers only receiving support from a few ministers on the political right.

Kollek was particularly infuriated by statements made in support of the settlers by a senior Labor Party member, Arik Nahemkin. In the 1980s Nahemkin served as agriculture minister and as such headed a major government authority helping the settlers, the Israel Lands Authority (ILA). Nahemkin, an old guard party leader, praised the "excellent men of Ateret Cohanim." Kollek's experience with Ateret Cohanim was quite different—"excellent" was the last thing that came to his mind when he thought of the settlement group, and he blasted Nahemkin for supporting it. Nahemkin could not remain silent in the face of the mayor's accusations. "I didn't realize that you expected an answer from me on the subject, but if that is what you want, here it is," Nahemkin began his reply.[33] "I was responsible for the Israel Lands Authority, and met a number of times with representatives of Ateret Cohanim, and they impressed me. It must be remembered that this was before the intifada, when the relations between Jews and Arabs in Jerusalem were better than they are today. I didn't see anything wrong in helping (in accordance with the law and regulations) Jews to settle in all parts of the Old City."

Nahemkin then threw the ball back in Kollek's court, charging that the mayor could not pretend not to have known what was going on in the Old City all of those years. "In one instance, you opposed the transfer of a building and adjoining lot in the Muslim section of the Old City to the settlers, and I ordered the move halted. There is no better proof that you were in the picture, and aware what was happening."[34]

Kollek knew the political reality he faced on the issue of Jewish settlement in the Old City. But he still felt confident the new Rabin government would break with the pro-settler policies of previous governments. The new government's establishment of the Klugman Committee was the first step in that direction, in Kollek's eyes. The next step, for Kollek, was to push the government to implement the recommendations made in the committee's hard-hitting report. He turned to all the government ministers connected to the issue, demanding they take action. "I enjoin you to find a way so that at least some of the properties that there is a high probability were illegally declared abandoned be returned to their rightful owners as soon as possible," Kollek wrote to justice minister David Liba'i.[35] "The issue is of great public importance." Liba'i, however, chose to ignore Kollek. This particularly hurt the mayor. Liba'i had a reputation as a no-nonsense legal expert. He was a professor of law with a leftward leaning, and the mayor hoped he would be an excellent partner in fixing Israel's policy on settlement in the Old City. Instead, Liba'i remained silent on the issue.

Kollek was not one to give up quickly. He was enraged that the new government was not behind him on the east Jerusalem settlement issue. He was even more angry that the government's own internal inquiry into the matter showed without a doubt that previous governments had acted wrongly, but nothing was going to be done about it. The mayor's dream, which he frequently expressed to those close to him, was that the properties wrongly taken from Arabs in the Old City and Silwan would be returned. For him, such a move would go a long way toward putting right Israel's policy in east Jerusalem. So he continued to fight.

In February 1993, four months after the Klugman inquiry finished its work, Kollek was still trying to find someone in the government who would listen. The mayor sent off another letter to Liba'i.[36] This time he tried a different tack. He figured that after having failed to appeal to Liba'i's judicial sense, he was left with no choice but to appeal to the minister's political instincts. "If we are interested in showing the Arab residents in the city that something has indeed changed in the policies of the government," we must return the homes taken by Elad to their former Arab residents, Kollek began his letter to Liba'i.[37] But then he turned from the issue of the homes in Silwan to the general ill-will felt by east Jerusalem Arabs. "Even the gestures that were made to the Arabs of the territories, were not made to those of the city," Kollek complained.

Kollek next went to police minister Moshe Shahal.[38] "It seems to me, that after the [Klugman] inquiry found the announcement of the properties in Silwan as abandoned was done illegally, the situation must immediately be returned to how it was," the mayor told Shahal, in a meeting at the Police Ministry. "The Arab families that lived in the homes for dozens of years must be allowed to move back. This would be major step toward giving co-existence a chance in east Jerusalem."

The municipal elections were only eight months away. To Kollek's thinking, the authorities' failure in the past to deal fairly with the city's Arab residents had kept them away from the voting stations. A success now, just before the elections, would bring Arab voters out in large numbers, he thought. Kollek was in desperate need of an electoral boost, and he looked to the Arabs of east Jerusalem to find it.

Kollek turned next to the outspoken and widely respected state comptroller, Miriam Ben-Porat. Having fared poorly with the government, he hoped he might find support in a senior civil servant with clout. The mayor sent a thick folder to Ben-Porat's office in March 1993, containing key documents from the Klugman Report and copies of the mayor's letters to government ministers.[39] The two also met several times to discuss the report. "There is great importance to correcting the injustice done to several of the Arab residents of the city, and it must be done quickly," Kollek told Ben-Porat.[40] "Leaving things as they are today, I fear, will only lead to greater tensions. Dealing with the issue is essential if we are to continue to stake a claim to co-existence in Jerusalem." Kollek pleaded with the comptroller to intervene, but got nowhere.

Kollek continued to lobby ministers, Knesset members, and others he believed might have influence on the prime minister and be able to bring about the dramatic shift in policy he wanted. From energy and infrastructure minister Amnon Rubenstein to MK Efriam Sneh— with whom the mayor took counsel on many issues involving east Jerusalem—to state prosecutor Dorit Banish, Kollek left no possible avenue for change untested.[41]

"I again turn to you on the subject of the expropriation of properties in east Jerusalem and the settlement of Jews in crowded Arab areas, which was carried out under the previous government,"[42] Kollek wrote in a letter to the prime minister in April 1993. "The inquiry uncovered serious wrongdoing by those involved in the purchase and occupation of the properties, . . . suspicions of criminal wrongdoing and conflict-of-interest." Kollek maintained that in the Klugman Report the state in effect "admitted that the pronouncement of certain [Arab] properties as abandoned was done illegally, but afterwards failed to take a stand with regard to the implications of the admission."

Kollek told Rabin it was his responsibility as prime minister to show the leadership necessary to correct the situation. "It is up to the government which you head to take a decision at the earliest possible moment, returning the situation to how it was, and allowing the [Arab] families to again live in the homes taken from them. As mayor, I believe such a move is of the utmost importance to correcting the great injustice that was done . . . Even doing so in just a few cases will be politically very meaningful, which will help us in the future battle for the unity of Jerusalem under Israeli authority." Four months later, following his lobbying effort with other government ministers, Kollek again turned to Rabin. But, to Kollek's great disappointment, the prime minister appeared in no hurry to take the necessary steps.[43]

For all his lobbying to give some teeth to the Klugman Report, Kollek was only able to achieve a single change in government policy toward Arab properties in east Jerusalem. Kollek convinced Rabin to order the custodian of absentee properties to stop declaring Arab properties abandoned when the owner lived abroad but the property was legally rented by an Arab tenant. That was all Kollek succeeded in changing. The Klugman Report clearly showed that the settlers forced Palestinians out of their homes in east Jerusalem and that many in the Israeli government had supported the settlers in their effort. Confronted with this, Israeli leaders on both the political right and left refused to do anything about it.

12

A Path to Peace Not Taken

"And my people shall abide in peaceful habitation, and in secure dwellings, and in a quiet resting place" (Isaiah 32:18). From this passage is taken the name of the first Jewish neighborhood to be built outside Jerusalem's Old City—Mishkenot Sha'ananim, Hebrew for "the quiet resting places." The year was 1860. A Jewish philanthropist from England donated the money for the project. He had difficulty, however, finding Jewish families to move into the twenty apartments. Even the high walls and iron fence surrounding the two single-story buildings that made up the "neighborhood" were not enough to convince families they would be safe leaving the confines of the Old City.

But eventually they did come—a group of poor Jewish families who, despite their concerns about bandits and thieves, were happy to have new homes. Each was given a two-room apartment, with a small plot of land outside where they could raise vegetables. From the neighborhood, the families could look out over the Hinnom Valley to Mount Zion, Jaffa Gate, and the Old City walls.

In 1948, when Jerusalem was divided, Mishkenot Sha'ananim was abandoned by its Jewish residents. The neighborhood, situated just on the Israeli side of the high walls and barbed-wire fence that separated West and East Jerusalem, was in too dangerous a place to live. After the Six Day War, the Jerusalem Foundation made the renovation of Mishkenot Sha'ananim one of its first major projects. The two single-story buildings were turned into an exclusive private guest residence. Famous artists from around the world were invited to stay there, taking inspiration from the old world architecture and spectacular view of the Old City.

Kollek also found another use for Mishkenot Sha'ananim. He chose a quiet patio or one of the small conference rooms to periodically bring together some of his closest aides and a few well-respected Israeli officials, and at times even foreign dignitaries, to discuss the subject closest to his heart—the future of Jerusalem. The forums began almost immediately after the Six Day War, and they continued until Kollek's last days in office. The meetings were semi-secret. Kollek hoped this would encourage participants to speak openly.

Kollek was following a well-worn tradition when he called experts from Israel and around the world together periodically in search of a magic formula for the city's future. From the end of the Ottoman period forward, various foreign and local interests had presented peace proposals for the city. Each had cut up Jerusalem and its environs in one way or another in search of the perfect symmetry for the multiethnic city. In 1994, sixty-two "positions" on the Jerusalem question were outlined in a study conducted by the Jerusalem Institute of Israel Studies.[1]

After the 1967 war, one of the first Israelis to suggest a comprehensive plan for Jerusalem was Meron Benvenisti, a close associate of Kollek who served first as the mayor's adviser on the Arab population and then as his deputy. At the time he presented the plan, Benvenisti was Kollek's adviser. He had consulted with Kollek as well as other Israeli officials about the plan, which was apparently the first to address in detail concrete avenues for reaching an understanding on Jerusalem between Israel and its Arab neighbors. Many of the ideas raised in the Benvenisti plan remain the subject of debate to the present day.

Benvenisti tried to find a way of satisfying both Israel's and the Arabs' demands in Jerusalem. The basic premise of his plan was that Israel should grant Jerusalem's Arab residents limited self-rule. "Deal with the problem from a municipal point of view," Benvenisti wrote.[2] "At the same time, I am suggesting small corrections in the area of Jerusalem of which Israel is sovereign, along the eastern side of the municipal border. I don't believe that such corrections would considerably change the existing situation for Israel," while they might appease the Arabs. Israel should return to Jordan the road along the Mount of Olives linking Abu Dis (just outside the municipal boundary) with Lions Gate of the Old City, according to Benvenisti. Just a short stretch of the road was within the municipal border. "The road could easily be linked to Azariya and Jericho. It goes through areas where there are no Jewish property interests, directly to Lions Gate and the Temple Mount." Allowing Jordan to control the road would give the Hashemite Kingdom a direct link with Haram al-Sharif, which, according to Benvenisti, was the Muslim world's central interest in Jerusalem. Benvenisti, just a year after the Six Day War, was already speaking in terms of Israel's returning the West Bank to Jordan. The question for him was only how, within such an agreement, Israel could hold onto east Jerusalem.

Benvenisti also recommended that Israel return to Jordan some of the outlying Arab villages that Israel had included in Jerusalem's postwar boundaries. "At first appearance, this item in the proposal constitutes a deviation from the principle of complete Israeli sovereignty. But I believe it is an essential part of the overall plan, and in fact is only a 'sweetener' [for the Jordanians] that has no real importance to us."

Nearly three decades later—with the opening of negotiations between Israel and the Palestinians—the same principle of minor border changes on the Mount of Olives raised by Benvenisti and the Kollek forum remains a topic of debate between the sides. Only now the issue is how to link the Palestinian Authority, not Jordan, with Haram al-Sharif. Benvenisti was writing at a time when the Palestinians were not yet a major political force. He and most other Israeli officials saw the Jordanians as Israel's potential partners in peace. Benvenisti's proposal was directed toward them. While Jordan has since lost its central role on the Jerusalem issue, many of the principles put forth in Benvenisti's proposal still hold. Israel's partner has simply changed from the Jordanians to the Palestinians.

The eight-page proposal also raised the idea of establishing a joint Arab-Israeli umbrella municipality for Jerusalem and adjoining

Arab villages and cities, including Bethlehem. The umbrella municipality would have five submunicipalities which would represent the
different areas and populations. The concept of a joint umbrella
municipality with submunicipalities has been used ever since in the
quest to find a solution to the Jerusalem question. Benvenisti went
into much detail, defining the exact area each submunicipality
would have, the authority of the submunicipalities and umbrella
municipality, and even the membership of the councils for the mu-
nicipalities, including the number of seats to be held by Jews, Muslims, and Christians.

He gave the Jews a strong majority of the seats in the umbrella
council. Of a total of 51 seats on the umbrella council, 33 were
to come from the Jewish subcouncil, which had 31 Jewish members,
1 Armenian member, and 1 Muslim member; 11 from the Arab
subcouncil, with 9 Muslim and 2 Christian members; 3 from the
Bethlehem city council, with 2 Christian and 1 Muslim member; the
Beit Jala city council with 1 Christian member; and 3 representatives
from the villages. That left 31 Jews, 14 Muslims, and 6 Christians on
the umbrella council. Benvenisti did not feel any need to explain why
the Arabs would ever accept an arrangement that would leave them
with a small minority of representatives. The umbrella council he
proposed was to be responsible for local issues, ranging from urban
planning to waste and water services. Benvenisti even went as far
as to suggest a name in Arabic for the umbrella council: Balidiyat
Urshalim al-Quds, reflecting both the Hebrew and Arabic names for
the city.

Benvenisti asked that his report be kept secret, and for good reason. Despite Israel's confidence after the Six Day War, it was willing
to show only one face to the world when it came to Jerusalem—that
the city, east and west, must forever remain united under Israeli rule.
In the introduction to the report, Benvenisti was careful to write that
his proposal was "personal." He understood the sensitivity of the Jerusalem issue. But the initiative from which the report arose was that
of the government. Benvenisti and other local and national officials
had met under the direction of the government on several occasions

to consider possible solutions for Jerusalem, as well as for the West Bank and Gaza.

About a year after its completion, Benvenisti's report was leaked to the Israeli press. It created a wave of criticism of the government for even considering making concessions on Jerusalem. The proposal was then filed away and largely forgotten. Israeli officials at every level of government knew that publicly raising any proposal suggesting that Israel share authority with the Palestinians in Jerusalem was an act of political suicide for themselves and their party. No Israeli government until that of Prime Minister Rabin in 1993 again seriously addressed possibilities for a political solution to the tensions surrounding Jerusalem. And even the Rabin government did so only after being forced by Palestinian leaders, and with what appeared to be no real intention of trying to arrive at an agreement on the city's future.

It was this vacuum that Kollek tried to fill by frequently calling secret meetings to discuss the city's future. Kollek spoke with everyone he could about ways to solve the "Jerusalem question," as the conflict over the city's future was termed. The mayor "would try to pull together anyone he could get his hands on to discuss Jerusalem," one former aide explained. Most of the meetings involved only Israeli and foreign figures, not Arabs. Professor Bernard Lewis, a leading Middle East expert and close friend of Kollek, frequently attended the discussions. Benvenisti was a central figure in these forums, as was David Farhi, a senior adviser to foreign minister Moshe Dayan. Conspicuously absent were government representatives. Even Farhi attended on a private basis and made sure it was clear that he was not speaking for the government. The concern that the proceedings would become public was great.

One such secret meeting was held in late February 1974 at Mishkenot Sha'ananim, the frequent venue for Kollek-led discussions on Jerusalem's future.[3] The cold winter weather left little choice but to hold the gathering inside. The forum was all-Israeli:

Tamar Eshel, Aharon Sarig, and Yoram Bar-Sela, senior aides of the mayor, as well as Baruch Yekutieli, the Jerusalem municipality legal adviser, and Farhi. The discussion was unique in that it was one of the few held at Kollek's initiative at which a detailed record was kept of the proceedings.

The meeting came on the heels of the Yom Kippur War, which took a harsh toll on Israel's national ego. Ultimately, in military terms, Israel won the war, but the early battlefield successes of the Arab states and the postwar revelations of questionable decision-making by Israeli military and political leaders sparked much soul-searching in the Jewish state. Among other things, that soul-searching prompted new thinking in Israel about the country's relations with its Arab neighbors and the Palestinians.

It was in such an atmosphere that Kollek opened the meeting, proclaiming, "For years now we have been dealing in a non-serious manner with different ways of thinking about Jerusalem. The time has come to organize these thoughts, and decide on a course of action." Yekutieli was next, "We still don't know when the Jerusalem question will be raised, even though it is clear that it will be dealt with in the future. Therefore, it is necessary to come up with models and conceptions that we will be able to 'sell' when the time comes. In the meantime, we can also see what ideas can be begun to be implemented already right now. I'm not ignoring the fact that this is likely to spark 'a war between the Jews.' But that should not prevent us from pressing ahead." The participants knew Jerusalem was a sensitive issue. Any action—even the simple step of holding a discussion on Jerusalem's future—if it became public threatened to spark harsh reaction.

Kollek and the other participants were determined not to be intimidated. Yekutieli continued:

I would like to raise two possible scenarios. The first is when we are faced with the return of Judea and Samaria, and the setting of a clear border wherever that may be. The second is the situation today with de facto open borders [with the West Bank]. I have made a very simplistic analysis. Too much importance should not be given to the establishment of a border in the building of a model. At the same time, it is clear that it is easier to build a model in the second scenario. I am talking about holy Jerusalem, spiritual Jerusalem, religious Jerusalem, with all that this entails for Islam and Christianity. The point is that we need to identify what we are talking about in terms of territory. Are we talking only about Jerusalem inside the Old City walls, or also the Mount of Olives, or maybe also Bethlehem and Rachel's Tomb, or even Ma'arat Hamachpela? It is clear that the wider you make the geographic-territorial area under discussion the more problems you face.

Let's take for an example the Vatican, and its special status. In relation to ourselves, it is possible to differentiate between the different theological possibilities for those who will have authority among the religious leaders, or the Christian and Muslim representatives, or national leaders who in effect represent the religions. In my opinion, representatives from the religious hierarchy are preferable.

Let's look at another possibility—the establishment of a board of directors with a chairman that is rotated. The board of directors will have authority with regard to the spiritual center. At first, it will operate according to understanding that will later take on formal status. I don't mean to remove Israel as one of the bodies involved in this center, even though it is preferable that at the initial stage it not be involved.

At one time the possibility was even raised that Jerusalem would not be like most other cities, but instead that the entire Jerusalem district would be a sort of D.C. in the United States, like Brasilia, Mexico City, and such, perhaps a sort of federal district that is more than a normal city.

A few years ago another possibility was raised, involving forming a greater Jerusalem from Ramallah to Beit Jala, with the purpose of expanding Jerusalem and including the entire area in interconnected relations that would create an interdependence between all parts. This model is a sort of Association of Cities that would be difficult to split up. It would seem that we have already missed the boat with this model, although it could perhaps still be considered.

My point is that we need to begin to take steps now; otherwise we will find that the reality is such that our hands will be completely tied. My feeling is that we should move in the direction of establishing a sort-of Federal District. I believe this can be done without complicating things with the issue of the Old City. One possibility is to establish now a legal body with more authority than the municipality has today. In the first stage, only Jerusalem should be considered, and not the cities around Jerusalem. We all should keep in mind that the more things are done in quiet, the better chance they have for success. That's how we were successful with the "open bridge policy."

David Farhi took the discussion one step further:

Baruch gave a good example of one of our successes, the open bridge policy. Such a possibility works in a situation that is unclear, in which it is possible to motivate the "occupied" population. Another way is through common interests, which has also been proven by past experience. We must keep in mind that the [Yom Kippur] war has changed the situation. The Arabs are today in a situation far better than they had before the war—the world powers are involved, the oil crisis and other factors have played into their hands. It seems to me that today, the Christian world is moving toward accepting a situation in which the Christians would not receive full sovereignty . . . The problem with the Muslims is different. The Muslim world is united in the demand for Islamic sovereignty in Jerusalem, over all the city and not just the Temple Mount. We therefore find ourselves facing different demands from the Christians and Muslims.

I suggest two courses of action. First, politically the country must decide what its position is, where it wants to arrive on the Jerusalem issue. Second, in the micro-political realm, where it is possible and necessary to take action to move forward this policy it must be done . . . We must keep in mind that the Arabs see the municipality as being less political than the government, and we should take advantage of this by giving the municipality more responsibility for the Arab population. This would solve many problems.

Yekutieli felt pressed to explain in more detail his view. All the talk about sovereignty had him worried. "I agree with David's two-tier approach of first setting the national priorities with regard to Jerusalem, and then deciding what immediate action can be taken. But from my point of view, we must be careful in our discussion of sovereignty. Maybe I have made myself misunderstood. I do not support giving up sovereignty to either the Muslims or Christians. But there are other steps that fall short of granting sovereignty that can and should be taken."

Kollek spoke next, at first addressing Farhi's characterization of the improved position of the Arab states.

I don't think we need to get all worked up about the atmosphere that exists today. All the Arab leaders today are declaring what they want, but when it comes to Jerusalem, I am certain that they are full of doubt that they will get what they want. They know full well that we will not give in on Jerusalem.

In addition, we can't forget that the Arabs are themselves in a very complicated state. They are filled with tension and fear, as for example about [former Egyptian President Gamal Abdel] Nasser . . . As a result, I believe, they are prepared to accept the situation as it is today. Neither the Arabs here, or in Jordan, are looking for a final solution at this stage . . . Maybe it will also be good for us if the PLO enters the region and in its path brings a wave of terror that will cause many deaths and the fleeing of many Arabs, and that the day may not be far off when there will be an outbreak of fighting between Israel and the PLO, and we will have no choice but to reconquer the West Bank, and there will be less Arabs there because many of them will have fled.

We also need to take positive action. The municipality will soon carry out a major infrastructure project in the Old City; the park outside Damascus Gate is to be improved; the whole-

sale market by the [east Jerusalem] bus station is to be renovated. These actions and others like them will show that we
have no intentions of giving up on Jerusalem.

In general, I believe that if a war does not break out in the
next three months, which I don't think will happen, that the
Arabs in Jerusalem and the West Bank will realize that despite
the pronouncements being made today, the Arab world is not
really very interested in them.

Kollek then turned the floor back over to Farhi, who added an international perspective to the mayor's analysis.

The PLO has now taken a new course. The thinking in the PLO
today goes like this: "We can't enter into direct negotiations
with Israel, because this would mean giving in on our goals. On
the other hand, we can't agree to the return of Jordanian rule [in
the occupied territories]. Thus our best choice is to agree to
the establishment of a Palestinian quasi-state that is run by the
local Palestinian leadership and which we will use as a jumping
board to a full-fledged state at a later date. [Egyptian President
Anwar] Sadat has apparently already agreed to support this position and has even met with several [Palestinian] leaders from
Nablus about the matter. They have been told that when the
negotiations begin, the local delegation will be headed by
Hakhmat el-Mizri from Nablus.

As for Jordan, there is disagreement between the King on one
side and his brothers and uncle on the other. Those that dis-
agree with the King are telling him, "Why are you so concerned
about the establishment of a Palestinian state? Those who establish it will not be able to make it work without Jordan's support, and will come running to us [the Jordanians] for help."

Farhi went on to emphasize that the Yom Kippur War "hurt Israel's image as unbeatable." At the same time, the Yom Kippur War
strengthened Sadat's hand relative to other Arab leaders, according
to Farhi, who said that this must be used to Israel's advantage in ad-
vancing a peace plan. Yekutieli then broke in and argued that "expe-

rience shows that during periods that are characterized by a level of shock much more can be done than during quiet times. We have failed to take advantage of the situation to improve our situation in Jerusalem. We must take action now—move ahead on development plans in east Jerusalem, give Jerusalem's Arab residents more rights and privileges. But first we need to decide where we want things to lead. I think we are forgetting this very important point."

Tamar Eshel, Kollek's foreign affairs adviser, agreed.

But we can't forget that we are dependent on the government, which until now has forbidden us from formerly setting up any sort of team of experts to consider Jerusalem's future, for fear of politically dangerous leaks. I don't think the situation has changed any today. The government isn't going to back our plans, it isn't going to pass any of the legislation we are looking for with regard to the Christian and Muslim holy places, or anything else. What the municipality can do is push forward development plans in Arab neighborhoods of east Jerusalem that will give the residents there the feeling the municipality cares. I suggest top priority be given to projects that are high visibility. The municipality can also initiate a long-term plan. But we must keep in mind that any plan will ultimately be dependent on the government, as even basic development projects require its financial backing.

Kollek had the final word in the discussion. He was brief and to the point. "The Christians are not the problem. We can come to agreement with them. The central problem is the Muslim Arabs, and Muslim Arab nationalism. That is the major problem we face. I think the suggestions made here about better defining what steps the municipality can take without waiting for the government were positive, and must be followed up."

Kollek was clearly concerned about the future of Israeli rule in east Jerusalem. He and his close aides foresaw the day when Israel would be pushed to give up at least some authority to the Arabs in east Jerusalem, and he was desperate to find a way out, to discover the means of putting off the international pressure and demands of Arab residents.

Kollek plowed ahead in this quest, seemingly undisturbed by the lack of government backing for his initiatives. In 1977, a decade after the Six Day War, the mayor offered his "four principles for continued progress towards a city of tolerant co-existence." The principles were outlined in an article in *Foreign Affairs* the mayor published that year.[4] But they offered nothing new—just a regurgitation of old ideas about a unified Jerusalem under Israeli rule that had been discussed over the past decade.

1. There shall be free access to all the Holy Places and they shall be administered by their adherents.
2. Everything possible shall be done to ensure unhindered development of the Arab way of life in the Arab section of the city and to ensure the Arabs a practical religious, cultural, and commercial governing over their own lives. The same holds true, of course, for the various Christian communities.
3. Everything possible should be done to ensure equal governmental, municipal, and social services in all parts of the city.
4. Continuing efforts should be made to increase cultural, social, and economic contacts among the various elements of Jerusalem's population.[5]

That in its first ten years of rule Israel had failed to even meet these basic principles—particularly the points regarding equal services and unhindered development in the Arab sector—speaks poorly for Israel's policy toward east Jerusalem. Kollek himself seemed resigned to a reality in which Jerusalem would continue to be a center of conflict. He spoke in the article about biding time, making life as good as possible until that day, still too far off to see, when peace is reached in Jerusalem. "Despite all our efforts, it is obvious that the Arabs in Jerusalem still do not accept being included within Israel's frontiers. But then it must not be forgotten that the city's Arabs complained about occupation when the Turks, the British and the 'Jordanian Bedouin' were in control. And they called it 'occupation' even then!" wrote Kollek.[6]

Buried in Kollek's 1977 proposal is the idea of setting up boroughs in east Jerusalem as a way of meeting the Palestinians' demands for authority. A decade later, the boroughs idea would become the center of Kollek's proposal for a solution to the Jerusalem question.

> For some time now, I have envisioned a future structure in Jerusalem under which the city would be governed through a network of boroughs. Each borough would have a great deal of autonomy over its own municipal services and its life style. It would decide its own needs and priorities. It would be modeled not on the boroughs of New York but on those of London, which have their own budgets and a great deal of independence.
>
> Of course, the borough idea is not a panacea. The Arabs will want the Temple Mount to be in their borough, and no Jew would agree to that. But the proposal does suggest an approach under which many of the aspects of everyday life can be delegated to local authorities, and the people of the various neighborhoods can feel some increasing control over their own lives and decisions.[7]

Kollek's borough's proposal was a direct takeoff from the plan detailed by Benvenisti just after the Six Day War. However, the mayor spoke specifically, although only in passing, of "local autonomy," a concept which is not mentioned in the Benvenisti proposal. Kollek said that "by increasing their local autonomy, we hope to diminish any feeling among Jerusalem's Arabs that their way of life is threatened by Israeli sovereignty. We want to create a secure future for Arabs within the capital of Israel." A decade of experience ruling east Jerusalem had made Kollek more guarded than his adviser concerning the feasibility of increased self-rule in east Jerusalem becoming the basis of an overall peace agreement. "We can only look at the situation realistically: If, at worst, Muslim and Jewish differences prove irreconcilable, we will have to live in tension for a long time. All the more reason to care for the city as much as we can to ensure its welfare and well-being in spite of the strains and stresses. If, at best, Jews and Arabs find accommodations that are acceptable to the aspirations of all three faiths, no one would argue that what we are doing for Jerusalem today has been irrelevant."[8] It is as if Kollek sees his four-point proposal, with the added measure of boroughs, as a Band-Aid, meant to help hold together a wounded Jerusalem until it is finally healed. He seemed resigned to a reality in which a final resolution to the conflict over Jerusalem was a distant dream.

Four years later, Kollek tried again. At the beginning of "Jerusalem: Present and Future," published in the summer 1981 issue of *Foreign Affairs*, Kollek asked, "In view of the political complexities of Jerusalem, what is the most desirable course of action that Israel's national authorities should take in regard to the city that is of such central concern to Jews, Christians, and Muslims?"[9] He provided the solution in the third paragraph. "What Israel must do in Jerusalem is very clear. We must recognize that Jerusalem will be among the last items on the agenda as the Middle East's problems are solved, and we must strive in the meantime to make the quality of life for all people in the city as attractive as we possibly can."

This is the post–Camp David Kollek speaking. Egyptian President Anwar Sadat had already paid his historic visit to Jerusalem. Egypt and Israel had found a way to work out their differences. But when it came to Jerusalem, the Israeli position remained the same: there would be no compromise. Sovereignty in the city is Israel's, and only Israel's. At best, the local Arab population will be given increased control over their local affairs—deciding where a new road will run or how many kindergartens will be opened—but nothing more. Kollek, and Israel, knew that this stance offered no opportunity for reaching agreement with either the local population or Arab states on Jerusalem.

In the first years after the Six Day War, there were Arab partners in the dialogues conducted by city hall on Jerusalem. But the Arab participants were few in number, and the discussion with them normally concentrated on day-to-day issues of life in Jerusalem, and not on larger political questions. The Arab figures were generally seen as aligned with Jordan and not with any of the Palestinian nationalist movements. They included newspaper publishers Othmann Halack of *An-Nahar* and Mohamad Abu Zuloff of *Al-Quds,* Dr. Yasser Eibed, Khalid Khutoub, Dr. Jamal Nasser, and Anwar Nusseiba.

Abu Zuloff set up his newspaper with the encouragement of Kollek. The mayor saw the emergence of a new Arabic paper in east Jerusalem as something that would demonstrate Israel's openness toward the Arab population. Kollek developed close personal relations with Abu Zuloff and other of these Arab figures. He saw these relationships as important to creating ties between Jews and Arabs in Jerusalem.

In the early 1980s Kollek managed to arrange a series of meetings between Anwar Nusseiba, the former Jordanian defense minister who lived in Jerusalem, and then foreign minister Shimon Peres. Yossi Beilin, a close associate of Peres who went on to become one of the draftsmen of the Oslo Accord, was also involved in the contacts with Nusseiba. Kollek also set up a meeting in Jericho between Nusseiba and then Israeli President Chaim Herzog. The point of all these meetings was first to send a message to King Hussein that Israel was willing to talk about coming to an agreement on Jerusalem. At the same time, Israel wanted to better understand the Jordanian position. But with the outbreak of the intifada, Israel discovered that it was the Palestinians, and not the Jordanians, who were the Israelis' major rival for power in Jeruslem. The Palestinians, however, largely ignored Kollek. Sari Nusseiba, a leading PLO figure in the city, turned down an invitation in 1990 to meet with the mayor. "I don't see any reason to meet with Kollek. He is all the time meeting with people and talking, but nothing ever comes of it," Nusseiba explained at the time. That was the reputation the mayor acquired for himself—of a local leader who might be well-intentioned when it comes to Palestinian rights in Jerusalem, but who cannot get results. Nusseiba and other Palestinian leaders in the city were talking with everyone else, including various Israeli political and academic forums, but not with city hall. They did not think it would do any good, and they were probably right.

The intifada shook Kollek's view of things, as it did for many Israeli leaders. The reality of a massive, grassroots resistance movement against Israeli rule in east Jerusalem, the West Bank, and Gaza took them by surprise. "The world's perception of the Arab-Israeli conflict and indeed much of its substance have been significantly altered by recent events in the West Bank, the Gaza Strip, and Jerusalem. Eleven months of unrest and King Hussein's severing of the links between Jordan and the West Bank have created a new and fluid situation," wrote Kollek, in the opening lines of an article in *Foreign Affairs* published in the winter of 1988, which created a major stir in Israel and abroad.[10] "These events are focusing the world's attention on the need for new policies after twenty years of waiting in vain for Arab governments or Palestinian representatives to come to the peace table."

From the outset, Kollek puts the blame on the other side. But the mayor was not out to attack. He watched as his dreams of peace and coexistence between Arab and Jew in Jerusalem literally went up in the smoke of burning tires, firebombs, and torched vehicles. The Palestinian uprising threw into question Israeli policy throughout the occupied territories. But it hit Israeli policy hardest in Jerusalem. Israel had never formally claimed the West Bank and Gaza as theirs. But with regard to east Jerusalem, they proclaimed aloud and repeatedly that it would remain forever part of Israel. "Jerusalem, the united, eternal capital of Israel, and all the Jewish people," became the slogan of Israeli leaders from across the political spectrum. To even suggest that Israel give up sovereignty of east Jerusalem, or any part of east Jerusalem, was to commit political suicide.

Kollek did not go that far in *Foreign Affairs,* even though from the reaction of the Israeli public one would think he had. What he put forth in the paper, "Sharing United Jerusalem," was indeed quite simple: to allow Arab neighborhoods of east Jerusalem greater control of their local affairs. The idea was not even new. He had raised it in his 1977 *Foreign Affairs* piece. By 1988, "community councils" already existed in three Arab neighborhoods: Beit Safafa, Beit Hanina, and A-Tur. He was now taking that idea a step further, by suggesting that the councils were not just a better way to run city affairs but also had political significance. Kollek did not mince words:

Thinking about new policies for Israel's relations with Arab states and with the Palestinians should start with Jerusalem. On the one hand, there is wide agreement that Jerusalem must be the last item on the agenda of any negotiations, because whatever is decided on the fate of the West Bank will affect arrangements in Jerusalem. On the other hand, Jerusalem's importance is such that no negotiations can even begin as long as any one of the parties is persuaded that there is no possible reconciliation of the various interests concerning Jerusalem. After 21 years of administering Jerusalem as one city, we know that all communities, but in particular the Arab ones, need a much larger measure of self-administration, autonomy or functional sovereignty . . .

Changes are long overdue. They could and should be implemented independently of political developments elsewhere, and without waiting to see what will be the future of the West Bank and Gaza. The future of Jerusalem is to remain united and the capital of Israel, and the overall sovereignty of Israel. There is, however, room for functional division of authority, for internal autonomy of each community and for functional sovereignty. This would go a long way toward showing that a Jerusalem united and shared is not an obstacle to negotiations; on the contrary, it would be a significant contribution to the creation of a climate conducive to constructive bargaining.

Kollek calls this his "modest proposal." A careful look shows he was offering little more than was already proposed. In 1968 Benvenisti had talked of "submunicipalities." Kollek instead preferred the term *minhalot* or neighborhood councils. The neighborhood councils in east Jerusalem would give the Arab population greater control of their day-to-day lives. But in the 1988 *Foreign Affairs* article, Kollek used more politically-charged terminology to describe his views. He spoke of "autonomy" and "functional sovereignty." He even suggested "a sharing of internal security with a municipal police force." Another new twist to the proposal was only hinted at in the article: allowing the Muslims to raise their own flag at Haram al-Sharif. "The flags that may fly from the mosques of the Temple Mount will not make Jerusalem less Jewish or more Muslim. Jerusalem is great enough for a few flags beside that of the State of Israel," Kollek wrote.

The mayor wanted to have it both ways, as did many Israeli leaders when it came to Jerusalem. He wanted Israel to remain in overall control of Jerusalem but to keep the peace by giving the local Arab population a large degree of autonomy in running their own affairs. "We must be firm in declaring that the unity of Jerusalem, the capital of Israel, is beyond negotiation. But we must be sufficiently confident to announce that everything else is negotiable as a matter of course," Kollek wrote. Kollek was suggesting that Israel would move ahead and unilaterally take steps to improve the political and economic conditions of Arabs in east Jerusalem. He expressed the need to create a situation *now* that would be conducive to coexistence and understanding in Jerusalem. The only problem was that he had said it all before and done little to make it happen. Again this time, the vision was there, but not the power, or perhaps will, to turn it into reality.

Kollek pushed his vision with world leaders he believed would have the most to say in determining Jerusalem's future. For the mayor, that meant primarily Americans. Kollek was never an official representative of any Israeli government. But his influence and status was such that there was not a head of state who would not visit the mayor during a state visit to Israel. This meeting with the mayor of Jerusalem became part of the protocol of foreign dignitaries even after Kollek left office. Similarly, when Kollek was abroad, he was the guest of leaders worldwide. He did not hesitate to take advantage of these meetings to try to push forward his views about how the Jerusalem question could be resolved.

In November 1988, Kollek met with U.S. Secretary of State George Shultz in Washington, D.C. Shultz at the time was about to be replaced by James Baker. Kollek used the meeting to push Shultz once more on such issues as moving the U.S. Embassy from Tel Aviv to Jerusalem.[11] But knowing that Shultz was on his way out, the mayor made initial inquiries about Baker and what the secretary thought his successor's policy in the Middle East would be. When Baker took over, Kollek was quick to send off a letter to the State Department congratulating him on the appointment.[12] Kollek, of course, also took the opportunity to present the new secretary with his view on the peace process and Jerusalem.

Dear Mr. Secretary,

. . . Thank you for stating during your confirmation hearings that Jerusalem should remain a united city.

Since Jerusalem may well take up more of your time and efforts than any other city in the world, I would like to tell you why I think that the time will be well spent. If Jews and Arabs can live in peace in a united Jerusalem, with all its particular difficulties, then peace is not an impossible dream anywhere in the world. The past twenty-one years have proved that peaceful co-existence is a reality in Jerusalem, even though vulnerable to outside pressures, as the past months have regrettably shown.

Recent international developments, resulting mainly from the efforts of the outgoing U.S. administration and of your predecessor in office, have created an atmosphere in which the peace between Israel and Egypt has a chance of being expanded to all the Middle East. If people of good will employ themselves toward this goal, Jerusalem may become the cornerstone of the peaceful settlement of the Arab-Israeli conflict, and a catalyst for peace in the region.

The recent worldwide "Peace Offensive" could not be assigned a more attractive or potentially effective and rewarding target than Jerusalem. Advances over Jerusalem could have positive repercussions all over the world, but certainly all over the Middle East. On the other hand, any attempt to re-divide Jerusalem could be a major defeat for the perception of any possible peace in the region and in the world.

Jerusalem would not be the first item on the agenda of any negotiations because the final form of the complex arrangements in the city may to a great extend depend on the agreements on the fate of the West Bank. But it would be a crucial item

I hope that the opportunity will present itself for you to visit here in the near future and to observe the potential for a concentrated campaign for peace in the region based on the united city of Jerusalem. If your schedule in the foreseeable future does not include a trip here, I would be grateful for an opportunity to call on you in Washington. I shall be in the United States towards the end of May, and could visit you during that period at virtually any time.

With all good wishes in your new—and vital—position.
Respectfully yours,
Teddy Kollek

Kollek, writing on January 20, 1989, over a year into the intifada, was still pushing the theme that Jerusalem must at all costs remain a united city. But there is a noteworthy new twist. The mayor usually emphasized that Jerusalem is such a complicated issue to solve that it must be put last on the agenda of peace talks. In the letter to Baker, however, the mayor toys with the idea that reaching an agreement, or at least an understanding, on Jerusalem would give a forward thrust to other issues in the Arab-Israel conflict. "Advances over Jerusalem could have positive repercussions all over the world," the mayor suggests. And elsewhere in the letter, "If Jews and Arabs can live in peace in a united Jerusalem, with all its particular difficulties, then peace is not an impossible dream anywhere in the world."

Kollek had a grand vision of peace, and he continued to present it to anyone who would listen. "In these days when all Israelis are united in their deep concern over recent American statements on Jerusalem, I am encouraged to write you as I recall the privilege I had taking Mrs. Bush and you through the city on your visit in Jerusalem in 1986," Kollek wrote U.S. President George Bush in March 1990.[13] The mayor was a friendly and outspoken character. He had an easy time developing good relations with many influential figures, including U.S. presidents. This was crucial for him at times such as this when the Israeli government was at odds with the U.S. administration. At the time, the controversial issue was settlements. The Likud government, with Ariel Sharon as housing minister, was bulldozing ahead with developing new Jewish settlements in administered territories. The United States was opposed to the settlements, and not just in the West Bank and Gaza but also in east Jerusalem, which it also considered an occupied territory whose future would be decided in negotiations.

Kollek wanted Bush to refrain from drawing this parallel between settlements in the West Bank and those in east Jerusalem. "I am aware of the policy of the United States toward the city of Jerusalem, namely 'that the city remain united but that its status be determined in the negotiations,'" Kollek wrote Bush.[14] "In my opinion there is no conflict between this policy and the actual state of affairs. While there is a difference between Israel's thinking that united Jerusalem is and shall remain the capital of Israel under Israel's sovereignty and American policy that leaves the city's ultimate status open, no conflict needs to arise from the existence of the new urban neighborhoods that have gone up in the last 22 years."

Kollek's logic was fantastic. He presented himself as understanding that the city's future would ultimately have to be decided at the negotiating table, but also maintaining that in the meantime Israel should be able to build new Jewish neighborhoods in east Jerusalem. That these new Jewish neighborhoods would set the tone for the negotiations, because it would be impossible to ignore the presence of tens of thousands of Jewish families living in areas included in the city in 1967, Kollek does not appear to see.[15] "No question mark should be permitted to hover over the new Jerusalem neighborhoods," he wrote.[16]

It seems hard to believe that Kollek really expected the United States to buy this argument. To the credit of the then-ruling Likud government, it can be said that it was at least willing to go head to head with the United States over the settlement issue and "tell it like it is." The Likud wanted to hold onto the West Bank, so it built there. It also wanted to hold on to east Jerusalem, so it built there too and stated openly that while it was in power, Jerusalem would not be the subject of negotiations. Kollek tried to have it both ways—continued Israeli housing construction for Jews in east Jerusalem and U.S. support, or at least acquiescence, for this effort.

President Bush tried to bring Kollek down to earth, but gently, as one elder statesman to another.[17]

Dear Mr. Mayor,

I would like to thank you . . . for sharing your insights with me. There is much that we hold in common. As you note, the basis of our position remains that Jerusalem must never again be a divided city. We did not approve of the status quo before 1967; in no way do we advocate a return to it now. This was and is the policy of the United States, and it is my policy. Our efforts in the peace process are in no way designed to promote the division of Jerusalem. We would oppose any such effort.

It is also our view that the final status of this most special of cities should be decided by negotiation and that this negotiation would be facilitated if we were well along that path toward peace. There is thus no intention on our part to focus now on the final status of Jerusalem. It is our view, just as it has been the view of the United States since 1967, that all sides should be taking steps to get to negotiations and avoiding steps that could prejudice the prospects for these negotiations. It is the pursuit of peace that ought to take priority, for only with peace can Jerusalem be truly open and whole.

Thank you again for taking the time to write me. Barbara joins me in sending our best wishes to you and your family. Sincerely,
George Bush

Bush and Kollek met two months later in Washington. Again Kollek talked of ensuring that Jerusalem remain a united city and appealed to the president not to place the new Jewish neighborhoods in east Jerusalem in the same category as the settlements in the West Bank. "The fact is that the Arab and Jewish populations are proportionally the same today as they were in 1967," Kollek told Bush.[18] Israeli Ambassador Moshe Arad was also present, as were national security adviser Brent Scowcroft and White House chief of staff John Sununu. Bush and the other Americans listened intently to the mayor. The U.S. president even asked him several questions concerning current affairs in Jerusalem. But the questions seemed to be out of courtesy. The Americans had already heard the mayor's position before, and he was offering nothing new this time around. He continued to want it all—for the United States to support Israeli development in east Jerusalem while continuing to function as an intermediary between Israel and its Arab neighbors and the Palestinians.

Bush and company were not convinced. They viewed Kollek as a friendly element in the Israeli scene, and worded the statement released after the meeting accordingly. "The President expressed his personal admiration for Mayor Kollek," the statement began.[19] "The long-standing opposition of the United States to settlement activity in the territories occupied by Israel in 1967 is well known. So too is the position of the United States supporting a united Jerusalem whose final status is determined by negotiations."[20] The Americans put it nicely. If they had been frank, they would have said simply that, "We aren't buying Kollek's, or Israel's, vision of the path to peace in Jerusalem." For its part, Israel continued to ignore the United States and moved ahead with the same policy it had implemented in east Jerusalem since 1967, ignoring the criticism from abroad, and problems from within, that this policy was causing.

A popular song sung by Jews at the Passover holiday each year recounts a long list of "what ifs" with regard to the history of Moses leading the Israelites out of slavery in Egypt. "What if God had lead us out of slavery, but not parted the Red Sea?" "What if God had parted the Red Sea, but not given us the Ten Commandments?" and the list goes on and on. A similar list of "what ifs" could easily be drawn up to recall Israeli rule in east Jerusalem, although instead of miracle after miracle, we would have failure after failure, or missed opportunity after missed opportunity. What if Teddy Kollek had insisted on building homes for Arabs in Jerusalem and not just Jews? What if Teddy Kollek had set up more Arab neighborhood councils, instead of just talking about it? What if Israel had applied the idea of "self-segregation" not just to Jewish residents but also to Arab residents? What if Israel hadn't expropriated so much Arab land in east Jerusalem? What if Israel had not tried to artificially sever the connection between the West Bank and east Jerusalem? The revised version of this song also goes on for pages.

The questions are unavoidable. Kollek and his close associates in local and national Israeli governments for decades outlined a vision for peace in Jerusalem. They took their ideas to foreign leaders and governments. But the actions they took flew in the face of this vision.

Instead of fostering peace, they laid the groundwork for increased tensions and conflict.

What about those who have come since? In the summer of 1998 they put forward their vision of the future of Jerusalem. The Palestinians were not even mentioned. Nor was the Palestinian Authority. It was as if the new mayor, Ehud Olmert, and government, headed by Prime Minister Binyamin Netanyahu, wanted to turn back the clock to the time before the signing of the Oslo Accord. On June 18, 1998, an Israeli government-appointed commission issued recommendations for expanding Jerusalem's borders into the West Bank.[21] Just how much Jerusalem was to expand the Israeli government left for a later date to decide.[22] Serious questions also remained as to whether the government intended to go through with the recommendations. Indeed, the only decision taken by the Netanyahu government in June 1998, when it accepted the recommendations, was to set up several committees to plan for strengthening Israel's control over Jerusalem. Committees were set up to discuss expanding the city's borders; setting up an umbrella local government for metropolitan Jerusalem; encouraging industry to relocate to Jerusalem; and even establishing a tram-car system in the city.[23] No concrete decisions were taken, notwithstanding the headlines worldwide proclaiming that Israel was on the verge of annexing areas around Jerusalem.

But the Netanyahu government's actions were significant. They showed that Israel was regressing to the days when it dreamed, and planned, to expand Jerusalem as far east as Jericho. The map, "Jerusalem Metropolitan Area" (see page 265) shows two ideas for expanding Jerusalem discussed in recent years by Israeli officials. The first, the "Outer Ring," was raised in the pre-Oslo days and defined a metropolitan Jerusalem including Jericho to the east and Beit Shemesh to the west. The second, the "Inner Ring," reflects what Netanyahu's committees apparently had in mind. There is a logic to these maps. In an imaginary Jerusalem that is not a center of the Arab-Israeli conflict, real urban planning needs argue for finding ways to coordinate, and even integrate, development in the Jerusalem region. It makes sense for Ma'ale Adumim and Jerusalem, and even Beit Jala and Jerusalem, to work together and not function as isolated units. If it was this imaginary Jerusalem that Israel had in mind when it made its June 1998 recommendations, perhaps it could be excused for appearing not to grasp the consequences of what it was considering. But this was not the case. With over three decades of experience ruling the reunited Jerusalem, Israel should have known better.

Epilogue

Is it too late? That is the major question today, thirty-two years since Israel reunified Jerusalem. Has the hatred grown too strong? Have the divisions between the parties vying for Jerusalem become so great that continued fighting is inevitable? The answer, from one perspective, appears easy. In the post-Cold War era, the conflict over Jerusalem is just another regional dispute whose time for resolution has arrived. But for all those who argue for the end of history, there are also those who remind us of the clashes of civilizations. That makes for a much less optimistic view.

In the preceding chapters we have presented a gloomy picture. We have tried to stick with the facts as we know them, but our opinion also comes through. It is our belief that Israeli policy in east Jerusalem has been misguided. That opinion, like all opinions, is open to debate, and one of our motives for writing this book was to spur a renewed exchange of opinions on Jerusalem.

But there is also a reality that must be faced, and about which there is no debate. Indeed, we can defer to former Mayor Teddy Kollek and his successor, Ehud Olmert, on this point. Kollek and Olmert came from opposing political traditions and have sharply opposing views concerning how Israel should govern Jerusalem. But they agree on one point: Palestinian residents of Jerusalem live in conditions that are far inferior to those of their Jewish neighbors, and the Israeli government is to blame. Israel has failed to properly maintain Arab east Jerusalem, leaving its neighborhoods to deteriorate and residents with no choice but to leave the city, while nearby the government has built beautiful new Jewish neighborhoods to encourage Jews from Israel and around the world to move onto land expropriated from Arabs.

Many speak up in defense of Israel's policy toward east Jerusalem.

They begin by reminding us of Judaism's religious and historic ties to Jerusalem, of how Jews have been the majority in Jerusalem since the nineteenth century, and how the Arabs rejected the U.N.'s proposal to make the city an international protectorate and, after conquering east Jerusalem in 1948, evicted all the Jewish residents and ransacked Jewish property. Kollek expressed this argument well: "Jews care intensely about Jerusalem. The Christians have Rome and Canterbury and even Salt Lake City; Muslims have Mecca and Medina. Jerusalem has great meaning for them also. But the Jews have only one Jerusalem and only the Jews have made it their capital. That is why it has so much deeper a meaning for them than anybody else."[1]

These arguments should not be belittled. But their underlying weakness must also be recognized. They give the false impression that history somehow bestows on Israel the last word about Jerusalem, and that Jerusalem belongs to Israel and only Israel. We say to those who adhere to this position: at least recognize where your argument has led. Do not believe the propaganda—the rosy picture Israel tries to show the world of life in Jerusalem since the 1967 reunification. Israel has treated the Palestinians of Jerusalem terribly. As a matter of policy, it has forced many of them from their homes and stripped them of their land, all the while lying to them and deceiving them and the world about its honorable intentions. And what makes all this so much more inexcusable is that there was no reason for it. Governing Jerusalem properly would not have jeopardized Israel's claim to the city. Indeed, it likely would have eased the growing conflict over Jerusalem's future. That massive error in judgment, we believe, is the tragedy of Israel's rule in east Jerusalem since 1967.

Notes

Much of this book is based on documents the authors obtained in the course of their work and research. Unless indicated, documents referred to are in the authors' possession, either in their original form or in a copy. The documents are in Hebrew, unless otherwise stated. Many of the documents cited come from the personal archive of Teddy Kollek. The archive, kept in the basement of the Israel Museum in Jerusalem, includes a wide range of papers, correspondence, and memoranda by not only the mayor but also other Israeli leaders and various non-Israelis. "KA" indicates that the document was taken from the Kollek archive. The other major source for this book was the authors' first-hand experience. In the notes, we have made reference to our presence only where it is particularly relevant to either understanding the subject at hand or our knowledge of the subject.

1. The Vision and the Reality

1. "Address of Israel's Prime Minister, Levi Eshkol, to the Chief Rabbis and Spiritual Leaders of Israel's Religious Communities," in *The Jerusalem Question and Its Resolutions: Selected Documents,* ed. Ruth Lapidoth and Moshe Hirsch (London: Martinus Nijhoff Publisher, in cooperation with The Jerusalem Institute for Israel Studies, 1994), p. 163.
2. Ibid.
3. "In 1845, the Prussian Consul in Jerusalem, Dr. Schultz, estimated the City's population as 7,120 Jews, 5,000 Muslim Arabs, and 3,390 Christian Arabs," the political cartographer Martin Gilbert wrote in *Jerusalem Illustrated History Atlas,* 3rd ed. (London: Books Britain, 1994).
4. *Jerusalem Statistical Yearbook, 1996,* ed. Maya Ghoshen and Na'amah Shahar (Jerusalem: Jerusalem Institute for Israel Studies), p. 30.
5. "Letter from Israel's Foreign Minister, Abba Eban, to the U.N. Secretary-General, July 10, 1967," *The Jerusalem Question,* p. 171.
6. Ibid.
7. *Jerusalem Statistical Yearbook, 1996,* pp. 46–50.
8. *Jerusalem Statistical Yearbook* annually details the poor conditions of Arabs compared to Jews in Jerusalem.
9. Kollek sent this speech to Samuel Sorin, executive vice-president of the

Jewish Community Centers of Greater Philadelphia, to be read at a Jerusalem Day event in that city in 1983. English. KA.
10. Ibid.

2. Mr. Jerusalem

1. Letter from Kollek to Samuel Sorin, February 9, 1984. KA.
2. The man taking the post was Amir Cheshin.
3. Minutes from a meeting at the home of city manager Aharon Sarig. Cheshin was also present at the meeting. KA.
4. *The Jerusalem Question and Its Resolutions: Selected Documents,* ed. Ruth Lapidoth and Moshe Hirsch (London: Martinus Nijhoff Publisher, in cooperation with The Jerusalem Institute for Israel Studies, 1994), p. xxvi.
5. "Development Plans for the Arab Sector," Internal Jerusalem Municipality Report, City Planning Department, July 1986. KA.
6. Ibid.
7. Ibid.
8. Efriam Sneh, "The Arabs of East Jerusalem: Positions and Trends," May 23, 1988. KA.
9. "Advisor to the Mayor of Jerusalem: 'Kollek Filed Away Critical Report on Services to Arab Population,'" *Ha'aretz* newspaper, May 4, 1994.
10. Untitled handwritten memo from Kollek adviser Shai Doron to deputy mayor Amos Mar-Haim, August 24, 1992, detailing the mayor's conversation with Prime Minister Rabin. KA.
11. Ibid.
12. Letter from Kollek to finance minister Avraham Shohat, September 18, 1992. KA.
13. Letter from Kollek to Rabin, December 4, 1992. KA.
14. Letter from Kollek to Rabin, December 29, 1992. KA.
15. Letter from Kollek to housing minister Binyamin Ben-Eliezer, November 15, 1992. KA.

3. When Giants Sleep

1. The account of this meeting was taken from the notes of Bill Hutman, who attended the meeting in his role as a reporter for the *Jerusalem Post.* The *Post* ran a front-page story on the meeting the next day. The Associated Press picked up the story, but little else was made of it at the time.
2. "Potential Housing Construction in Jerusalem," City Planning Department, Planning Policy Division, August 1993. KA.
3. *Jerusalem Statistical Yearbook, 1996,* ed. Maya Ghoshen and Na'amah Shahar (Jerusalem: Jerusalem Institute for Israel Studies), p. 30.
4. "Alternatives for Jerusalem's Future Road Needs," compiled for the municipality by the Jerusalem-based Economic Consulting and Planning Ltd.

and classified in the mayor's office as secret. The date is no longer legible on the document, but the report itself states that it was based on research done in the latter part of 1970 and apparently was written soon after this. KA.

5. "Recommendations of the Sub-Committee [of the Ministerial Committee on Jerusalem] on Development in Jerusalem," June 6, 1975. KA.

6. Letter from Kollek to justice minister Haim Tsadok, chairman of the Ministerial Committee on Jerusalem, June 28, 1976. KA.

7. The actual decision to uproot the orchard was taken by the quasi-government Jewish National Fund. The JNF wanted to replace the orchard with its own trees, so the villagers would not be able to claim users' rights to the land.

8. The urban planner was the well-known Jerusalemite Shlomo Hayat.

9. The plan was outlined in a letter by its authors, Kollek, Yitzhak Levy of the Israel Lands Authority, and Yosef Sharon, the Housing Ministry director-general, to the government, March 29, 1970. KA.

10. Minutes from the Ministerial Committee on Jerusalem, May 12, 1970. KA.

11. Letter from Kollek to Prime Minister Golda Meir, May 18, 1970. KA.

12. Untitled Israel Defense Ministry report, July 29, 1988. KA.

13. Ibid.

14. Minutes of the meeting in the office of Israeli attorney-general Meir Shamgar, May 19, 1970. KA.

15. Letter from Housing Ministry deputy director-general S. Peleg to Meron Benvenisti, December 20, 1970, stating that the government would provide partial funding for the Nusseiba housing project. At the time, only 100 units were slated for the project. The government insisted that 50 units go to Arab families evicted from their homes because of the clearing of the plaza in front of the Western Wall and the renovation of the Jewish Quarter. The other 50 units were to be sold on the open market, "with priority given to candidates approved by the municipality and housing ministry." KA.

16. Letter from Shamgar to Kollek, August 27, 1970. KA.

17. "Proposed Building Program for Neveh Ya'acov," Internal Housing Ministry memo, September 24, 1970. KA.

18. "Proposed Building Program for East Talpiot," Internal Housing Ministry memo, September 25, 1970. KA.

19. See, for instance, *Documents on Israel* (Jerusalem: Palestinian Academic Society for the Study of International Affairs, December 1996), pp. 247–291.

20. *The Jerusalem Question and Its Resolutions: Selected Documents,* ed. Ruth Lapidoth and Moshe Hirsch (London: Martinus Nijhoff Publisher, in cooperation with The Jerusalem Institute for Israel Studies, 1994).

21. Letter from Kollek to Foreign Ministry official Ziyama Dibon, October 26, 1970.

22. Minutes of the meeting in the office of attorney-general Meir Shamgar, June 29, 1970. KA.

23. The actual negotiations were conducted by Jerusalem deputy mayor Avraham Kahila and Housing Ministry director-general Shmaryahu Cohen. KA.

24. Interior minister Yitzhak Peretz led the opposition to the plan. Several days before the plan was brought before the board, Peretz called Kollek into his office and told him he would prevent its approval.

25. "Municipal Area of Jerusalem, 1952–1993," *Jerusalem Statistical Yearbook, 1996,* p. 3.

26. Ibid.

27. "Israel Government Official Publications," no. 1425, 1968, p. 688.

28. Ibid., no. 1443, 1968, p. 1238.

29. Ibid., no. 1656, 1970, p. 2808.

30. Ibid., no. 2614, 1980, p. 1305.

31. Ibid., no. 3,877, 1991, p. 2479.

32. "Proposed Program for Building at East Talpiot," Israeli Housing Ministry internal memo, September 25, 1970. KA.

33. "Proposed Program for Building at Neveh Ya'acov," Israeli Housing Ministry internal memo, September 24, 1970. KA.

34. Minutes of the meeting between foreign minister Moshe Dayan and Kollek at King David Hotel, December 31, 1972.

35. *Jerusalem Statistical Yearbook, 1996.*

4. A Question of Trust

1. Memo from Kollek to deputy mayor Amos Mar-Haim and city treasurer Ya'acov Efrati, September 8, 1993. The memo details Kollek's meeting with finance minister Avraham Shohat. KA.

2. Interview by the authors with former Shin Bet head Ya'acov Pery on April 8, 1996.

3. Cheshin attended the meeting and wrote the minutes, which the authors reviewed.

5. Mr. Arafat, Can You Lend Me a Hand?

1. "Unclear How Long the Lines Will Be," *Ha'aretz* newspaper, September 3, 1993.

2. Ibid.

3. Ibid.

4. Teddy Kollek, "Jerusalem: Present and Future," *Foreign Affairs,* summer 1981, p. 1045.

5. Cheshin attended both of those meetings and took minutes for Kollek.

6. Letter from Aharon Sarig to Kollek, December 27, 1992. KA.

7. "Unclear How Long the Lines Will Be." The figure was provided by Israel's Central Election Committee to the Office of the Mayor's Adviser on Arab Affairs.

6. The Eagle Has Landed

1. Interview with Aharon Sarig.
2. Ibid.
3. Ibid.
4. Ibid.
5. Ibid.
6. Ibid.
7. Ibid. Ya'acov Gabai, who later was appointed head of east Jerusalem public schools by the Jerusalem municipality, also confirmed this account in an interview with the authors.
8. Ibid.
9. Ibid.
10. Interview with Ya'acov Gabai.
11. Ibid.
12. Untitled municipal working paper, dated October 1, 1992. An identical working paper, dated June 8, 1992, also exists. Apparently, city officials simply used data they compiled at the end of the previous school year as the basis for their discussions. But they put a new date on the material to make it appear to Gal that it was current. The Gal-initiated discussions continued until the end of October, according the official minutes of the last of those meetings on October 22, 1992. KA.
13. Ibid.
14. Interview with Victor Gabai.
15. We have not revealed the name of this school and its administrators, given the continued sensitivity of their willingness to cooperate with Israel.
16. *Our Town* (Jerusalem: The Jerusalem Municipality Education Department and Ministry of Education and Culture, Education Programs Division, 1993).
17. Ibid.
18. Ibid.
19. Interview with Victor Gabai.
20. Memorandum from Amir Cheshin to Jerusalem Mayor Ehud Olmert, December 9, 1993. A copy of the memorandum, returned by Olmert to Cheshin, contains a handwritten note by the mayor: "To: Nissim Solomon; Amir Cheshin; Victor Gabai. I asked you to prepare a memorandum assessing this situation. Has this been done? Please prepare and present to me immediately. Ehud."
21. Ibid.

7. The Forgotten Ones

1. Amir Cheshin was present at this meeting.
2. Amir Cheshin was present at this meeting.
3. The agreement was defined in an exchange of letters, June 14, 1967, between Israeli Foreign Ministry official Michael Comay and UNRWA commissioner-general Lawrence Michelmore. The authors did not review the actual letters but rather obtained an undated Israeli Foreign Ministry statement describing the agreement. KA.
4. Letter from Shahal to prime minister, defense minister, and mayor, August 7, 1985. KA.
5. Untitled Israeli Energy Ministry report, June 24, 1986. KA.
6. Minutes of the meeting between Kollek, U.S. ambassador Thomas Pickering, and U.S. consul Morris Driefer, March 18, 1986. KA.
7. Minutes of the meeting of Ministerial Committee on Jerusalem, February 14, 1973. KA.
8. Ibid.
9. Ibid.
10. Minutes of the meeting between Kollek and defense minister Moshe Dayan, December 31, 1972. KA.
11. "Decision of the Ministerial Committee [on Jerusalem]," February 13, 1973. KA.
12. Ibid.
13. "National Insurance Institute Regulations," p. 1063.
14. Ibid.
15. Letter from Kollek to Efriam Shilo, August 1986. KA.
16. Ibid.
17. Letter from Efriam Shilo to Kollek, October 1986. KA.

8. Security Breach

1. "Information on Terror Casualties in Jerusalem, 1967–1988," undated Jerusalem municipality memo, authored by Kollek's assistant Shmuel Eyal, apparently based on information he received from Jerusalem police. KA.
2. Ibid.
3. Ibid.
4. Ibid.
5. Ya'acov Pery, head of Shin Bet during the intifada, said this in an interview with the authors.
6. Letter from Kollek to Prime Minister Shimon Peres, June 4, 1986. KA.
7. Ibid.
8. Letter from Kollek to police minister Haim Bar-Lev, January 19, 1987. KA.

9. Ibid.

10. Our account of the meeting on February 16, 1988, is based on detailed official minutes, as well as interviews with participants Ya'acov Pery, then head of Shin Bet, and Aharon Sarig, then Jerusalem municipality director-general. KA.

11. Ibid.

12. Ibid.

13. Ibid.

14. Ibid.

15. Ibid.

16. Ibid.

17. Ibid.

18. Official minutes of the meeting on March 2, 1988, in the office of police minister Haim Bar-Lev. KA.

19. Ibid.

20. Ibid.

21. Ibid.

22. "All Departments—In the Framework of Budget and Work Plans," internal Jerusalem municipality memo, by city manager Michael Gal, October 5, 1992. KA.

9. Damage Control

1. Letter from Kollek to Jerusalem Committee members, March 2, 1988. KA.

2. Letter from Kollek to Jerusalem Foundation members, March 4, 1988. KA.

3. "Jerusalem: A Divided City Again," *Chicago Tribune,* February 10, 1988.

10. A First Friendship

1. Avi Melamed personally oversaw this project for the Jerusalem municipality, from its initiation. The following account is based on his notes.

11. No Judenrein in Jerusalem

1. Letter from Kollek to Prime Minister Yitzhak Shamir, December 8, 1991. KA.

2. Ibid.

3. Ibid.

4. "Strengthening Israel's Position in Jerusalem," memo from Kollek to Rabin, July 16, 1992. KA.

5. Ibid.

6. Amir Cheshin was a member of the commission.
7. The findings were outlined in the commission's "Report on Settlement in East Jerusalem," October 9, 1992; it is more widely known in Israel as the Klugman Report.
8. Ibid., p. 17.
9. Ibid., appendix 6.
10. Ibid.
11. "Financial Assistance to Institutions in the Old City," internal Housing Ministry memo, included as attachment to Klugman Report.
12. Ibid.
13. Letter from Rueven Shalom, Housing Ministry director-general, to the Klugman Commission, August 26, 1992, included as attachment to the Klugman Report. The commission had ordered Shalom to provide the figures.
14. Ibid.
15. Klugman Report, appendix 6, "Assistance to Institutions in the Old City."
16. Klugman Report, p. 11.
17. "Absentee Property Law (1950)," *Israel Law Book,* no. 37, p. 86.
18. Official minutes of the meeting convened by housing minister Ariel Sharon, October 22, 1990.
19. "Klugman Report," p. 17, which states, "properties were declared absentee based upon information . . . brought to the custodian by the [settler] groups. The validity of this information . . . was never checked by the custodian. He never visited the properties."
20. Klugman Report, p. 24.
21. Ibid.
22. Official minutes of the meeting convened by housing minister Ariel Sharon, October 22, 1990.
23. Klugman Report, p. 11.
24. Ibid., p. 12.
25. Ibid.
26. "Letter of Appointment" from Housing Ministry director-general Arye Bar to Purchasing Committee member and Housing Ministry official Shalom Bagad, July 25, 1991. The letter was among the material submitted to the Klugman Commission by the Housing Ministry.
27. "Purchasing of Homes in East Jerusalem," letter from Housing Ministry director-general Arye Bar to Housing Ministry Programs Department head Eitan Lahovsky, July 20, 1992.
28. "High Court Rulings," vol. 92 , no. 1 (1992), p. 1827.
29. Letter from Gidon Avni, the Israel Antiquities Authority chief archaeologist of the Jerusalem District, to housing minister Ariel Sharon, March 17, 1992.

30. "Sharon Doesn't Stop at the Red Light," *Ma'ariv* newspaper, June 5, 1968.
31. "The Antiquities Authority: Agreement Reached with Ateret Cohanim on the Archaeological Dig by Herod's Gate," *Ha'aretz*, May 29, 1998.
32. "Sharon and Olmert Push Ateret Cohanim Plan at Herod's Gate," *Kol Ha'ir*, May 5, 1998.
33. Letter from Arik Nahemkin to Kollek, September 24, 1992. KA.
34. Ibid.
35. Letter from Kollek to justice minister David Liba'i, December 13, 1992. KA.
36. Letter from Kollek to justice minister David Liba'i, February 4, 1993. KA.
37. Ibid.
38. Official minutes of the meeting between Kollek and police minister Moshe Shahal, February 4, 1993. KA.
39. Letter from state comptroller Miriam Ben-Porat to Kollek, March 11, 1993. KA.
40. Ibid.
41. Letters from Kollek to state attorney Dorit Banish, August 4, 1993; minister of energy and infrastructure Amnon Rubenstein, April 30, 1993; Efriam Sneh, April 15, 1993; police minister Moshe Shahal, February 4, 1993, and foreign minister Shimon Peres, February 4, 1993. KA.
42. Letter from Kollek to Prime Minister Yitzhak Rabin, April 14, 1993.
43. Official minutes of the meeting between Kollek and Rabin, August 5, 1993. KA.

12. A Path to Peace Not Taken

1. *Whither Jerusalem? Proposals and Positions Concerning the Future of Jerusalem,* ed. M. Hirsch, D. Housen-Couriel, R. Lapidoth (London: Martinus Nijhoff Publisher in cooperation with The Jerusalem Institute for Israel Studies, 1995).
2. Memorandum from Meron Benvenisti to Foreign Ministry director-general Mordechai Gazit, July 2, 1968. KA. The quotes concerning Benvenisti's plan also come from the memorandum.
3. Official minutes of the meeting, compiled by Aharon Sarig, February 21, 1974. KA. All quotes from this meeting are taken from the minutes.
4. Teddy Kollek, "Jerusalem," *Foreign Affairs,* summer 1977.
5. Ibid., p. 704.
6. Ibid., p. 712.
7. Ibid., p. 710.
8. Ibid., p. 715.
9. Teddy Kollek, "Jerusalem: Present and Future," *Foreign Affairs,* winter 1981.

10. Teddy Kollek, "Unified Jerusalem," *Foreign Affairs,* winter 1988/1989, p. 156.
11. Official minutes of the meeting between Kollek and U.S. secretary of state George Shultz. KA.
12. Letter from Kollek to U.S. secretary of state James A. Baker, April 12, 1991. English. KA.
13. Letter from U.S. President George Bush to Kollek, March 13, 1990. English. KA.
14. Ibid.
15. Ibid.
16. Ibid.
17. Letter from U.S. President George Bush to Kollek, March 13, 1990. English. KA.
18. Official minutes of the meeting, authored by Kollek adviser Gabi Padon, May 3, 1990. KA.
19. "Statement by the Press Secretary," The White House, Office of the Press Secretary, May 3, 1990. KA.
20. Ibid.
21. "Report of the Committee for Strengthening Jerusalem," The Prime Minister's Office, Office of the Director General, June 18, 1993. KA.
22. Ibid.
23. Ibid.

Epilogue

1. Teddy Kollek, "Jerusalem," *Foreign Affairs,* summer 1977, p. 715.

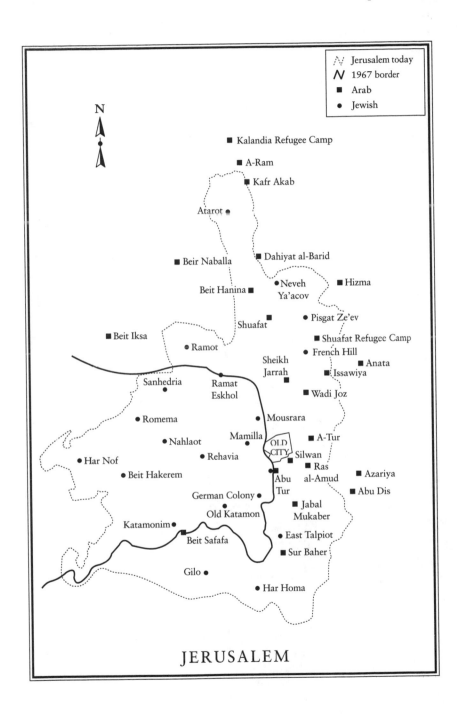

JERUSALEM

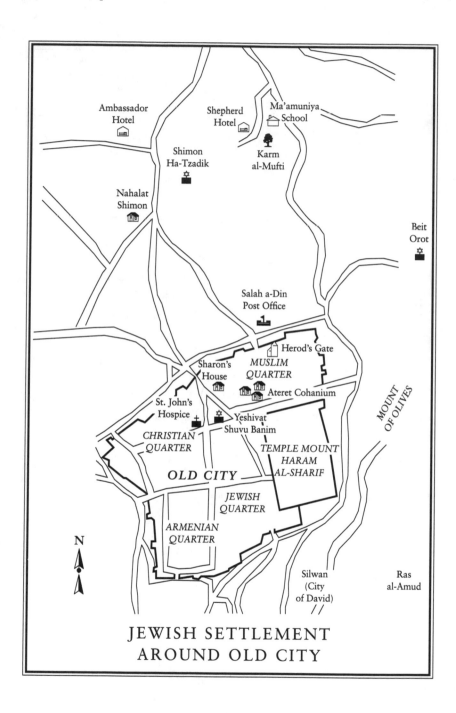

Ambassador
Hotel

Shepherd
Hotel

Ma'amuniya
School

Shimon
Ha-Tzadik

Karm
al-Mufti

Nahalat
Shimon

Beit
Orot

Salah a-Din
Post Office

Herod's Gate

Sharon's
House

*MUSLIM
QUARTER*

St. John's
Hospice

Ateret Cohanium

Yeshivat
Shuvu Banim

*CHRISTIAN
QUARTER*

*MOUNT
OF OLIVES*

*TEMPLE MOUNT
HARAM
AL-SHARIF*

OLD CITY

*JEWISH
QUARTER*

N

*ARMENIAN
QUARTER*

Silwan
(City
of David)

Ras
al-Amud

JEWISH SETTLEMENT
AROUND OLD CITY

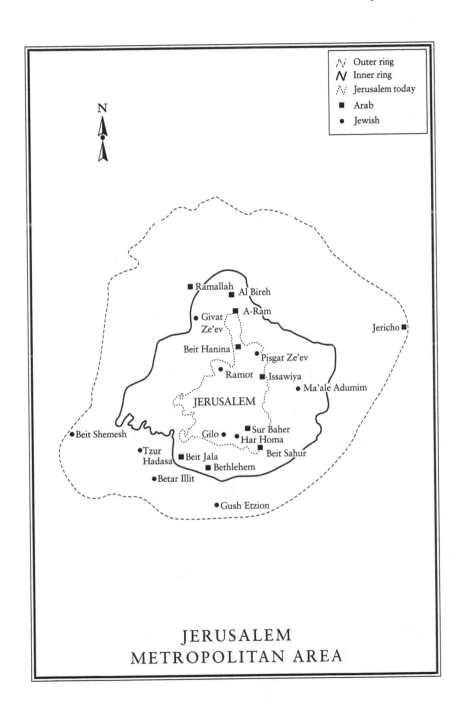

JERUSALEM
METROPOLITAN AREA

JORDANIAN PROPOSAL FOR EXPANSION
OF EAST JERUSALEM BORDERS

Index

Abadiya neighborhood, 126
Abassi, Mussa, 211, 212
Absentee Property Law, 215, 216–217, 224
Abu Assaleh, Hassan, 35, 36
Abu Dis, 63–64, 127, 150, 227
Abu Ghosh, Fouzi, 109–110
Abu Tarek, 81, 179–180
Abu Toumah, Jamil, 121
Abu Tur neighborhood, 61, 114, 148, 174, 192, 198–199
Abu Zuloff, Mohamad, 238
Akbat al-Sariya neighborhood, 116
al-Aksa mosque, 184
Allenby Bridge, 26, 176
Alon, Yigal, 105
Alpert Music Center for Youth, 192
American Colony, 16, 69
Amit, Meshulam, 121, 166, 170
Amman, Jordan, 74, 91, 102, 106, 122
Ammunition Hill, 99
Amouri, Sayid, 53
Antoniya private school, 104
Arab Affairs Office, 85, 152–153, 155, 200
Arabic language, 178
Arad, Moshe, 246
Arafat, Yasser, 71, 89, 97–99, 120
A-Ram neighborhood, 54, 94, 127
Arens, Moshe, 195
Army, Israeli, 68, 71, 73, 77, 80, 96, 127
Art and culture centers, 10–11
Asana neighborhood, 158
al-Ashab, Husni, 105
Askalan village, 146
Association of Cities proposal for border definitions within Jerusalem, 231–232
Atara L'Yoshna settlement group, 216, 218
Atarot Airport, 39
Atarot Industrial Zone, 40, 41, 57

Ateret Cohanim settlement group, 215–220
A-Tur neighborhood, 158, 188, 240
Azariya neighborhood, 63–64, 65, 94, 127, 134–136, 149, 150, 151, 188, 227
A-Zayim neighborhood, 127

Baker, James, 242, 244
Balidiyat Urshalim al-Quds proposal, 228
Banais village, 146
Banish, Dorit, 223
Bank of Israel, 72
Bank of Jerusalem, 150
Barakat, Fayik, 163, 164
Baran, Ze'ev, 50–51
Bar-Lev, Haim, 161, 166, 167, 169–170, 173–174
Bar-Sela, Yoram, 230
Barzacci, Elinoar, 29, 30, 35, 37, 51
Basic Law, 20–21
Bedouins, 201, 236
Be'eri, David, 211, 212, 217–218
Begin, Menachem, 20, 212
Beilin, Yossi, 239
Beit Hanina neighborhood, 19–20, 45, 52–55, 57, 65, 104, 116, 146, 147, 150, 169, 240
Beit Jala, 137, 228, 231, 249
Beit Orot Yeshiva, 219, 220
Beit Safafa neighborhood, 136–137, 147, 177–180, 182, 241
Beit Sahur neighborhood, 58, 59, 62, 137
Beit Shemesh, 248
Ben-Eliezer, Binyamin, 219
Ben-Gurion, David, 27
Ben-Porat, Miriam, 222–223
Benvenisti, Meron, 41–42, 95, 97, 100, 226–229, 237
Bethlehem, 57, 58, 62, 122, 136–137, 144, 229, 231
Bialik, Haim, 103

Biblical Zoo, 192
al-Bireh village, 137
Border definitions within Jerusalem, 227, 230–232, 248
British Mandate, 49, 73, 74, 160, 237
Building permits and fees, 44, 50, 77, 80, 137, 139. See also Housing construction
Bush, Barbara, 244, 246
Bush, George, 244, 245–247

Christian Quarter, Old City, 159, 213
Church of the Holy Sepulcher, 137, 139, 159
Citizenship rights, 43, 60, 62, 64–65; welfare benefits and, 148–149, 152. See also Identification and traveling papers; Visas
City Council of Jerusalem, 87, 91–92, 94
Civics education, 106, 107
Civil Administration, 127, 128–129, 131–132, 135–136, 153
Civil guard, 171
Cohen, Guela, 212–213
Cohen, Haim, 96
Cohen, Yossi, 204, 208
Community planning, 21, 45, 49
Constantinople, 73
Curfews, 171, 173

Dabash, Hader, 77–78, 79
Dajala, Ahmad, 77–78, 79
Dahiyat al-Barid neighborhood, 116
Damascus Gate, 13, 80, 104, 195, 196, 233
Dan, Matti, 217, 218
Daniel, Danny, 200
Dar el-Aytam school, 116
Darwish, Darwish, 67–70
Darwish, Mordechi, 18
Darwish, Ziyad, 146, 147
David, King, 5–6, 211–224
Davidson, Meir, 218
Dayan, Moshe, 63–64, 149–150, 229
Dead Sea, 68
Debt collection, 173–174
Defense Ministry, 41, 131
Democratic Front for the Liberation of Palestine, 168
a-Din, Salah, 68

Dome of the Rock, 184
Driefer, Morris, 142

East Jerusalem Chamber of Commerce, 163–164, 165
East Talpiot neighborhood, 22, 36, 39, 45, 48, 55, 56, 59, 60, 163, 192, 199; Jabal Mukaber–East Talpiot project in Arab-Jewish relations, 199–210
Eban, Abba, 7–9
Education Ministry (Israel), 103, 105–108, 111–112, 117
Education Ministry (Jordan), 102, 105, 122
Education Ministry (Palestinian Authority), 122–123
Education system, 9, 10–11, 16, 22, 24, 25, 73–74, 101–102; departments, 84, 86, 156; Jordanian control of, 101, 102, 105–106, 107–108; following 1967 war, 101–105; Arabs in, 103, 105–106, 114, 188; Palestinians in, 103–104, 114; censorship of textbooks and curriculum, 106, 107, 117, 118–120, 122; intifada violence and strikes, 108–115. See also Schools; Teachers and principals
Efrat, Yona, 143
Egypt, 238
Eibed, Yasser, 238
Eindenhaur Fund (Germany), 200
Einsmeister, Meir, 125, 126, 129
Elad settlement group, 211–212, 216, 217, 218, 222
Elections and voting, 91–92, 94, 96–100, 222; Arab vote, 92–94, 95, 96–97, 99, 100; Palestinian vote, 97
Electricity, 21, 124, 137–145
Energy Ministry (Israel), 141, 142–143
Energy Ministry (Jordan), 142
Eshel, Tamar, 230, 235
Eshkol, Levy, 5
Even Rosh settlement company, 217
Expropriation of Arab land, 38–44, 46–48, 49, 52, 55, 56, 59–60, 92, 97, 169, 201, 204, 247, 248, 250, 251; in east Jerusalem, 56–57, 58, 59; vs. use of state land, 149–150; for Jewish settlement movement, 211–224
Ezra, Gidon, 166, 170

Farhi, David, 229, 230, 232–233, 234
Fatah, 82, 83
Fawaka, Mohammed, 77–78, 79
Frankel, Ya'acov, 72
Freij, Elias, 137
French Hill neighborhood, 19, 22, 55, 57, 192
Frères College for Boys, 48, 49, 104, 116

Gabai, Victor, 112, 113, 114–115
Gal, Michael, 24–25, 111, 116, 126, 129, 155, 156, 182–184, 186
Garbage collection, 21, 25, 124, 125–129, 169, 171, 174
Gaza/Gaza Strip, 23, 80, 155, 172, 192, 239–240; schools, 119, 120, 122; refugee camps, 130; municipal services in, 136; street violence and rioting in, 143, 158, 159; Jewish settlement movement in, 212, 214; housing and development projects, 244–245
Geneva Convention, 47, 48
Ghabi, Rateb, 102
Gidada, Luigi, 48
Gilo neighborhood, 33, 55, 56, 59, 62, 192
Ginat, Yossi, 17
Givat Hamatos neighborhood, 59

Haas Promenade, 192
Hadassah University Hospital, 152, 153
Halack, Othmann, 238
Hamad, Fatmah, 152–153
Hamas, 82, 83, 145, 209
Haram al-Sharif, 118, 184–186, 227, 241 See also Temple Mount
Harel, Yossi, 205
Har Homa neighborhood, 55, 57–59, 60, 62
Hashemite Kingdom. See Jordan
Hazak, Rueven, 94–95
Health services, 9, 14, 16, 24, 152–153, 206
Hebrew language, 106, 107, 113, 117, 175, 178

Hebron, 14, 81
Herod's Gate, 111, 112, 188
Herzog, Chaim, 239

Hillel, Shlomo, 181
Hinnom Valley, 15, 57, 184, 225
Housing and development, 14, 19, 22, 23, 27, 31–32, 38–39, 41–43, 51–55, 65–66, 97, 127; shortages, 42–43, 63, 93–94; in east Jerusalem, 42–45, 49–50, 55–56, 58, 62–65, 130, 138–139, 219, 233–235, 244–247; in Arab neighborhoods, 149–151, 219, 220; in West Bank, 149–151; in Jewish neighborhoods, 212, 218–219; in Gaza, 244. See also Kollek, Teddy: housing and development policies; Zoning plans
Housing construction: restrictions, 29, 30–35, 36–37; potential units designation, 31, 37, 50; limitation system, 50–53, 54–55, 89. See also Building permits and fees
Housing Ministry (Israel), 22, 42, 53, 54, 138, 215–219
Hussein, King of Jordan, 142, 234, 239, 240
Husseini, Adnan, 185
Husseini, Faisal, 69, 70, 87, 88–89, 90, 97, 98, 204
el-Husseini, Mohammed Ali, 144

Ibrahimiyya College, 104, 116
Identification and traveling papers, 23, 64–65, 66, 74, 92, 127–129, 135, 150, 152, 153, 176. See also Citizenship rights; Visas
Income Tax Authority, 76
Industrial growth, 38, 39, 41, 48, 57
Interior Ministry (Israel), 23, 162
Intifada, 12, 23, 68, 70, 87, 88, 131, 143, 154, 176–177, 196, 204; commercial strikes called by, 170–173, 164, 165–166, 168, 169, 170, 181; collapse of the mukhtar system and, 77–81; street violence tactics, 80, 160, 161–162, 163, 170, 186, 188–189; municipal services and, 82–83, 134, 135; promotes anarchy in schools, 108–115, 170; Israeli strategy against, 159, 166–167, 170, 173, 175; effect on Jewish-Arab relations, 200, 220; effect on PLO-Israeli relations, 239–240; effect on Israeli policy on east Jerusalem, 239–241. See also

Intifada *(continued)*
  Palestine Liberation Organization
  (PLO); Street violence and rioting; Ter-
  rorism
Islamic fundamentalist groups, 83, 88,
  144, 145
Israel Aircraft Industries (IAI), 39, 40, 41
Israel Electric Corporation, 138, 139,
  140–141, 142–143, 144
Israeli Defense Force, 56, 96
Israel Lands Authority (ILA), 42, 59, 220
Israel Museum, 192
Issat, Hassin, 204–205
Issawiya neighborhood, 19, 22, 67–68,
  69, 70, 71, 72, 81–83, 86, 175

Jabal Mukaber–East Talpiot project in
  Arab-Jewish relations, 199–210
Jabal Mukaber neighborhood, 20, 22,
  100, 103, 129, 158, 162–163, 188, 199
Jaffa Gate, 13, 15, 104, 159, 184, 225
Jericho, 119, 137, 227, 248
"Jerusalem: Present and Future" (Kollek),
  238
Jerusalem Committee, 186
Jerusalem District Electric Company
  (JDEC), 137–145
Jerusalem Film Center, 192
Jerusalem Foundation, 16, 153, 186, 191,
  192, 193, 225
Jerusalem Fund, 200
Jerusalem Institute of Israel Studies, 155,
  226
Jerusalem National Park, 192
Jewish Quarter, Old City, 49, 61–63,
  144
Jewish Quarter Redevelopment Company,
  215–216
Jews Only segregationist policy, 60–62
Jordan, 26, 43, 46, 68, 74, 91, 99, 175,
  176, 227; occupation and rule in Jerusalem, 7, 8, 9, 48, 49, 93, 134, 150, 160,
  198, 227, 237, 239; control of education system in Jerusalem, 101, 102,
  105–106, 107, 115, 120–122; status of,
  following Six Day War, 101; provision
  of municipal services to Jerusalem, 130,
  131, 136, 138, 142, 144; Jewish settlement movement and, 216; occupation

and rule in the occupied territories,
  233–234. *See also* Six Day War
Judea, 149, 230
Judean Desert, 68
Judenrein, 211–224

Kafr Akab neighborhood, 50–52, 81
Kahila, Avraham, 51
Kalandia B industrial area, 39, 40
Kalandia refugee camp, 39–40
Kaminker, Sara, 30
Karmani, Ronan, 177
al-Khatib, Omar (aka Abu Khalid), 97–98
Khutoub, Khalid, 238
Klugman, Haim/Klugman Report, 214–
  215, 218, 221–224
Knesset, 20, 89, 95, 96, 120, 151, 166,
  181, 219; Labor and Welfare Committee, 151; Jewish settlement movement
  and, 212–213
Kollek, Teddy, 18, 20, 27–28, 70, 86, 127,
  204, 227, 250; provision of municipal
  services in east Jerusalem, 10–11, 12–
  13, 21, 98, 135–138, 141–142, 153–
  155, 156–157, 169, 188, 190; intifada
  and Palestinian terrorism and, 12, 160–
  161, 163–164, 166–167, 169, 173, 174,
  186–190, 193–194, 196–197, 203,
  239–240; revitalization of Arab sector,
  14–15, 16–18, 24, 27–28, 98; awareness of Arab circumstances in east Jerusalem, 21–23, 25–26, 28, 125, 189–
  190, 242; housing and development policies, 34–35, 38–39, 40–42, 44–45, 51,
  52–54, 62, 63, 149, 189, 190, 214,
  244–247, 248; policy on east Jerusalem,
  42, 44–45, 45–46, 47–49, 229, 235–
  236; separatist policy of, 61, 213, 215,
  248; demographic superiority policy,
  62, 63, 64; fundraising programs, 71–
  72, 153, 186, 191–193; defeat in 1993
  election, 72, 89, 97–100, 120; desire for
  civil order, coexistence and unification,
  83–84, 91, 107, 110–111, 118, 156–
  157, 163, 169, 180–182, 186–190, 194;
  boroughs/neighborhood councils proposal, 85–86, 90, 237–238, 240–241,
  247; relations with Palestine Liberation
  Organization, 88–90, 97, 233, 239; vot-

ing policy, 91–92, 93, 94, 99; campaign strategies, 94–96, 99; Labor Party and, 95, 96; education policy, 106, 107, 110–112, 113, 114, 118, 119, 189, 190; commercial strikes and, 170, 173–174, 188; street violence and, 179–180, 184, 185, 188, 202–203; publicity campaigns, 190–191, 242; provision of municipal services in east Jerusalem, 193, 194, 233–234, 236; concerns for safety of his person, 194–196; desire for civil order, coexistence and unification, 203, 213, 222, 226, 230, 236, 240–245, 247; Jewish settlement movement and, 213–214, 220–224; on Muslim Arab nationalism, 235; proposed self-rule in east Jerusalem, 236–238, 241–242; population ratio and concept of demographic balance, 246
Krauss, David, 166, 168–169
el-Kurd, Eid, 80

Labor Party, 16, 20, 24, 97, 99, 125, 151, 167, 212; victory in election of 1992, 26, 27–28; Arab vote and, 93, 94; Kollek and, 95, 96; education system and, 121–122; Jewish settlement movement and, 220
Land Day, 169, 170
Law of Return, 152
Lebanon, 182
Levy, Rafi, 17
Lewis, Bernard, 229
Liba'i, David, 221, 222
Liberty Bell Garden, 192
Libraries, 16, 20, 45
Likud Party/government, 20, 89, 94, 120, 125, 166, 244, 245; elections and, 93, 95–96; Jewish settlement movement and, 212, 213, 214, 219, 220
Lions Gate, 158, 159, 227

Ma'ale Adumim neighborhood, 248
Ma'alot Dafna neighborhood, 44, 56
Ma'amuniya Girls High School, 102, 108, 113, 219
Ma'arat Hamachpela, 231
Mabedi, George, 102
Magaleh Orot settlement group, 216

Mahane Yehuda market bombing, 160
Majdal village, 146

Mamilla neighborhood, 15–16, 57
Mar-Haim, Amos, 29
Martin Luther School, 116
el-Mashrua ("The Project") housing development, 150
Mea Shearim neighborhood, 175
Meir, David, 57, 58
Meir, Golda, 33, 39
Meretz Party, 30, 181, 219
Merhav, Reuven, 24–26
Mevasseret Tsion, 35
Military industries, 40–41
Ministerial Committee on Jerusalem, 20, 39, 48, 149, 150, 151, 154
Mishkenot Sha'ananim neighborhood, 184, 225–226, 229
el-Mizri, Hakhmat, 234
Mofeid, Abu, 134–135
Mordechai, Yitzhak, 96
Mordot Moria settlement company, 217
Mount of Olives, 7, 48, 49, 63, 100, 104, 134, 158, 227, 231; Jewish settlement movement in, 215, 219
Mount Scopus, 48, 68
Mount Zion, 39, 225
Mousrara market, 13
Mukhtars/mukhtar system, 73–75, 76–81, 84–85, 136, 179, 200
Municipal services and infrastructure, 23–26, 42, 49, 54, 62–64, 68–69, 156, 188, 233–234, 250; village committees and, 81, 82–83, 85–86; vs. political issues, 82–83; departments, 84–85, 155–156; in Arab neighborhoods, 124–129, 155, 207–208; effect of strikes on, 169; threat of discontinuation during intifada, 171, 173–174. See also specific types of services
Municipal umbrella proposal for Jerusalem, 227–228, 248
Murder, 200; of Palestinians by Jews, 81–82, 185; of Jews by Palestinians, 83, 160, 177, 179, 202, 209, 219; of Palestinians by Palestinians, 202. See also Street violence and rioting; Terrorism

Muslim Arab nationalism, 235
Muslim holy sites, 118–119
Muslim Quarter, Old City, 79, 97, 213,
    218, 219

Nablus, 152, 234
Nackman, Michael, 72
Nahamia House community center, 198
Nahemkin, Arik, 220–221
Namir, Ora, 151
Nasser, Gamal Abdel, 233
Nasser, Hannah, 144
Nasser, Jamal, 238
Nathan, Abi, 97
National Insurance Institute (NII), 22–23,
    26, 148–153
Natur, Mihktal, 109, 111
Nazlat Abu-Sweh village, 83
Netanyahu, Binyamin, 59, 96, 219, 248
Neveh Ya'acov development, 19–20, 33,
    39, 45, 55, 56, 57, 60, 62, 169, 192,
    203
New Gate, 104
1948 War of Independence, 6–7, 136,
    138, 146, 180, 198, 217, 251
1967 war, 13, 15, 39–40, 44, 46, 47, 56,
    160, 198, 251; deportations and evic-
    tions following, 63, 87; education sys-
    tem following, 101–105; reunification
    of Jerusalem following, 138, 180, 251;
    expropriation of Arab land following,
    212, 217. See also Six Day War
Nizamiyya school, 116
Nusseiba, Mohammed, 65
Nusseiba, Anwar, 65, 140, 142, 144, 238–
    239
Nusseiba, Sari, 87, 239
Nusseiba Housing Project, Beit Hanina,
    43, 65

Old City, 6, 7, 9, 13, 14, 37, 39, 49, 56,
    57, 104, 134, 183, 184, 188, 194, 225,
    226; segregation in, 61–62; Arabs en-
    couraged to move from, 149–151; inti-
    fada and street violence in, 158–159,
    163, 169, 196; security issues, 181, 183;
    Jewish settlement movement in, 215,
    217, 219–221; border definition, 231
Old City Wall, 192

Olmert, Ehud, 89, 95, 97–98, 100, 120–
    122, 125, 204, 208, 220, 248, 250
Orient House (PLO headquarters), 69, 88,
    89
Oron, Haim, 219
Oslo Peace Accord, 71, 89, 90, 119, 123,
    208, 239, 248
Ottoman rule in Jerusalem, 73, 226, 236
"Our Town" education program, 117–
    118

Palestine Liberation Organization (PLO),
    69, 71, 76, 88, 89, 144–145, 188, 204,
    233, 234, 239; city elections and, 91–
    92, 93, 97; education system and, 115,
    120, 122; street violence and terrorism,
    158, 160–161; Jewish settlement move-
    ment and, 216. See also Intifada, Pales-
    tinian Authority
Palestinian Authority (PA), 119, 120, 121,
    122, 227, 248
Palestinian containment policy, 57, 58, 59,
    60, 98. See also Population ratio
    (Arabs-Jews) in Jerusalem
Palestinian leadership, 87–90, 97, 167,
    204
Palestinian nationalist groups, 91, 107,
    120, 122, 146, 160–161, 164–165, 166,
    176, 181, 202, 238
Parks and recreation facilities, 11, 20, 23,
    39, 45, 49, 55, 67, 198–199. See also
    Sports and social facilities
Peled, Rafi, 202, 203
Peres, Shimon, 39–40, 161, 239
Pery, Ya'acov, 17, 166, 167, 168
Philadelphia, the (restaurant), 13
Pickering, Thomas, 41, 46–47, 142
Pisgat Ze'ev neighborhood, 19–20, 55, 57,
    62, 125–126, 129, 192
Pluga village, 146
Police, 22, 26, 143, 167, 183; intifada ac-
    tivism and, 68, 71, 77, 78, 80, 167–168,
    171, 174–175, 177, 178, 200–201; riot-
    ing and, 81–82, 158–159, 161, 176,
    179–180, 185–186, 188, 202–203; stu-
    dent protests and, 108–115; paramili-
    tary, 110, 179, 196, 212, 218; border,
    132, 147, 166, 170, 175, 178, 179,
    195–197; strikes and, 164, 170–173;

brutality, 169–170, 175; proposed municipal sharing of, 241
Police Ministry (Israel), 166
Population ratio (Arabs-Jews) in Jerusalem, 10, 16, 19, 30, 31–35, 38, 62–63, 149, 182, 246; policy of demographic balance, 43, 49, 55, 62, 63, 64. *See also* Palestinian containment policy
Postal service, 75–76, 145–148
Public housing. *See* Housing and development; Housing construction
Public works projects, 38, 49, 81, 125

Rabin, Yitzhak, 26–28, 71, 96, 214, 219, 221, 223, 224, 229
Rachel's Tomb, 231
Rafidiya Hospital, Nablus, 152
el-Rahman, Abed, 139
Ramallah, 14, 55, 62, 122, 136, 137, 231
Ramat Rachel neighborhood, 57
Ramot Alon neighborhood, 192
Ramot Eshkol neighborhood, 44, 55, 56
Ramot neighborhood, 55, 56, 177
Ras al-Amud neighborhood, 81, 83, 219, 220
Rashidiya Boys High School, 102, 105, 108, 111
Recreation facilities. *See* Parks and recreation facilities; Sports and social facilities
Refugee camps, 23, 39–40, 130–134, 158, 194
Rehavia neighborhood, 17, 126
Rejectionist front groups, 144
Rioting. *See* Street violence and rioting
Roads. *See* Streets and roads
Romach, Shimon, 95
Rothman, Jay, 200
Rubenstein, Amnon, 223
Russian Compound, 80, 109, 112, 164, 165

Sadat, Anwar, 234, 238
Samaria, 230. *See also* West Bank
Sanitation services, 84, 156, 162. *See also* Sewage systems
Sarig, Aharon, 17, 87, 99, 100, 102, 103, 107, 125, 170, 230
Savir, Uri, 89
Sawana neighborhood, 116

Sawarha, 81, 201
Schmidt private school, 104, 116
Schools, 18, 19, 21, 22, 25, 45, 49, 55, 207–208; recreation facilities at, 67; closure of, 82, 102, 111, 112, 117, 170, 173; private, 103–105, 107–109, 113, 115–117, 119, 122; public, 103–107, 109, 114–117, 122, 123; Christian, 104, 109, 122; Muslim, 104, 109, 122; Arab, 108, 109–110, 113–120, 122–123; student protests, 108–115, 188; construction of, 114; Christian Arab, 116; "unofficially recognized," 119. *See also* Education system; Teachers and principals
Scowcroft, Brent, 246
Secrecy, 166, 206, 216, 228–229, 232
Security establishment, 26, 161–162, 166, 186, 194–196, 203–204, 205; strategy against intifada, 166–181; Jewish settlement movement and, 218. *See also* Police; Shin Bet internal security force
Seidman, Danny, 219
Self-rule in east Jerusalem, 119, 226–227, 234, 237–238, 240–241
Self-segregation policy, 61–62, 247
Settlement movement of Jews in Arab neighborhoods, 211–224
Sewage systems, 19, 24, 25, 70, 81, 84, 124, 162, 169, 207. *See also* Sanitation services
Shabiba movement, 68, 70–71, 82
Shahaf, David, 153
Shahal, Moshe, 26, 141, 222
Shahin, Mohammed, 79–80
Shamgar, Meir, 41, 42, 43, 44, 48–49
Shamir, Yitzhak, 16, 213–214
"Sharing United Jerusalem" (Kollek), 84, 240
Sharon, Ariel, 16, 58, 217–220, 244
Sheikh Abdallah School, 112
Sheikh Jarrah neighborhood, 16, 67
Sheikh Sa'ad neighborhood, 128, 129
Shema'ah neighborhood, 39
Shilo, Efriam, 154–155
Shin Bet internal security force, 17, 77, 80, 87, 94, 143, 166, 183; intifada and, 167–168, 169, 173, 174, 181; Kollek and, 194–196

Shohat, Avraham, 26, 71–72
Shuafat–Beit Hanina zoning plan, 52–54
Shuafat neighborhood, 19–20, 45, 52–55, 57, 62, 100, 114, 138, 139, 169, 188
Shuafat refugee camp, 23, 130–134, 194
Shuafat Ridge neighborhood, 56
Shukri, Abu, 13
Shultz, George, 242
Silwani, Khalil, 175
Silwan village, 83, 145, 162, 176, 221, 222; Jewish settlement movement in, 211, 212, 213, 215, 218
Sivan, Amiram, 17, 18
Six Day War, 5, 7, 9, 13–15, 20, 33, 91, 99, 104, 159, 237; lack of municipal services following, 129–130; unification of Jerusalem following, 198; expropriation of Arab land following, 201, 212; renovation of Jewish properties following, 225, 226; division of Jerusalem following, 227, 228. See also 1967 war
Smuggling, 176
Sneh, Efriam, 23–24, 223
Solomon, Gershon, 184
Sports and social facilities, 11, 21, 22, 23, 67–68, 70–72, 81, 198–199. See also Parks and recreation facilities
St. John's Hospice, 213, 216
St. Joseph private school, 104, 116
Streets and roads, 18, 19, 20, 21, 24, 25, 35, 82, 169, 207; naming of, 145–148
Street violence and rioting, 40, 61, 68, 70–71, 77, 78, 80–82, 143, 158–159, 161, 169, 175, 176, 180, 185–186, 188, 197, 200–203, 209; firebombs, 68, 77, 80, 162; student protests, 108–115, 188; effect on businesses, 165–166; by Jews, 177–180; affected by events outside Jerusalem, 182; Israeli preparation for, 182–184; at Temple Mount, 184–186. See also Intifada; Murder; Terrorism
Strikes, 77, 80, 104, 106; at schools, 108, 168, 170; commercial, 164, 165–166, 168, 169, 170, 171–173, 181, 188
Student protests, 108–115, 188
Suicide bombings, 83, 209
Sununu, John, 246
Sur Baher neighborhood, 29, 35–37, 59, 62, 77, 78, 188, 201
Suwana neighborhood, 104

Synagogues, 18, 19, 49
Syrian Patriarch, 49

a-Tawil, Ramin, 92–93
Taxes, 22, 40–41, 77, 93, 105–106, 127, 131, 151
Taziz, Ali, 163–165
Teachers and principals, 22, 102–103, 107, 120; violence and strikes in schools and, 108, 113, 114, 115; training courses, 114, 117. See also Education system; Schools
Tear gas, 176, 197
Tehiya Party, 213
Tel Aviv, 6, 20, 114, 117, 137, 242
Telephone service, 148
Temple Mount, 7, 12, 26, 101, 159, 188, 227, 232, 237, 241; riot (1990), 184–186
Temple Mount Faithful group, 184–185
Terner, Ya'acov, 218
Terrorism, 159–160, 162, 177, 179, 200; car bombs, 160; demolition of homes of terrorists, 173, 174; Palestinian, 182, 195, 209, 219. See also Intifada; Murder; Street violence and rioting
"The Program," 45, 49
"The Project" Arab housing development, 150
Tiberias, 117
Tobol, Leor, 177
Tourists, 160, 162, 163, 169, 188, 196
Tower of David Museum, 184
Transportation, 26, 33, 248
Transport Ministry, 42
Trash collection. See Garbage collection
Tsadik, Walik, 206
Tsur, Yitzhak, 94–95
Turkey. See Ottoman rule in Jerusalem
Twite, Robin, 200, 201
Tzamaret Habira neighborhood, 19
Tzion Square bombing, 160

el-Umma school, 116
Umm Rashrash village, 146
Umm Tuba neighborhood, 62, 126
Unions, 102, 144–145
United Nations, 7, 10, 23, 46, 185, 251; Security Council, 20, 46; Relief and Works Agency (UNRWA), 104–105, 130–135, 138

United States, 41, 46–47, 142, 242–243, 244–247; Oslo Peace Accord signed in, 71, 119
Urban planning. *See* Housing and development

el-Vabala school, 116
Vatican, 48, 104, 231
Village committees, 69–70, 72–73, 81, 82, 84, 90; municipal services and, 81, 82–83, 85–86
Visas, 65, 80. *See also* Citizenship rights; Identification and traveling papers
Voting. *See* elections and voting

Wadi Joz neighborhood, 14–15, 16, 66, 218–219; Jewish settlement movement in, 215, 220
Wadi Kadoum neighborhood, 158
Wakf (Muslim religious authority in Jerusalem), 39, 49, 104, 115. *See also* Muslim interests in Jerusalem
Wallace, Mike, 196–197
al-Wardiya private school, 104
War of Independence. *See* 1948 War of Independence
Water system, 9, 21, 84, 124, 129–137, 171, 174

Welfare benefits, 9, 26, 64, 105, 148–153, 171; citizenship rights and, 148–149, 152
West Bank, 23, 26, 43, 46, 65, 80, 81, 104, 155, 176, 192, 239, 240, 241; schools, 119, 120, 122, 123; municipal services in, 127–129, 136; refugee camps, 130; welfare benefits in, 148–151; police authority in, 159; military law in, 172, 173; Jewish settlement movement in, 212, 214; border definition, 227, 230–231, 248; housing and development projects, 244–246
Western Wall, Jerusalem, 7, 124, 183, 185
Wenlor, Uri, 17, 58–59

Yaffa village, 146
Yehudai, Yosef, 158–159, 164–165, 166, 171, 172
Yekutieli, Baruch, 230–321, 232, 233, 234
Yom Kippur War, 230, 232, 234

Zionism, 6, 55, 113
Zoning plans, 29, 32, 37, 49, 50, 51, 52, 53, 54, 55, 88–89, 130. *See also* Housing and development